Michael Wolff is the author of *Fire and Fur*  that for the first time told the inside stor
He has received numerous awards for his
Magazine Awards. The author of seven p
a regular columnist for *Vanity Fair*, *New Yo*
British *GQ* and other magazines and newspap
and has four children.

'Michael Wolff's new book, *Siege*, is a deliciously catty look inside the White House, full of wicked anecdotes and gossipy gold. It's like sitting in a hairdresser's listening to a fabulously indiscreet conversation beside you. It's The Kardashians: White House edition' *Telegraph*

'A mordant, readable tell-all designed to show how Trump, simply by being Trump, has made himself the perfect wrecking ball, blasting holes through an array of institutions' *New York Times*

'Michael Wolff is back and not with a whimper. The latest instalment of his Trump chronicles picks up where *Fire and Fury* ended' *Guardian*

'Bannon's frequently shrewd observations make it clear why Wolff finds him irresistible. The author is mostly interested in Trump's psychology. He is adept at documenting the president's lunacy, and Bannon is frequently an able fellow shrink' *Washington Post*

'This book confirms that Trump should never have been allowed to hold power in the first place' The *i*

'Once again, the dirt is abundant. Donald Trump insults everyone in his orbit, repeatedly, viciously, and – always privately – they return the favor ... *Siege* is overflowing with such titillating material, which is sure to make it another tour de force for the Trump resistance' *Vanity Fair*

'Utterly gripping' *GQ*

SIEGE

Trump Under Fire

MICHAEL WOLFF

ABACUS

First published in Great Britain in 2019 by Little, Brown
This paperback edition published in 2020 by Abacus

1 3 5 7 9 10 8 6 4 2

A CIP catalogue record for this book
is available from the British Library.

ISBN 978-0-349-14430-6

Printed and bound in Great Britain by Clays Ltd, Elcograf S.p.A.

Papers used by Abacus are from well-managed forests
and other responsible sources.

Abacus
An imprint of
Little, Brown Book Group
Carmelite House
50 Victoria Embankment
London EC4Y 0DZ

An Hachette UK Company
www.hachette.co.uk

www.littlebrown.co.uk

To the Memory of My Father
Lewis A. Wolff

Contents

Author's Note

Shortly after Donald Trump's inauguration as the forty-fifth president of the United States, I was allowed into the West Wing as a sideline observer. My book *Fire and Fury* was the resulting account of the organizational chaos and constant drama—more psychodrama than political drama—of Trump's first seven months in office. Here was a volatile and uncertain president, releasing, almost on a daily basis, his strange furies on the world, and, at the same time, on his own staff. This first phase of the most abnormal White House in American history ended in August 2017, with the departure of chief strategist Stephen K. Bannon and the appointment of retired general John Kelly as chief of staff.

This new account begins in February 2018 at the outset of Trump's second year in office, with the situation now profoundly altered. The president's capricious furies have been met by an increasingly organized and methodical institutional response. The wheels of justice are inexorably turning against him. In many ways, his own government, even his own White House, has begun to turn on him. Virtually every power center left of the far-right wing has deemed him unfit. Even some among his own base find him undependable, hopelessly distracted, and in over his head. Never before has a president been under such concerted attack with such a limited capacity to defend himself.

His enemies surround him, dedicated to bringing him down.

* * *

I am joined in my train-wreck fascination with Trump—that certain knowledge that in the end he will destroy himself—by, I believe, almost everyone who has encountered him since he was elected president. To have worked anywhere near him is to be confronted with the most extreme and disorienting behavior possible. That is hardly an overstatement. Not only is Trump not like other presidents, he is not like anyone most of us have ever known. Hence, everyone who has been close to him feels compelled to try to explain him and to dine out on his head-smacking peculiarities. It is yet one more of his handicaps: all the people around him, however much they are bound by promises of confidentiality or nondisclosure agreements or even friendship, cannot stop talking about their experience with him. In this sense, he is more exposed than any president in history.

Many of the people in the White House who helped me during the writing of *Fire and Fury* are now outside of the administration, yet they are as engaged as ever by the Trump saga. I am grateful to be part of this substantial network. Many of Trump's pre–White House cronies continue to both listen to him and support him; at the same time, as an expression both of their concern and of their incredulity, they report among one another, and to others as well, on his temper, mood, and impulses. In general, I have found that the closer people are to him, the more alarmed they have found themselves at various points about his mental state. They all speculate about how this will end—badly for him, they almost all conclude. Indeed, Trump is probably a much better subject for writers interested in human capacities and failings than for most of the reporters and writers who regularly cover Washington and who are primarily interested in the pursuit of success and power.

My primary goal in *Siege* is to create a readable and intuitive narrative—that is its nature. Another goal is to write the near equivalent of a real-time history of this extraordinary moment, since understanding it well after the fact might be too late. A final goal is pure portraiture: Donald Trump as an extreme, almost hallucinatory, and certainly cautionary, American character. To accomplish this, to gain the perspective and to find the voices necessary to tell the larger story, I provided anonymity to any source who requested it. In cases where I have been told—on the promise of no attribution—about an unreported event or private conversation or remark, I have made every effort to confirm it with other sources or documents. In some cases, I have witnessed the events or conversations described herein. With regard to the Mueller investigation, the narrative I provide is based on internal documents given to me by sources close to the Office of the Special Counsel.

Dealing with sources in the Trump White House has continued to offer its own set of unique issues. A basic requirement of working there is, surely, the willingness to infinitely rationalize or delegitimize the truth, and, when necessary, to outright lie. In fact, I believe this has caused some of the same people who have undermined the public trust to become private truth-tellers. This is their devil's bargain. But for the writer, interviewing such Janus-faced sources creates a dilemma, for it requires depending on people who lie to also tell the truth—and who might later disavow the truth they have told. Indeed, the extraordinary nature of much of what has happened in the Trump White House is often baldly denied by its spokespeople, as well as by the president himself. Yet in each successive account of this administration, the level of its preposterousness—even as that bar has been consistently raised—has almost invariably been confirmed.

In an atmosphere that promotes, and frequently demands, hyperbole, tone itself becomes a key part of accuracy. For instance, most crucially, the president, by a wide range of the people in close contact with him, is often described in maximal terms of mental instability. "I have never met anyone crazier than Donald Trump" is the wording of one staff member who has spent almost countless hours with the president. Something like this has been expressed to me by a dozen others with firsthand experience. How do you translate that into a responsible evaluation of this singular White House? My strategy is to try to show and not tell, to describe the broadest context, to communicate the experience, to make it real enough for a reader to evaluate for him- or herself where Donald Trump falls on a vertiginous sliding scale of human behavior. It is that condition, an emotional state rather than a political state, that is at the heart of this book.

SIEGE

1

BULLSEYE

The president made his familiar stink-in-the-room face, then waved his hands as though to ward off a bug.

"Don't tell me this," he said. "Why are you telling me this?"

His personal lawyer John Dowd, in late February 2018, little more than a year into Trump's tenure, was trying to explain that prosecutors were likely to issue a subpoena for some of the Trump Organization's business records.

Trump seemed to respond less to the implications of such a deep dive into his affairs than to having to hear about it at all. His annoyance set off a small rant. It was not so much about people out to get him—and people were surely out to get him—but that nobody was defending him. The problem was his own people. Especially his lawyers.

Trump wanted his lawyers to "fix" things. "Don't bring me problems, bring me solutions," was a favorite CEO bromide that he often repeated. He judged his lawyers by their under-the-table or sleight-of-hand skills and held them accountable when they could not make problems disappear. His problems became *their* fault. "Make it go away" was one of his frequent orders. It was often said in triplicate: "Make it go away, make it go away, make it go away."

The White House counsel Don McGahn—representing the White

House rather than, in a distinction Trump could never firmly grasp, the president himself—demonstrated little ability to make problems disappear and became a constant brunt of Trump's rages and invective. His legal interpretation of proper executive branch function too often thwarted his boss's wishes.

Dowd and his colleagues, Ty Cobb and Jay Sekulow—the trio of lawyers charged with navigating the president through his personal legal problems—had, on the other hand, become highly skilled in avoiding their client's bad humor, which was often accompanied by menacing, barely controlled personal attacks. All three men understood that to be a successful lawyer for Donald Trump was to tell the client what he wanted to hear.

Trump harbored a myth about the ideal lawyer that had almost nothing to do with the practice of law. He invariably cited Roy Cohn, his old New York friend, attorney, and tough-guy mentor, and Robert Kennedy, John F. Kennedy's brother. "He was always on my ass about Roy Cohn and Bobby Kennedy," said Steve Bannon, the political strategist who, perhaps more than anyone else, was responsible for Trump's victory. "'Roy Cohn and Bobby Kennedy,' he would say. 'Where's my Roy Cohn and Bobby Kennedy?'" Cohn, to his own benefit and legend, built the myth that Trump continued to embrace: with enough juice and muscle, the legal system could always be gamed. Bobby Kennedy had been his brother's attorney general and hatchet man; he protected JFK and worked the back channels of power for the benefit of the family.

This was the constant Trump theme: beating the system. "I'm the guy who gets away with it," he had often bragged to friends in New York.

At the same time, he did not want to know details. He merely wanted his lawyers to assure him that he was winning. "We're killing it, right? That's what I want to know. That's *all* I want to know. If we're not killing it, you screwed up," he shouted one afternoon at members of his ad hoc legal staff.

From the start, it had become a particular challenge to find top lawyers to take on what, in the past, had always been one of the most vaunted of legal assignments: representing the president of the United States. One high-profile Washington white-collar litigator gave Trump a list of twenty issues that would immediately need to be addressed if he were to take on the case. Trump refused to consider any of them. More than a dozen major firms had turned down his business. In the end, Trump was left with a ragtag group of solo practitioners without the heft and resources of big firms. Now, thirteen months after his inauguration, he was facing personal legal trouble at least as great as that faced by Richard Nixon and Bill Clinton, and doing so with what seemed like, at best, a Court Street legal team. But Trump appeared to be oblivious to this exposed flank. Ratcheting up his level of denial about the legal threats around him, he breezily rationalized: "If I had good lawyers, I'd look guilty."

Dowd, at seventy-seven, had had a long, successful legal career, both in government and in Washington law firms. But that was in the past. He was on his own now, eager to postpone retirement. He knew the importance, certainly to his own position in Trump's legal circle, of understanding his client's needs. He was forced to agree with the president's assessment of the investigation into his campaign's contact with Russian state interests: it would not reach him. To that end, Dowd, and the other members of Trump's legal team, recommended that the president cooperate with the Mueller investigation.

"I'm not a target, right?" Trump constantly prodded them.

This wasn't a rhetorical question. He insisted on an answer, and an affirmative one: "Mr. President, you're not a target." Early in his tenure, Trump had pushed FBI director James Comey to provide precisely this reassurance. In one of the signature moves of his presidency, he had fired Comey in May 2017 in part because he wasn't satisfied with the enthusiasm of the affirmation and therefore assumed Comey was plotting against him.

Whether the president was indeed a target—and it would surely have taken a through-the-looking-glass exercise not to see him as the bullseye of the Mueller investigation—seemed to occupy a separate reality from Trump's need to be reassured that he was not a target.

"Trump's trained me," Ty Cobb told Steve Bannon. "Even if it's bad, it's great."

Trump imagined—indeed, with a preternatural confidence, nothing appeared to dissuade him—that sometime in the very near future he would hear directly from the special counsel, who would send him a comprehensive and even apologetic letter of exoneration.

"Where," he kept demanding to know, "is my fucking letter?"

* * *

The grand jury empanelled by Special Counsel Robert Mueller met on Thursdays and Fridays in federal district court in Washington. Its business was conducted on the fifth floor of an unremarkable building at 333 Constitution Avenue. The grand jurors gathered in a nondescript space that looked less like a courtroom than a classroom, with prosecutors at a podium and witnesses sitting at a desk in the front of the room. The Mueller grand jurors were more female than male, more white than black, older rather than younger; they were distinguished most of all by their focus and intensity. They listened to the proceedings with "a scary sort of attention, as though they already know everything," said one witness.

In a grand jury inquiry, you fall into one of three categories. You are a "witness of fact," meaning the prosecutor believes you have information about an investigation at hand. Or you are a "subject," meaning you are regarded as having personal involvement with the crime under investigation. Or, most worrisome, you are a "target," meaning the prosecutor is seeking to have the grand jury indict you. Witnesses often became subjects, and subjects often became targets.

In early 2018, with the Mueller investigation and its grand jury maintaining a historic level of secrecy, no one in the White House could be sure who was what. Or who was saying what to whom. Anyone and everyone working for the president or one of his senior aides could be talking to the special counsel. The investigation's code of silence extended into the West Wing. Nobody knew, and nobody was saying, who was spilling the beans.

Almost every White House senior staffer—the collection of advisers who had firsthand dealings with the president—had retained a lawyer. Indeed, from the president's first days in the White House, Trump's tangled legal past and evident lack of legal concern had cast a shadow on those who worked for him. Senior people were looking for lawyers even as they were still learning how to navigate the rabbit warren that is the West Wing.

In February 2017, mere weeks after the inauguration, and not long after the FBI had first raised questions about National Security Advisor Michael Flynn, Chief of Staff Reince Priebus had walked into Steve Bannon's office and said, "I'm going to do you a big favor. Give me your credit card. Don't ask me why, just give it to me. You'll be thanking me for the rest of your life."

Bannon opened his wallet and gave Priebus his American Express card. Priebus shortly returned, handed the card back, and said, "You now have legal insurance."

Over the next year, Bannon—a witness of fact—spent hundreds of hours with his lawyers preparing for his testimony before the special counsel and before Congress. His lawyers in turn spent ever mounting hours talking to Mueller's team and to congressional committee counsels. Bannon's legal costs at the end of the year came to $2 million.

Every lawyer's first piece of advice to his or her client was blunt and unequivocal: talk to no one, lest it become necessary to testify about what you said. Before long, a constant preoccupation of senior staffers in the Trump White House was to know as little as possible. It was a wrong-side-up world: where being "in the room" was traditionally the most sought after status, now you wanted to stay out of meetings. You wanted to avoid being a witness to conversations; you wanted to avoid being witnessed being a witness to conversations, at least if you were smart. Certainly, nobody was your friend. It was impossible to know where a colleague stood in the investigation; hence, you had no way of knowing how likely it was that they might need to offer testimony about someone else—you, perhaps—as the bargaining chip to save themselves by cooperating with the special counsel, a.k.a. flipping.

The White House, it rapidly dawned on almost everyone who worked there—even as it became one more reason *not* to work there—was the scene of an ongoing criminal investigation, one that could potentially ensnare anyone who was anywhere near it.

* * *

The ultimate keeper of the secrets from the campaign, the transition, and through the first year in the White House was Hope Hicks, the White House communications director. She had witnessed most everything.

She saw what the president saw: she knew what the president, a man unable to control his own running monologue, knew.

On February 27, 2018, testifying before the House Intelligence Committee—she had already appeared before the special counsel—she was pressed about whether she had ever lied for the president. Perhaps a more accomplished communications professional could have escaped the corner here, but Hicks, who had scant experience other than working as Donald Trump's spokesperson, which, as often as not, meant dealing with his disregard of empirical truth, found herself as though in a sudden and unexpected moral void trying to publicly parse the relative importance of her boss's lies. She admitted to telling "white lies," as in, somehow, less than the biggest lies. This was enough of a forward admission to require a nearly twenty-minute mid-testimony conference with her lawyers, distressed by what she might be admitting and by where any deconstruction of the president's constant inversions might lead.

Not long after she testified, another witness before the Mueller grand jury was asked how far Hicks might go to lie for the president. The witness answered: "I think when it comes to doing anything as a 'yes man' for Trump, she'll do it—but she won't take a bullet for him." The statement could be taken as both a backhanded compliment and an estimate of how far loyalty in the Trump White House might extend—probably not too far.

Almost no one in Trump's administration, it could be argued, was conventionally suited to his or her job. But with the possible exception of the president himself, no one provided a better illustration of this unprepared and uninformed presidency than Hicks. She did not have substantial media or political experience, nor did she have a temperament annealed by years of high-pressure work. Always dressed in the short skirts that Trump favored, she seemed invariably caught in the headlights. Trump admired her not because she had the political skills to protect him, but for her pliant dutifulness. Her job was to devote herself to his care and feeding.

"When you speak to him, open with positive feedback," counseled Hicks, understanding Trump's need for constant affirmation and his almost complete inability to talk about anything but himself. Her attentiveness to Trump and tractable nature had elevated her, at age twenty-nine, to the top White House communications job. And practically speaking, she acted as his de facto chief of staff. Trump did not want his administration to be staffed by professionals; he wanted it to be staffed by people who attended and catered to him.

Hicks—"Hope-y," to Trump—was both the president's gatekeeper and his comfort blanket. She was also a frequent subject of his prurient interest: Trump preferred business, even in the White House, to be personal. "Who's fucking Hope?" he would demand to know. The topic also interested his son Don Jr., who often professed his intention to "fuck Hope." The president's daughter Ivanka and her husband, Jared Kushner, both White House senior advisers, expressed a gentler type of concern for Hicks: sometimes they would even try to suggest eligible men.

But Hicks, seeming to understand the insular nature of Trumpworld, dated exclusively inside the bubble, picking the baddest boys in it: campaign manager Corey Lewandowski during the campaign and presidential aide Rob Porter in the White House. As the relationship between Hicks and Porter unfolded in the fall of 2017, knowing about the affair became an emblem of Trump insiderness, with special care taken to keep this development from the proprietary president. Or not: other people, assuming that Porter's involvement with Hicks would not at all please Trump, were less than discreet about it.

* * *

In the heightened enmity of the Trump White House, Rob Porter may have succeeded in becoming the most disliked person by everyone except perhaps the president himself. A square-jawed, 1950s-looking guy who could have been a model for Brylcreem, he was almost a laughable figure of betrayal and perfidy: if he *hadn't* stabbed you in the back, you would be forced to acknowledge how unworthy he considered you to be. A sitcom sort of suck-up—"Eddie Haskell," cracked Bannon, citing the early television icon of insincerity and brownnosing featured in *Leave It to Beaver*—he embraced Chief of Staff John Kelly, while at the same time poisoning him with the president. Porter's estimation of his own high responsibilities in the White House, together with the senior-most jobs that the president, he let it be known, was promising him, seemed to put the administration and the nation squarely on his shoulders.

Porter had, before the age of forty, two bitter ex-wives, at least one of whom he had beaten, and both of whom he had cheated on at talk-of-the-town levels. During a stint as a Senate staffer, the married Porter had an affair with an intern, costing him his job. His girlfriend Samantha Dravis had moved in with Porter in the summer of 2017, while, quite unbeknownst to her, he was seeing Hicks. "I cheated on you because you're not attractive enough," he later told Dravis.

In a potentially criminal break of protocol, Porter had gained access to his raw FBI clearance reports and seen the statements of his ex-wives. His most recent ex-wife had also written a blog about his alleged abuse, which, while it did not name him, clearly fingered him. Concerned about the damaging impact his former wives could have on his security review, he recruited Dravis to help him smooth his relationship with both women.

Lewandowski, Hicks's former boyfriend, caught wind of the Hicks-Porter relationship and began working to expose it; by some reports, he got paparazzi to follow Hicks. Though Porter's history of abuse was slowly making its way to the surface as a result of the FBI investigation, the Lewandowski campaign against Hicks cut through many other efforts to cover up Porter's transgressions.

Dravis, in the autumn of 2017, heard the Lewandowski-pushed rumors of the Hicks-Porter relationship. After finding Hicks's number listed under a man's name in Porter's contacts, Dravis confronted Porter, who promptly threw her out. Moving back in with her parents, she began her own revenge campaign, openly talking about Porter's security clearance issues, including to people inside the White House counsel's office, saying he had protection at the highest levels in the White House. Then, along with Lewandowski, Dravis helped leak the details of the Hicks-Porter romance to the *Daily Mail*, which published a story about it on February 1.

But Dravis, joined by Porter's former wives, decided that, outrageously, he had come out looking *good* in the *Daily Mail* account—he was part of a glam power couple! Porter called Dravis to taunt her: "You thought you could get me!" Dravis and his former wives all then publicly revealed their abuse at his hand. His first wife said he kicked and punched her; she even produced a photograph of her black eye. His second wife informed the media that she had filed an emergency protective order against him.

The White House, or at least Kelly—and likely Hicks—had been aware of many of these claims and, effectively, covered them up. ("You usually have enough competent people for White House positions to weed out the wife beaters, but you couldn't be so choosy in the Trump White House," said one Republican acquaintance of Porter's.) The furor that erupted around Porter and his troubling gross-guy history not only annoyed Trump— "He stinks of bad press"—it further weakened Kelly. On February 7, after both of his former wives gave interviews to CNN, Porter resigned.

A publicity-shy Hicks—Donald Trump put a high value on associates who did not steal his press opportunities—suddenly found her love life in the glare of intense international press scrutiny. Her affair with the discredited Porter highlighted her own odd relationship with the president and his family, as well as the haphazard management, interpersonal dysfunctions, and general lack of political savvy in the Trump court.

* * *

The affair was, curiously, among the least of Hicks's problems. Indeed, for Hicks the Porter scandal became perhaps a *better* cloud under which to leave the administration than what almost everybody in the West Wing assumed was the real cloud.

On February 27, a reporter at the Washington insider newsletter *Axios*, Jonathan Swan, a favorite conduit for White House leaks, reported that Josh Raffel was leaving the White House. In a novel arrangement, Raffel had come into the White House in April 2017 as the exclusive spokesperson for the president's son-in-law Jared Kushner, and his wife, Ivanka, bypassing the White House communications team. Raffel, who, like Kushner, was a Democrat, had worked for Hiltzik Strategies, the New York public relations firm that represented Ivanka's clothing line.

Hope Hicks, who had also worked for the Hiltzik firm—perhaps best known for having long represented the film producer Harvey Weinstein, caught, in the fall of 2017, in an epochal harassment and abuse scandal and cover-up—had originally had the same role as Raffel but at a higher level: she was the personal spokesperson for the president. In September,

Hicks had been elevated to White House communications director, with Raffel as her number two.

The trouble had arisen the previous summer. Both Hicks and Raffel had been on Air Force One in July 2017 as the news broke about Donald Trump Jr.'s meeting in Trump Tower during the campaign with Russian government go-betweens offering dirt on Hillary Clinton. During the flight back to the United States after the G20 summit in Germany, Hicks and Raffel aided the president in his efforts to issue a largely false story about the Trump Tower meeting, thus becoming part of the cover-up.

Even though Raffel had been at the White House for a little more than nine months, the *Axios* report said that his departure had been under discussion for several months. That was untrue. It was an abrupt exit.

The next day, just as abruptly, Hope Hicks—the person in the White House closest to the president—resigned as well.

The one person who perhaps knew more than anyone else about the workings of the Trump campaign and the Trump White House was suddenly out the door. The profound concern inside the White House was the reasonable supposition that Hicks and Raffel, both witnesses to and participants in the president's efforts to cover up the details of his son and son-in-law's meeting with the Russians, were subjects or targets of the Mueller investigation—or, worse, had already cut a deal.

The president, effusive in his public praise for Hicks, did not try to talk her out of leaving. In the weeks to come he would mope about her absence—"Where's my Hope-y?"—but, in fact, as soon as he got wind that she might be talking, he wanted to cut her loose and began, in a significant rewrite, downgrading her status and importance on the campaign and in the White House.

Yet here, from Trump's point of view, was a hopeful point about Hicks: as central as she was to his presidency, her duties really only consisted of pleasing him. She was an unlikely agent of grand strategy and great conspiracies. Trump's team was made up of only bit players.

* * *

John Dowd may have been reluctant to give his client bad news, but he well understood the danger of a thorough prosecutor with virtually unlimited resources. The more a determined team of G-men sifts, strips, and inspects, the greater the chance that both methodical and casual crimes will be revealed. The more comprehensive the search, the more inevitable the outcome. The case of Donald Trump—with his history of bankruptcies, financial legerdemain, dubious associations, and general sense of impunity—certainly seemed to offer prosecutors something of an embarrassment of riches.

For his part, however, Donald Trump yet seemed to believe that his skills and instincts were at least a match for all the thoroughness and resources of the United States Department of Justice. He even believed their exhaustive approach would work in his favor. "Boring. Confusing for everybody," he said, dismissing the reports of the investigation provided by Dowd and others. "You can't follow any of this. No hook."

One of the many odd aspects of Trump's presidency was that he did not see being president, either the responsibilities or the exposure, as being all that different from his pre-presidential life. He had endured almost countless investigations in his long career. He had been involved in various kinds of litigation for the better part of forty-five years. He was a fighter who, with brazenness and aggression, got out of fixes that would have ruined a weaker, less wily player. That was his essential business strategy: what doesn't kill me strengthens me. Though he was wounded again and again, he never bled out.

"It's playing the game," he explained in one of his frequent monologues about his own superiority and everyone else's stupidity. "I'm good at the game. Maybe I'm the best. Really, I could be the best. I think I am the best. I'm very good. Very cool. Most people are afraid that the worst might happen. But it doesn't, unless you're stupid. And I'm not stupid."

In the weeks after his first anniversary in office, with the Mueller investigation in its eighth month, Trump continued to regard the special counsel's inquiry as a contest of wills. He did not see it as a war of attrition—a gradual reduction of the strength and credibility of the target through sustained scrutiny and increasing pressure. Instead, he saw a situation to confront, a spurious government undertaking that was vulnerable to his attacks. He was confident he could jawbone this "witch hunt"—often tweeted in all-caps—to at least a partisan draw.

He remained irritated by efforts to persuade him to play the game in the usual Washington way—mounting a disciplined legal defense, negotiating, trying to cut his losses—rather than his way. This was disconcerting to many of the people closest to him, but it alarmed them more to see that as Trump's indignation and sense of personal insult rose, so did his belief in his own innocence.

* * *

By the end of February, in addition to the Mueller grand jury indictments of a group of Russian nationals for illegal activities involved with efforts by the Russian government to influence the U.S. election, Mueller had reached several levels into the Trump circle. Among those who were indicted or who had pled guilty to felonies were his former campaign manager Paul Manafort, his former national security advisor Michael Flynn, the eager-beaver junior adviser George Papadopoulos, and Manafort's business partner and campaign official Rick Gates. This series of legal moves could be classically read as a methodical, step-by-step approach to the president's door. Or, from the Trump camp's point of view, it could be seen as a roundup of the sorts of opportunists and hangers-on who had always trailed Trump.

The doubts about the usefulness of Trump's hangers-on was an implicit part of their usefulness: they could be shrugged off and disavowed at any time, which is what promptly happened at the least sign of trouble. The Trumpers swept up by Mueller were all declared wannabe and marginal players. The president had never met them, could not remember them, or had a limited acquaintance with them. "I know Mr. Manafort—I haven't spoken to him in a long time, but I know him," declared a dismissive Trump, pulling a line from the "who dat?" page of his playbook.

The difficulty in proving a conspiracy is proving intent. Many of the president's inner circle believed that Trump, and the Trump Organization, and by extension the Trump campaign, operated in such a diffuse, haphazard, gang-that-couldn't-shoot-straight manner that intent would be very difficult to establish. What's more, the Trump hangers-on were so demonstrably subpar players that stupidity could well be a reasonable defense against intent.

Many in the Trump circle agreed with their boss: they believed that whatever idiotic moves had been made by idiotic Trump hands, the Russia investigation was too abstruse and nickel-and-dime to ultimately stick. At the same time, many, and perhaps all, were privately convinced that a deep dive—or, for that matter, even a cursory inspection—of Trump's financial past would yield a trove of overt offenses, and likely a pattern of career corruption.

It was hardly surprising, then, that ever since the beginning of the special counsel's investigation, Trump had tried to draw a line in the sand between Mueller and Trump family finances, openly threatening Mueller if he went there. Trump's operating assumption remained that the special counsel was afraid of him, conscious of where and how his tolerance might end. Trump was confident that the Mueller team could be made to understand its limits, by either wink-wink or unsubtle threat.

"They know they can't get me," he told one member of his circle of after-dinner callers, "because I was never involved. I'm not a target. There's nothing. I'm not a target. They've told me, I'm not a target. And they know what would happen if they made me a target. Everybody understands everybody."

* * *

Books and newspaper stories about Trump's forty-five years in business were full of his shady dealings, and his arrival in the White House only helped to highlight them and surface even juicier ones. Real estate was the world's favorite money-laundering currency, and Trump's B-level real estate business—relentlessly marketed by Trump as triple A—was quite explicitly designed to appeal to money launderers. What's more, Trump's own financial woes, and desperate efforts to maintain his billionaire lifestyle, cachet, and market viability, forced him into constant and unsubtle schemes. In the high irony department, Jared Kushner, when he was in law school, and before he met Ivanka, identified, in a paper he wrote, possible claims of fraud against the Trump Organization in a particular real estate deal he was studying—a subject now of quite some amusement among his acquaintances at the time. Practically speaking, Trump hid in plain sight, as the prosecutors appeared to be finding.

In November 2004, for instance, Jeffrey Epstein, the financier later caught in a scandal involving underage prostitutes, agreed to purchase from bankruptcy a house in Palm Beach, Florida, for $36 million, a property that had been on the market for two years. Epstein and Trump had been close friends—playboys in arms, as it were—for more than a decade, with Trump often seeking Epstein's help with his chaotic financial affairs. Soon after negotiating the deal for the house in Palm Beach, Epstein took Trump to see it, looking for advice on construction issues involved with moving the swimming pool. But as he prepared to finalize his purchase for the house, Epstein discovered that Trump, who was severely cash-constrained at the time, had bid $41 million for the property and bought it out from under Epstein through an entity called Trump Properties LLC, entirely financed by Deutsche Bank, which was already carrying a substantial number of troubled loans to the Trump Organization and to Trump personally.

Trump, Epstein knew, had been loaning out his name in real estate deals—that is, for an ample fee, Trump would serve as a front man to disguise the actual ownership in a real estate transaction. (This was, in a sense, another variation of Trump's basic business model of licensing his name for commercial properties owned by someone else.) A furious Epstein, certain that Trump was merely fronting for the real owners, threatened to expose the deal, which was getting extensive coverage in Florida papers. The fight became all the more bitter when, not long after the purchase, Trump put the house on the market for $125 million.

But if Epstein knew some of Trump's secrets, Trump knew some of Epstein's. Trump often saw the financier at Epstein's current Palm Beach house, and Trump knew that Epstein was visited almost every day, and had been for many years, by girls he'd hired to give him massages that often had happy endings—girls recruited from local restaurants, strip clubs, and, also, Trump's own Mar-a-Lago. Just as the enmity between the two friends increased over the house purchase, Epstein found himself under investigation by the Palm Beach police. And as Epstein's legal problems escalated, the house, with only minor improvements, was acquired for $96 million by Dmitry Rybolovlev, an oligarch who was part of the close

Putin circle of government-aligned industrialists in Russia, and who, in fact, never moved into the house. Trump had, miraculously, earned $55 million without putting up a dime.

This was Donald Trump's world of real estate.

* * *

As though using mind-control tricks, Jared Kushner had become highly skilled at containing his deep frustration with his father-in-law. He stayed expressionless—sometimes he seemed almost immobile—when Trump went off the rails, unleashing tantrums or proposing dopey political or policy moves. Kushner, a courtier in a crazy court, was possessed of an eerie calmness and composure. He was also very worried. It seemed astounding and ludicrous that this fig-leaf technicality—"You're not a target, Mr. President"—could offer his father-in-law such comfort.

Kushner understood that Trump was surrounded by a set of mortal arrows, any of which might kill him: the case for obstruction; the case for collusion; any close look at his long, dubious financial history; the always-lurking issues with women; the prospects of a midterm rout and the impeachment threat if the midterm elections went against them; the fickleness of the Republicans, who might at any time turn on him; and the senior staffers who had been pushed out of the administration (Kushner had urged the ouster of many of them), any of whom might testify against him. In March alone, Gary Cohn, the president's chief economic adviser, Rex Tillerson, the secretary of state, and Andrew McCabe, the deputy director of the FBI—each man bearing the president deep contempt— were pushed from the administration.

But the president was in no mood to hear Kushner's counsel. Never entirely trusted by his father-in-law—in truth, Trump trusted no one except, arguably, his daughter Ivanka, Kushner's wife—Kushner now found himself decidedly on the wrong side of Trump's red line of loyalty.

As a family insider, Kushner, in a game of court politics so vicious that, in another time, it might have yielded murder plots, had appeared to triumph over his early White House rivals. But Trump invariably soured on the people who worked for him, just as they soured on him, not least because he nearly always came to believe that his staff was profiting at his expense. He was convinced that everyone was greedy, and that sooner or later they would try to take what was more rightfully his. Increasingly, it seemed that Kushner, too, might be just another staff member trying to take advantage of Donald Trump.

Trump had recently learned that a prominent New York investment fund, Apollo Global Management, led by the financier Leon Black, had provided the Kushner Companies—the family real estate group that had been managed by Kushner himself while his father, Charlie, was in federal prison—with $184 million in financing.

This was troubling on many levels, and it left a vulnerable Kushner open to more questions about the conflicts between his business and his position in the White House. During the transition, Kushner had offered Apollo's cofounder Marc Rowan, the job of director of the Office of Management and Budget. Rowan initially accepted the job, declining it only after Apollo chairman Leon Black objected to what would have to be disclosed about Rowan's and the firm's investments.

But the president-elect's concerns were elsewhere: he was more keenly and furiously focused on the fact that, in the constant search for financings that occur in mid-tier real estate companies like Trump's, Apollo had never extended itself for the Trump Organization. Now, it seemed baldly apparent, Apollo was backing the Kushners solely because of the family's connection to the administration. The constant accounting in Trump's head of who was profiting from whom, and his sense of what he was therefore owed for creating the circumstances by which everyone could profit, was one of the things that reliably kept him up at night.

"You think I don't know what's going on?" Trump sneered at his daughter, one of the few people he usually went out of his way to try to mollify. *"You think I don't know what's going on?"*

The Kushners had gained. He had not.

The president's daughter pleaded her husband's case. She spoke of the incredible sacrifice the couple had made by coming to Washington. And for what? "Our lives have been destroyed," she said melodramatically—and yet with some considerable truth. The former New York socialites had been reduced to potential criminal defendants and media laughing-stocks.

After a year of friends and advisers whispering that his daughter and son-in-law were at the root of the disarray in the White House, Trump once again was thinking they should never have come. Revising history, he told various of his late-night callers that he had *always* thought they never should have come. Over his daughter's bitter protests, he declined to intercede in his son-in-law's security clearance issues. The FBI had continued to hold up Kushner's clearance—which the president, at his discretion, could approve, his daughter reminded him. But Trump did nothing, letting his son-in-law dangle in the wind.

Kushner, with superhuman patience and resolve, waited for his opportunity. The trick among Trump whisperers was how to focus Trump's attention, since Trump could never be counted on to participate in anything like a normal conversation with reasonable back-and-forth. Sports and women were reliable subjects; both would immediately engage him. Disloyalty also got Trump's attention. So did conspiracies. And money—always money.

* * *

Kushner's own lawyer was Abbe Lowell, a well-known showboat of the D.C. criminal bar who prided himself on, and managed his clients' expectations and attention with, an up-to-the-minute menu of rumors and insights about what gambit or strategy prosecutors were about to dish up. The true edge provided by a high-profile litigator was perhaps not courtroom skill but backroom intelligence.

Lowell, adding to the reports Dowd had received, told Kushner that prosecutors were about to substantially deepen the president's—and the Trump family's—jeopardy. Dowd had continued to try to mollify the president, but Kushner, with intel supplied by Lowell, went to his father-in-law with reports about this new front in the legal war against him. Sure enough, on March 15 the news broke that the special counsel had issued a subpoena for the Trump Organization records: it was a deep and encompassing order, reaching many years back.

Kushner also warned his father-in-law that the investigation was about to spill over from the Mueller team, with its narrow focus on Russian collusion, to the Southern District of New York—that is, the federal prosecutor's office in Manhattan—which would not be restricted to the Russia probe. This was a work-around intended to circumvent the special counsel's restriction to Russia-related matters, but also an effort by the Mueller team to short-circuit any attempt by the president to disband or curtail its investigation. By moving parts of the investigation to the Southern District, Mueller, as Kushner explained to Trump, was ensuring that the investigation of the president would continue even without the special counsel. Mueller was playing a canny, or ass-protecting, game, while also following precise procedures: even as he focused on the limited area of his investigation, he was divvying up evidence of other possible crimes and sending it out to other jurisdictions, all of which were eager to be part of the hunt.

It gets worse, Kushner told Trump.

The Southern District was once run by Trump's friend Rudy Giuliani, the former mayor of New York. In the 1980s, when Giuliani was the federal prosecutor—and when, curiously, James Comey had worked for him—the Southern District became the premier prosecutor of the Mafia and of Wall Street. Giuliani had pioneered using a draconian, and many believed unconstitutional, interpretation of the RICO (Racketeer Influenced and Corrupt Organizations) Act against the Mob. He used the same interpretation against big finance, and in 1990 the threat of a RICO indictment, under which the government could almost indiscriminately seize assets, brought down the investment bank Drexel Burnham Lambert.

The Southern District had long been worrisome to Trump. After his election, he had an unseemly meeting with Preet Bharara, the federal prosecutor there, a move whose optics were alarming to all of his advisers, including Don McGahn and the incoming attorney general, Jeff Sessions. (The meeting foreshadowed the one Trump would shortly have with Comey, during which he sought a pledge of loyalty in return for job security.) His meeting with Bharara was unsatisfactory: Bharara was unwilling to humor him—or, shortly, even to return his calls. In March 2017, Trump fired him.

Now, said Kushner, even without Bharara, the Southern District was looking to treat the Trump Organization as a Mob-like enterprise; its lawyers would use the RICO laws against it and go after the president as if he were a drug lord or Mob don. Kushner pointed out that corporations had no Fifth Amendment privilege, and that you couldn't pardon a corporation. As well, assets used in or derived from the commission of a crime could be seized by the government.

In other words, of the more than five hundred companies and separate entities in which Donald Trump had been an officer, up until he became president, many might be subject to forfeiture. One potential casualty of a successful forfeiture action was the president's signature piece of real estate: the government could seize Trump Tower.

* * *

In mid-March, a witness with considerable knowledge of the Trump Organization's operations traveled by train to Washington to appear before the Mueller grand jury. Picked up at Union Station by the FBI, the witness was driven to the federal district court. From 10:00 a.m. to 5:00 p.m., two prosecutors on the Mueller team, Aaron Zelinsky and Jeannie Rhee, reviewed with the witness, among other issues, the structure of the Trump Organization.

The prosecutors asked the witness about the people who regularly talked to Trump, how often they met with him, and for what purposes. They also asked how meetings with Trump were arranged and where they took place. The witness's testimony yielded, among other useful pieces of information, a signal fact: all checks issued by the Trump Organization were personally signed by Donald Trump himself.

The Trump Organization's activities in Atlantic City were a particular subject of interest that day. The witness was asked about Trump's relationship with known Mafia members—not *if* he had such relationships, but the nature of the relationships prosecutors already knew existed. The prosecutors also wanted to know about Trump Tower Moscow, a project pursued by Trump for many years—pursued, in fact, well into the 2016 campaign—albeit never brought to fruition.

Michael Cohen, Trump's personal lawyer and a Trump Organization officer, was another significant topic. The prosecutors asked questions about the level of Cohen's disappointment at not being included in the president's White House team. They seemed to be trying to gauge how much resentment Cohen felt, which led the witness to infer that they wanted to estimate how much leverage they might have if they attempted to flip Michael Cohen against the president.

Zelinsky and Rhee wanted to know about Jared Kushner. And they wanted to know about Hope Hicks.

The two prosecutors also delved into the president's personal life. How often did he cheat on his wife? With whom? How were trysts arranged? What were the president's sexual interests? The Mueller investigation, and its grand jury, was becoming a clearing house for the details of Trump's long history of professional and personal perfidiousness.

When the long day was finally over, the witness left the grand jury room shocked—not so much by what the prosecutors wanted to know but by what they already knew.

* * *

By the third week of March, Trump's son-in-law had the president's full attention. "They can not only impeach you, they can bankrupt you" was Kushner's message.

Agitated and angry, Trump pressed Dowd for more reassurances, holding him accountable for the prior reassurances Trump had frequently demanded he be given. Dowd held firm: he yet believed that the fight was in its early stages and that Mueller was still on a fishing expedition.

But Trump's patience was finally at an end. He decided that Dowd was a fool and should go back into the retirement from which, Trump kept repeating, he had rescued him. Indeed, resisting that retirement, Dowd pleaded his own case, assuring the president that he could continue to provide him with valuable help. To no avail: on March 22, Dowd reluctantly resigned, sending another bitter former Trumper into the world.

2

THE DO-OVER

The day John Dowd was forced out, Steve Bannon was sitting at his dining-room table trying to forestall another threat to the Trump presidency. This one wasn't about a relentless prosecutor but rather a betrayed base. It was about the Wall that wasn't.

The town houses on Capitol Hill, middle-class remnants of the nineteenth century, are cramped up-and-down affairs of modest parlor floors, nook-y sitting rooms, and small bedrooms. Many serve as headquarters for causes and organizations that can't afford Washington's vast amount of standard-issue office real estate. Some double as housing for their organization's leaders. Many represent amateur efforts or eccentric pursuits, often a kind of shrine to hopes and dreams and revolutions yet to occur. The "Embassy" on A Street—a house built in 1890 and the former location of Bannon's Breitbart News—was where Bannon had lived and worked since his exile from the White House in August 2017. It was part frat house, part man cave, and part pseudo-military redoubt; conspiracy literature was scattered about. Various grave and underemployed young men, would-be militia members, loitered on the steps.

The Embassy's creepiness and dark heart were in quite stark contrast to Bannon's expansive and merry countenance. He might be in exile from the Trump White House, but it was an ebullient banishment, coffee-fueled or otherwise.

In the last few weeks, he had helped install his allies—and first-draft choices during the presidential transition—in central posts in the Trump administration. Mike Pompeo had recently been named secretary of state, John Bolton would soon become the national security advisor, and Larry Kudlow had been appointed director of the National Economic Council. The president's chief political aides were Corey Lewandowski and David Bossie, both Bannon allies, if not acolytes; both operated outside the White House and were frequent visitors at the Embassy. Many of the daily stream of White House defenders on cable television—the surrogates— were Bannon people carrying Bannon's message as well as the president's. What's more, his enemies in the White House were moving out, including Hope Hicks, H. R. McMaster, the former national security advisor, and the ever shrinking circle of allies supporting the president's son-in-law and daughter.

Bannon was often on the road. He was in Europe meeting with the rising populist right-wing groups, and in the U.S. meeting with hedge funders desperate to understand the Trump variable. He was also looking for every opportunity to try to convince liberals that the populist way ought to be their way, too. Early in the year, Bannon went to Cambridge to see Larry Summers, who had been Bill Clinton's Treasury secretary, Barack Obama's director of the National Economic Council, and, for a time, president of Harvard. Summers's wife refused to allow Bannon into their home, so the meeting happened at Harvard instead. Summers was mis-shaven and wearing a shirt that was missing a button or two, while Bannon was sporting his double-shirt getup, cargo pants, and a hunting jacket. "Both of them looked like Asperger guys," said one of the people at the meeting.

"Do you fucking realize what your fucking friend is doing?" yelled Summers about Trump and his administration. "You're fucking the country!"

"You elite Democrats—you only care about the margins, people who are rich or people who are poor," returned Bannon.

"Your trade mumbo jumbo will sink the world into a *depression*," thundered Summers.

"And you've exported U.S. jobs to China!" declared a delighted Bannon, always enjoying the opportunity to joust with a member of the establishment.

Bannon was—or at least saw himself to be—a fixer, power broker, and kingmaker without portfolio. He was a cockeyed sort of Clark Clifford, that political eminence and influence peddler of the 1960s and '70s. Or a wise man of the political fringe, if that was not an ultimate kind of contradiction. Or the head of an auxiliary government. Or, perhaps, something truly sui generis: no one quite like Bannon had ever played such a central role in America's national political life, or been such a thorn in the side of it. As for Trump, with friends like Bannon, who needed enemies?

The two men might be essential to each other, but they reviled and ridiculed each other, too. Bannon's constant public analysis of Trump's confounding nature—both its comic and harrowing components, the behavior of a crazy uncle—not to mention his indiscreet diatribes on the inanities of Trump's family, continued to further alienate him from the president. And yet, though the two men no longer spoke, they hung on each other's words—each desperate to know what one was saying about the other.

Whatever current feeling Bannon might have for Trump—his mood ranged from exasperation to fury to disgust to incredulity—he continued to believe that nobody in American politics could match Trump's midway-style showmanship. Yes, Donald Trump had restored *showmanship* to American politics—he had taken the wonk out of politics. In sum, he knew his audience. At the same time, he couldn't walk a straight line. Every step forward was threatened by his next lurch. Like many great actors, his innate self-destructiveness was always in conflict with his keen survival instincts. Some around the president merely trusted that the latter would win over the former. Others, no matter the frustration of the effort, understood how much he needed to be led by unseen hands— unseen being the key attribute.

With no one to tell him otherwise, Bannon continued, unseen, to conduct the president's business from his dining-room table on A Street.

* * *

That afternoon, a bipartisan Congress with surprising ease had passed the $1.3 trillion 2018 appropriations bill. "McConnell, Ryan, Schumer, and Pelosi," said Bannon about the Republican and Democratic congressional leadership, "in their singular moment of bipartisan magnanimity, put one over on Trump."

This legislative milestone was a result of Trump's disengagement and everybody else's attentive efforts. Most presidents are eager to get down into the weeds of the budget process. Trump took little or no interest. Hence the Republican and Democratic leadership—here supported by the budget and legislative teams in the White House—were able to pass an enormous spending bill that failed to fund Trump's must-must item, the holy grail Wall, that prospective two-thousand-mile monument meant to run the entire length of the border between the United States and Mexico. Instead, the bill provided only $1.6 billion for border security. The current bill was in effect the same budget bill that had been pushed forward at the end of the previous September, when the Wall had once again not been funded. In the fall, Trump had agreed to have the Republican-controlled Congress vote to extend the September budget bill. The *next* time it came up, the Wall would be funded or, he threatened, the government would be shut down.

Even the hardest-core Trumpers in Congress seemed content not to have to die on the actual battlefield of funding the Wall, since that would mean embracing or at least enduring an always politically risky shutdown. Trump, too, in his way, seemed to understand that the Wall was more myth than reality, more slogan than actual plan. The Wall was ever for another day.

On the other hand, it was unclear what the president understood. "We've gotten the budget," he privately told his son-in-law at the end of the March budget negotiations. "We've gotten the Wall, totally."

* * *

On Wednesday, March 21, the day before the final vote, Paul Ryan, the Speaker of the House, had come to the White House to receive the president's blessings on the budget bill.

"Got $1.6 Billion to start Wall on Southern Border, rest will be forthcoming," the president shortly tweeted.

The White House had originally asked for $25 billion for the Wall, although high-end estimates of the Wall's ultimate cost came in at $70 billion. Even then, the $1.6 billion in the appropriations bill was not so much for the Wall as for better security measures.

As the final vote neared, a gentlemen's agreement appeared to have been reached, one that extended to every corner of the government—with, it even seemed, Trump's own tacit support, or at least his convenient distraction. The understanding was straightforward: whatever their stripe, members of Congress would not blow up the appropriations process for the Wall.

There were, too, Republicans like Ryan—with the backing of Republican donors such as Paul Singer and Charles Koch—who were eager to walk back, by whatever increment possible, Trump's hard-line immigration policies and rhetoric. Ryan and others had devised a simple method for accomplishing this kind of objective: you agreed with him and then ignored him. There was happy talk, which Trump bathed in, followed by practical steps, which bored him.

That Wednesday, Trump made a series of calls to praise everyone's work on the bill. The next morning, Ryan, in a televised news conference to seal the deal, said, "The president supports this bill, there's no two ways about it."

Here were the twin realities. The Wall was the most concrete manifestation of Trumpian policy, attitude, belief, and personality. At the same time, the Wall forced every Republican politician to come to terms with his or her own common sense, fiscal prudence, and political flexibility.

It was not just the expense and impracticality of the Wall, it was having to engage in a battle for it. A government shutdown would mean a high-stakes face-off between the Trump world and the non-Trump world. Should this come to pass, it would potentially be as dramatic a moment as any that had occurred since the election of 2016.

If the Democrats wanted to harden the partisan division and were eager to find yet another example—perhaps the mother of all examples—of Trump at his most extreme, a shutdown over the Wall would hand them one. If the Republicans wanted to shift the focus from a full-barbarian Trump to, say, the tax bill the Congress had recently passed, shutting down the government would sweep that approach right off the table.

The White House, quite behind Trump's back, was aggressively working to pass the appropriations bill and avoid a shutdown. The vice president gave Trump the same assurance he had been given previously when a budget had been passed without full funding for the Wall: Pence said the bill provided a "down payment" for the Wall, a phrase whose debt-finance implications seemed to amply satisfy the president and which he repeated with great enthusiasm. Marc Short, the White House director of legislative affairs, and Mick Mulvaney, the director of the Office of Management and Budget, in a joint appearance in the White House briefing room that Thursday, shifted the debate from the Wall to the military. "This bill will provide the largest year-over-year increase in defense spending since World War II," said Mulvaney. "It'll be the largest increase for our men and women in uniform in salary in the last ten years."

* * *

The attempt to distract the Trumpian base with these bromides utterly failed. The hard-core cadre insisted on forcing the issue, and Bannon was delighted to serve as their general.

Within minutes of the budget bill's passage on March 22, Bannon, in the Embassy, began working the phones. Calling Trump's most ardent supporters, his goal was to "light him up." The effect was nearly immediate: an unsuspecting Trump started to hear from many of those on his noisy back bench, who were suddenly furious.

Bannon understood what moved Trump. Details did not. Facts did not. But a sense that something valuable might be taken from him immediately brought him up on his hind legs. If you confronted him with losing, he would turn on a dime. Indeed, turning on a dime was his only play. "It's not that he needs to win the week, or day, or even the hour," reflected Bannon. "He needs to win the *second*. After that, he drifts."

For the hard-core Trumpers, it was back to a fundamental through line of Trumpism: you had to constantly remind Trump which side he was on. As Bannon organized a howling protest from the president's base, he took stock of the Trump reality: "There simply is not going to be a Wall, ever, if he doesn't have to pay a political price for there not being a Wall."

If the Wall was not under way by the midterm elections in November, it would show Trump to be false and, worse, weak. The Wall needed to be real. The absence of the Wall in the spending bill was just what it seemed to be: Trump out to lunch. Trump's most effective message, the forward front of the Trump narrative—maximal aggression toward illegal immigrants—had been muted. And this had happened without him knowing it.

* * *

The night of the twenty-second, the Fox News lineup—Tucker Carlson, Laura Ingraham, and Sean Hannity—hammered the message: betrayal.

The battle was on. The Republican leadership on the Hill, along with the donor class, stood sober and pragmatic in the face of both political realities and the prospect of unlimited billions in government spending—with, certainly, no illusions that Mexico was going to pay for the Wall. Opposing them were the Fox pundits, righteous and unyielding in their appeal to the true emotion of Trumpism.

The personal transformation of Trump over the course of the evening was convulsive. All three Fox pundits delivered a set of electric shocks, each rising in current. Trump had sold out the movement. Or, worse, Trump had been outsmarted and outwitted. Trump, on the phone, roared in pain and fury. He was the victim. He had no one in his corner. He could trust no one. The congressional leadership: against him. The White House itself: against him. Betrayal? Almost everyone in the White House had betrayed *him*.

The next morning it got worse. Pete Hegseth, the most obsequious of the Fox Trump lovers, seemed, on *Fox & Friends*, nearly brought to tears by Trump's treachery.

Then, almost simultaneously with Hegseth's wailing, Trump abruptly—confoundingly—shifted position and tweeted that he was considering vetoing the appropriations bill. The same bill that, twenty-four hours before, he had embraced.

That Friday morning, he came down from the residence into the Oval Office in a full-on rage so violent that, for a moment, his hair came undone. To the shock of the people with him, there stood an almost entirely bald Donald Trump.

The president's sudden change of heart sent the entire Republican Party into a panic. If Trump carried out his threat not to sign the bill, he would bring on what they most feared: a shutdown. And he might well blame the shutdown on his own party.

Mark Meadows, the head of the House Freedom Caucus and a staunch Trump ally in Congress, called the president from Europe to say that after the vote on Thursday afternoon most members had left town for the congressional recess. Congress wouldn't be able to undo the previous day's vote, and the shutdown was due to commence in mere hours.

Mitch McConnell rushed Defense Secretary Jim Mattis into action to tell the president that American soldiers would not be paid the next day if he didn't sign the bill. This was a repeat performance: Mattis had issued a similar warning during a threatened shutdown in January.

"*Never . . . never . . . never . . . again*," Trump shouted, pounding the desk after each "never."

Once again he caved and agreed to sign the bill. But he vowed that next time there would be billions upon billions for the Wall or there really would be a shutdown. Really. *Really.*

* * *

Bannon had been here before, so many times.

"Dude, he's Donald fucking Trump," said Bannon, holding his head and sitting at his table in the Embassy the day after the president signed the bill.

Bannon was not confused: he had a clear understanding of how great a liability Trump could be to Bannon's own vision and career. To the nervous titters of the people around him, Bannon believed he was the man of populist destiny and not Donald Trump.

The urgency here was real. Bannon believed he represented the workingman against the corporate-governmental-technocratic machine whose constituency was the college-educated. In Bannon's romantic view, the workingman smelled of cigarettes, crushed your hand in his, and was hard as brick—and not from working out in a gym. This remembrance of things past, of (if it ever existed) a leveled world where a workingman was proud of his work and identity, was inspiring, Bannon believed, a global anger. It was a revolution—this worldwide unease and fear and day-by-day upending of liberal assumptions—and it was his. The global hegemon was in his sights. He was the man behind the curtain—and he might as well be in front of it, too—trying to snatch the world back from its postmodern anomie and restore something like the homogenized and neighborly embrace of 1962.

And China! And the coming Götterdämmerung! To Bannon, this was way-of-life stuff. China was the Russia of 1962—but smarter, more tenacious, and more threatening. American hedge funders, in their secret support of China against the interests of the American middle class, were the new fifth column.

How much of this did Trump understand? How much was Trump committed to the ideas that moved Bannon and, by some emotional osmosis, the base? Trump was more than a year in, and not a shovelful of dirt had yet been dug for the Wall, nor a penny allocated. The Wall and so much else that was part of Bannon's populist revolution—the details of which he had once listed on whiteboards in his White House office, expecting to check each one off—were entirely captive to Trump's inattention and wild mood swings. Trump, Bannon had long ago learned, "doesn't give a fuck about the agenda—he doesn't know what the agenda *is*."

* * *

In late March, after the gloom of the budget bill disaster had lifted, there was a brief, optimistic moment for the faithful in Trump's inner circle.

Chief of Staff John Kelly, fed up with Trump—just as Trump was fed up with him—seemed surely on the way out. Kelly had joined the White House, replacing Reince Priebus, Trump's first chief of staff, in August 2017, charged with bringing management discipline to a chaotic West Wing. But by mid-fall, Trump was circumventing Kelly's new procedures. Jared and Ivanka—with many of the new rules designed to curtail their open access to the president—were going over his head. By the end of the year, Trump was casually mocking his chief of staff and his penchant for efficiency and strict procedures. Indeed, both men were openly trashing each other, quite unmindful of the large audience for their slurs. For Trump, Kelly was a "twitcher" and "feeble" and ready to "stroke out." For Kelly, Trump was "deranged" and "mad" and "stupid."

The drama just got weirder.

In February, Kelly, a retired four-star general, grabbed Trump adviser Corey Lewandowski outside the Oval Office and pushed him up against a wall. "Don't look him in the eye," whispered Trump about Kelly after the incident, circling his finger next to his head in the crazy sign. The confrontation left everybody shaken, with Trump asking Lewandowski not to tell anyone, and Lewandowski, when talking to the people he did tell, saying that he had almost wet himself.

By March, Trump and Kelly were hardly speaking. Trump ignored him; Kelly sulked. Or Trump would drop pointed hints that Kelly should resign, and Kelly would ignore him. Everyone assumed the countdown had begun.

Various Republicans, from Ryan to McConnell to their right-wing adversary Mark Meadows, along with Bannon, had gotten behind a plan to push House majority leader Kevin McCarthy for chief of staff. Even Meadows, who hated McCarthy, was all for it. Here finally was a strategy: McCarthy, a top tactician, would refocus an unfocused White House on one mission—the midterms. Every tweet, every speech, every action would be directed toward salvaging the Republican majority.

Alas, Trump didn't want a chief of staff who would focus him. Trump, it was clear, didn't want a chief of staff who would tell him *anything*. Trump did not want a White House that ran by any method other than to satisfy his desires. Someone happened to mention that John F. Kennedy didn't have a chief of staff, and now Trump regularly repeated this presidential factoid.

* * *

The Mueller team, as it pursued the Russia investigation, continued to bump up against Trump's unholy financial history, exactly the rabbit hole

Trump had warned them not to go down. Mueller, careful to protect his own flank, took pains to reassure the president's lawyers that he wasn't pursuing the president's business interests; at the same time, he was passing the evidence his investigation had gathered about Trump's business and personal affairs to other federal prosecutors.

On April 9, the FBI, on instructions from federal prosecutors in New York, raided the home and office of Michael Cohen, as well as a room he was using in the Regency Hotel on Park Avenue. Cohen, who billed himself as Trump's personal lawyer, sat handcuffed for hours in his kitchen while the FBI conducted its search, itemizing and hauling away every electronic device its agents could find.

Bannon, coincidentally, also stayed at the Regency on his frequent trips to New York, and he would sometimes bump into Cohen in the hotel's lobby. Bannon had known Cohen during the campaign, and the lawyer's mysterious involvement in campaign issues often worried him. Now, in Washington, seeing the Cohen news, Bannon knew that another crucial domino had fallen.

"While we don't know where the end is," said Bannon, "we can guess where it might begin: with Brother Cohen."

* * *

On April 11, three weeks after the president signed the budget bill, Paul Ryan—one of the government's most powerful figures given the Republican lock on Washington—announced his plan to leave the Speakership and depart Congress.

"Listen to what Paul Ryan is saying," said Bannon, sitting at his table in the Embassy early that morning. "It's over. Done. Done. And Paul Ryan wants the fuck off the Trump train today."

Ryan had been telling almost anyone who would listen that as many as fifty or sixty House seats would be lost seven months hence in the midterm elections. A Ryan lieutenant, Steve Stivers, chairman of the National Republican Congressional Committee, was estimating a loss of ninety to one hundred seats. At this gloomy hour, it seemed more than possible that the Democrats would eliminate their twenty-three-seat deficit and gain a majority greater than the one the Republicans held now. Except, unlike the Republicans, theirs would be a unified party—or at least one that was unified against Donald Trump.

Ryan and Stivers were hardly the only ones seeing such a result. Mitch McConnell was telling donors not to even bother contributing to House races. The money should go to the Senate campaign, where prospects for holding the Republican majority were significantly brighter.

This was, for Donald Trump, in Bannon's view, the most desperate moment in his political career, arguably even worse than the revelation of the *Access Hollywood* grab-them-by-the-pussy tape. He was already on the ropes legally, with Mueller and the Southern District bearing down; now, looking at a likely wipeout in the midterm elections, he was in serious political jeopardy as well.

But Bannon's usual ebullience quickly returned. As he talked his way out of his funk, he became nearly joyful. If the establishment—Democrats, Republicans, moderate thinkers of every sort—believed that Donald Trump needed to be run out of town, then Bannon relished the prospect of defending him. For Bannon, this was the mission, but it was also sport. Bannon thrived on the possibility of upset. His own leap to the world stage had come because the Trump campaign was so deep in hopelessness that he was allowed to take it over. Then, on November 9, 2016, against all odds and expectations, Trump, riding Bannon's campaign—with Bannon's primacy soon one of the bitterest pills for Trump to swallow—won the presidency. Now, even with almost every indicator for the November elections looking bleak, Bannon believed he could yet see how Republican losses could be held to under the twenty-three seats needed to save the House majority. Still, it was going to be a grinding fight.

"When Trump calls his New York friends after dinner and whines that he doesn't have a friend in the world, he's kind of right," said a mordant Bannon.

Bannon viewed the case against Donald Trump as both inherently political—his enemies willing to do whatever it took to bring him down—and essentially true. He had little doubt that Trump was guilty of most of what he was accused of. "How did he get the dough for the primary and then for the general with his 'liquidity' issues?" asked Bannon with his hands out and his eyebrows up. "Let's not dwell."

But for Bannon there were two sides in American politics—not so much right and left, but right brain and left brain. The left brain was represented by the legal system, which was empirical, evidentiary, and methodical; given the chance, it would inevitably and correctly convict Donald Trump. The right side was represented by politics, and therefore by voters who were emotional, volatile, febrile, and always eager to throw the dice. "Get the deplorables fired up"—he slapped his hands in thunder-clap effect—"and we'll save our man."

Almost a year and a half on, all of the issues of 2016 remained as powerful and raw as ever: immigration, white man's resentment, and the liberal contempt for the working—or out-of-work—white man. The year 2018 was, for Bannon, the real 2016: the deplorable base had become the deplorable nation. "It's civil war," Bannon said, a happy judgment he often repeated.

The most resonant issue was Donald Trump himself: the people who elected him would be galvanized by the effort to take him from them. Bannon was horrified by mainstream Republican efforts to run the coming election on the strength of the recent Republican tax cut. "Are you kidding? Oh my fucking god, are you kidding?" This election was about the fate of Donald Trump.

"Let's have a do-over election. That's what the libs want. They can have it. Let's do it. Up or down, Trump or no Trump."

Impeachment was not to be feared, it was to be embraced. "That's what you're voting for: to impeach Donald Trump or to save him from impeachment."

The legal threat, however, might be moving faster than the election. And to Bannon—who knew more about the president's hankerings, mood swings, and impulse-control issues than almost anyone—you could not have produced a needier or more hapless defendant.

* * *

Since coming aboard in the summer of 2017, the president's legal team—Dowd, Cobb, and Sekulow—had delivered the message their client insisted upon hearing, that he was not a target and would shortly be exonerated. But the lawyers went even further with their feel-good strategy.

Presidents, faced with hostile investigations by the other coequal branches of government, Congress and the judiciary, invariably cite executive privilege both as a legitimate principle and as a dilatory tactic. It's a built-in bargaining chip. But Trump's lawyers, hoisted by how often they had to assure the president that he had nothing to fear, supported their confident assessment, to Trump's delight, by dispensing with any claim of executive privilege and willingly satisfying all the special counsel's requests. Trump, in all his dodginess, had become an open book. What's more, Trump himself, ever believing in the force and charm of his own personality, was, with his attorneys' apparent assent, eager to testify.

And yet, Bannon knew, it was still much worse. The president's lawyers had sent more than 1.1 million documents to the special counsel, aided by only a scant document production team. It was just Dowd, Cobb, and two inexperienced assistants. In major litigations, documents are meticulously logged and cross-referenced into elaborate and efficient database systems. Here, they shipped over much of the material merely as attachments, and kept minimal or no records of what exactly had been sent. Few in the White House knew what they had given up and thus what the special counsel had. And the haphazard approach didn't stop there. Dowd and Cobb neither prepared many of the witnesses who had worked for the White House in advance of their testimony to Mueller's team nor debriefed them after they testified.

Bannon was overcome by the hilarity and stupidity of this what-me-worry approach to federal prosecutors whose very reputations depended on nailing the president. Trump needed a plan—which, of course, Bannon had.

Bannon swore that he did not want to go back into the White House. He wouldn't ever, he said. The humiliations of working in Trump's administration had almost destroyed Bannon's satisfaction at having risen so miraculously to the top of the world.

Some, however, were not convinced by his protestations. They believed that Bannon actively fantasized that he would be brought back into the West Wing to save Trump—and that, not incidentally, this would be his ultimate revenge on Trump, saving him yet again. Bannon certainly believed that he was the only one who could pull off this difficult rescue, a reflection of his conviction that he was the most gifted political strategist of his time, and of his view that Trump was surrounded by only greater and lesser lummoxes.

Trump, Bannon believed, needed a wartime consigliere. And if, he mused, Jared and Ivanka were finally sent packing . . . But no, he insisted, not even then.

Moreover, Trump would not be able to tolerate it. Bannon understood that only Trump could save the day, or at least that Trump *believed* only he could save the day. No other scenario was possible. He would rather lose, would rather even go to jail, than have to share victory with someone else. He was psychologically incapable of not being the focus of all attention.

In the end, it was easier and more productive to give Trump advice at a distance than up close. It was a safer play to do what needed to be done without Trump himself actually being involved with, or even aware of, what was being done.

The morning Ryan announced his retirement from the House, Bannon was particularly eager to send some advice Trump's way. Setting up a deft bank shot, he invited Robert Costa, a reporter for the *Washington Post*, to visit him at the Embassy.

Bannon spent a good part of every day talking to reporters. On some days, perhaps most days, his blind-quote voice—hidden behind a familiar attribution such as "this account is drawn from interviews with current and former officials"—crowded out most other voices on the subject of whatever new crisis was engulfing the Trump administration. These quotes functioned as something like a stage whisper that Trump could pretend he didn't hear. Trump, in fact, was always desperately seeking Bannon's advice, though only if there was the slightest pretext for believing that it came from some place other than Bannon. Indeed, Trump was quite willing to hear Bannon say something in this or that interview and then claim he had thought of it himself.

Costa sat at Bannon's dining-room table for two hours, taking down Bannon's prescription for how to save Trump from himself.

Trump's stupidity, said Bannon, could sometimes be made into a virtue. Here was Bannon's idea: the president should make a retroactive claim of executive privilege. *I didn't know. Nobody told me. I was ill-advised.*

It was hard not to see Bannon's satisfaction in a prostrate Trump admitting to his own lack of guile and artfulness.

Bannon understood that this claim of retroactive executive privilege would have no chance of success—nor should it. But the sheer audacity of it could buy them four or five months of legal delay. Delay was their friend, possibly their only friend. They could work this claim of retroactive executive privilege, no matter how loopy, all the way to the Supreme Court.

For this plan to work, the president would have to get rid of his inept lawyers. Oh, and he would also have to fire Rod Rosenstein, the deputy attorney general who was overseeing the Mueller investigation. Bannon had been against the firing of Comey, and in the months after the appointment of the special counsel, he had fought the president's almost daily impulse to fire Mueller and Rosenstein, seeing this as the surest invitation to impeachment. ("Just don't pay attention to his crazy shit," he had urged everyone around the president.) But now they had run out of options.

"Firing Rosenstein is our only way out of here," Bannon told Costa. "I don't come to this lightly. As soon as they went to Cohen—that's what they do in Mob prosecutions to get a response from the true target. So you can sit there and get bled out—get indicted, go to grand juries—or you can fight it politically. Get it out of the law-and-order system where we are losing and are going to lose. A new DAG will review where we stand on this thing, which could take a couple of months. Delay, delay, delay—and shift it politically. Can we win? I have no fucking idea. But I know on that other path I'm going to lose. It's not perfect . . . but we live in a world of imperfect."

* * *

Costa's story, which was posted online later that day, described Bannon as "pitching a plan to West Wing aides and congressional allies to cripple the federal probe into Russian interference in the 2016 election, according to four people familiar with the discussions." But however many people

Costa had spoken to about the background machinations of Steve Bannon, what mattered was that he had spoken directly and at length to Bannon himself, who was using the *Washington Post* to pitch a plan to the president.

Bannon's three-part plan for Trump instantly made its way to the Oval Office. And the next morning, the president offered Kushner his view that he should fire Rosenstein, reinstate a claim of executive privilege, and get a tough-guy lawyer.

Kushner, pressing his own strategies, urged his father-in-law to move cautiously when it came to Rosenstein.

"Jared is spooked," said a scornful Trump later that day while on the phone to a confidant. "What a girl!"

3

LAWYERS

There was a running sweepstakes or office pool for the unhappiest person in the White House. Many had held the title, but one of the most frequent winners was White House counsel Don McGahn. He was a constant target for his boss's belittling, mocking, falsetto-voice mimicry, and, as well, sweeping disparagements of his purpose and usefulness.

"This is why we can't have nice things," McGahn uttered almost obsessively under his breath, quoting the Taylor Swift song to comment on whatever egregious act Trump had just committed (". . . because you break them," the song continues).

McGahn's background was largely as a federal election lawyer. Mostly he was on the more-money side—he was against, rather than for, aggressive enforcement of election laws. He served as the counsel to the Trump campaign. Before joining the Trump administration, McGahn had no White House or executive branch experience. He had never worked in the Justice Department or, in fact, anywhere in government. Formerly an attorney for a nonprofit affiliated with the Koch brothers, he was hyperpartisan: when Obama's White House counsel, Kathy Ruemmler, the previous occupant of McGahn's office, reached out to congratulate him and to offer to be a resource on past practices, McGahn did not respond to her email.

One of McGahn's jobs was to navigate what was possibly the most complicated relationship in modern government: he was the effective point person between the White House and the Department of Justice. Part of his portfolio, then, was to endure the president's constant rage and bewilderment about why the DOJ was personally hounding him, and his incomprehension that he could do nothing about it.

"It's my Justice Department," Trump would tell McGahn, often repeating this more than dubious declaration in his signature triad.

Nobody could quite be certain of the number of times McGahn had had to threaten, with greater or lesser intention, to quit if Trump made good on his threat to fire the attorney general, the deputy attorney general, or the special counsel. Curiously, one defense against the charge that the president had tried to fire Mueller in June 2017 in an effort to end the special counsel's investigation—as the *New York Times* claimed in a January 2018 scoop—was the fact that Trump was almost constantly trying to fire Mueller or other DOJ figures, doing so often multiple times a day.

McGahn's steadying hand had so far helped avert an ultimate crisis. But he had missed a number of intemperate, unwise, and interfering actions by the president that might, McGahn feared, comprise the basis of obstruction charges. Deeply involved with the conservative Federalist Society and its campaign for "textualist" judges, McGahn had long dreamed himself of becoming a federal judge himself, but given the no-man's-land he occupied between Trump and the Justice Department—not to mention Trump's sometimes daily attacks on the DOJ's independence, which McGahn had to accept or condone—he knew his future as a jurist was dead.

* * *

Fifteen months into Trump's tenure, the tensions between the administration and the Department of Justice had erupted into open conflict. Now it was war—the White House against its own DOJ.

Here was a modern, post-Watergate paradox: the independence of the Justice Department. The DOJ might be, from every organizational and statutory view, an instrument of the White House, and, as much as any other agency, its mission might appear to be driven by whoever held the presidency. That's what it looked like on paper. But the opposite was true, too. There was a permanent-government class in the Justice Department that believed an election ought to have no role at all in how the DOJ conducted itself. The department was outside politics and ought to be as blind as the courts. In this view, the Justice Department, as the nation's preeminent investigator and prosecutor, was as much a check on the White House, and ought to be as independent of the White House, as the other branches of government. (And within the Justice Department, the FBI claimed its own level of independence from its DOJ masters, as well as from the White House itself.)

Even among those at Justice and the FBI who had a more nuanced view, and who recognized the symbiotic nature of the department's relationship with the White House, there was yet a strong sense of the lines that cannot be crossed. The Justice Department and the FBI had, since Watergate, found themselves accountable to Congress and the courts. Any top-down effort to influence an investigation, or any evidence of having bowed to influence—memorialized in a memo or email—might derail a career.

In February 2018, Rachel Brand, the associate attorney general, a former Bush lawyer who had been nominated for the number three DOJ job by Obama, resigned to take a job as a Walmart lawyer. If Trump had fired Rosenstein during Brand's tenure, she would have become acting attorney general overseeing the Mueller investigation. She told colleagues she wanted to get out before Trump fired Rosenstein and then demanded that she fire Mueller. She would take Bentonville, Arkansas, where Walmart had its headquarters, over Washington, D.C.

For a generation or more, the arm's-length relationship between the White House and the Department of Justice often seemed more like a never-ending conflict between armed camps. Bill Clinton could hardly stomach his attorney general, Janet Reno, having to weather the blowback from her decisions regarding Ruby Ridge, a standoff and deadly overreaction between survivalists and the FBI; Waco, another botched standoff with a Christian cult; and the investigation of Dr. Wen Ho Lee, with the DOJ chastised for its reckless pursuit of a suspected spy. Clinton came very close to firing Louis Freeh, his FBI director, who openly criticized him, but managed to swallow his rage. Top people from the Bush White House, the FBI, and the Justice Department almost came to literal blows at the bedside of the ailing AG John Ashcroft—James Comey himself standing in the way of the White House representatives trying to get Ashcroft to renew a domestic surveillance program—with the White House finally having to back down. Under Obama, Comey, who by then was the FBI director, made a further grab for the FBI's independence from the Justice Department when he unilaterally decided to end and later reopen the Hillary Clinton email investigation—and, by doing so, arguably tossing the election to her opponent.

Enter Donald Trump, who had neither political nor bureaucratic experience. His entire working life was spent at the head of what was in essence a small family operation, one designed to do what he wanted and to bow to his style of doing business. At the time of his election, he was absent even any theoretical knowledge of modern government and its operating rules and customs.

Trump was constantly being lectured about the importance of "custom and tradition" at the Justice Department. As reliably, he would respond, "I don't want to hear this bullshit!"

He needed, one aide observed, "a hard, black line. Without a hard, black line that he can't cross, he's crossing it."

Trump believed what to him seemed obvious: the DOJ and FBI worked for him. They were under his direction and control. They must do exactly what he demanded of them; they must jump through his hoops. "He reports to me!" an irate and uncomprehending Trump repeated early in his tenure about both his attorney general Jeff Sessions and his FBI director James Comey. "I am the boss!"

"I could have made my brother the attorney general," Trump insisted, although in fact he did not even speak to his brother (Robert, a seventy-one-year-old retired businessman). "Like Kennedy." (Six years after John F. Kennedy appointed his brother Robert attorney general, Congress passed the Federal Anti-Nepotism Statute, called the "Bobby Kennedy law," to prevent exactly this sort of thing in the future—although that did not stop Trump from hiring his daughter and son-in-law as senior advisers.)

Efforts by anyone to explain the fine points of the relationship among various branches of government frustrated Trump and caused him to double down on his sense of righteousness and entitlement. He often felt that people were ganging up on him, which infuriated him even more. As had happened so many times before in his life, lawyers were out to get him. He couldn't get it out of his head: Comey, Mueller, Rosenstein, and McCabe were part of a club he did not belong to. "They talk to each other all the time," Trump would say. "They're totally in it together."

If the typical relationship between the president of the United States and his attorney general was necessarily cool, if not always strained, Trump had made it immeasurably worse. His public humiliation of Jeff Sessions—one of his first supporters in Congress—had turned Sessions into the Trump hater-in-chief. Trump was not only taunting Sessions, but threatening him, or, at least, as pointedly as possible, pressuring him to quit or to reverse his recusal. On several occasions the president directed McGahn to pressure Sessions to unrecuse himself. Trump urged many, if not all, of his aides to join this effort. Not long after Sessions had recused himself on Russia-related matters, the president directed Cliff Sims, a young West Wing staffer who had ingratiated himself with the president ("a weasel, who had weaseled his way in," in Bannon's description), and who, like Sessions, was from Alabama, to go to the attorney general's house on a Saturday morning and demand that he unrecuse himself. Bannon, in this instance, countermanded the president's directive to Sims.

If there was a world in which the attorney general, appointed by the president, might use his authority to take the tension between a president and the DOJ's prosecutors down a level or two, Jeff Sessions, swallowing almost daily abuse from the president, wasn't part of it. During one especially tense period, Sessions sent word back to the president that if he persisted with his badgering and threats, he would resign and recommend the president's impeachment.

* * *

In the days after the April 9 raid on Michael Cohen's office and home, the president was seething. Not only was the Justice Department against him, the DOJ was conspiring to strike him at his most vulnerable point—

his lawyer. Little matter that sometimes when Michael Cohen had, in the past, represented himself as Trump's "personal lawyer," Trump had meanly corrected, "He does PR for me."

And how had the Justice Department gotten its warrant to go after Cohen? On the one hand, Trump insisted the raid had nothing to do with him. It was all about Cohen's taxi business—and besides, the president declared, Cohen was mobbed up. On the other hand, he believed that the raid proved that the Justice Department had used any pretext to spread a net of wiretaps among people through whom the "deep state" might capture Trump's own conversations. In the Trump-centric view of the world, his own government—a permanent substructure of like-minded souls, somehow loyal to both Barack Obama and George Bush—was after him.

In a kind of curious and profound role reversal, many conservatives, in the past reflexively supportive of law enforcement, had become suspicious, if not paranoid, about government oversight and policing. As the Mueller investigation progressed, the conviction that the deep state existed and that it was out to get Trump had become embedded in right-wing culture; this conviction had been adopted, albeit begrudgingly, even by many standard-issue Republicans. It had become one of Fox News star Sean Hannity's main talking points, both on television and in private phone calls. "Sean's in crank land," observed Bannon, "but these are good bedtime stories for the president."

Likewise, many liberals, in the past antagonistic to the FBI, prosecutors, and the intelligence community, were now counting on government investigators to pursue Trump and his family relentlessly and, by so doing, protect democracy from ruin. On MSNBC, FBI agents had become gods. In the new liberal view of the world, figures in law enforcement, once deeply disdained, were enthusiastically embraced. People like James Comey, whose investigation of Hillary Clinton helped pave the way for Donald Trump's presidency, had become heroes of the Trump resistance.

* * *

On April 17, James Comey's book, *A Higher Loyalty*, was published. Comey and Stephen Colbert, the late-night comedian, clinked wineglasses (in fact, paper cups) on national television.

Among the book's other revelations, there were perhaps two notes that should have been especially worrisome for Donald Trump: its underlying theme of Trump's Mafia-like behavior, and the fact that Comey said nothing at all about the Trump Organization. If the former head of the FBI says you act like you're a Mafia don, that's a neon sign. And if he doesn't mention the organization at the center of your business and family life, then that's a tell: the organization is an FBI target.

Though the White House knew the book was coming, it was yet woefully unprepared for it—and unprepared for Trump's outsize reaction to it. Kellyanne Conway was quickly sent out to dispute the book, but instead focused on Comey's handling of the Clinton emails, quite implying that Comey had tipped the election to Trump—something you never wanted to say in the Trump White House, since the election could never be anything other than a decisive Donald Trump win.

An overriding characteristic of the Trump presidency was the fact that almost all conflicts became personalized. In this way, Comey, consumed by his own blood score after having been fired in such spiteful fashion, was a worthy adversary.

"Comey thinks I am stupid. I will show him how stupid I am if he thinks I'm stupid. I am so stupid I will screw all of them, that's how stupid I am," declared an oddly satisfied Trump in one late-night call to a New York friend. Comey's book, filled with his personal justifications, rather happily conformed to Trump's view that all feds were out of control and quite specifically after him. "I get these guys," Trump went on, seeing his enemies motivated by the same rapacity that motivated him. "I get it. Same old, same old. You go for the biggest name you can. I get that."

In some sense, Trump also saw the feds not in his role as president, an upholder of the nation's laws, but as a businessman who at any moment might catch their attention and run afoul of them. Throughout his long career in real estate, the feds had always been a danger to him and people like him. Federal prosecutors "are like cancer—colon cancer," Trump once told a friend who was having problems with the Justice Department.

But this did not mean, he pointed out, that he was, like many people he knew, afraid of the DOJ. There was a game here, one he believed he excelled at. He would simply be more intimidating than they were. "If they think *they* can get *you*, they will. If they think *you* might fuck *them*, they won't," he said, summing up his legal theory.

One of his most acute disappointments was the discovery that as president he could not control federal law enforcement. It was nearly beyond his comprehension that because he was president the feds were now a *greater* nuisance and threat.

The fault, however, was not his own. Nor was it the fault of the system or the structure of government. Trump placed the blame squarely on Jeff Sessions, his attorney general, repeatedly saying he should have given the AG job to Rudy Giuliani or Chris Christie, Trump's only two real pals in politics, "because they know how to play this game."

For good measure, Trump blamed the appointment of Sessions on Bannon, Sessions's longtime ally and supporter. "Fucked by him again. Fucked, fucked, *fucked*—so many times, so many times, so *many* times."

* * *

After John Dowd's departure, Trump turned his ire on Ty Cobb, the second of the over-the-hill lawyers the Trump White House had recruited in the summer of 2017, after failing to find top litigation teams. Trump heaped vast abuse on the sixty-eight-year-old attorney, not least because Cobb had a mustache. All mustaches annoyed Trump, but this one, with waxed ends, seemed particularly obnoxious to him. (In some not entirely clear logic of mockery, or possibly just a senior moment, Trump called Cobb—who bears the same name as a baseball great—Cy Young, the name of another baseball great.) And, to boot, the president was certain that Cobb was no match for the Mueller squad.

By early April, Trump had begun a daily series of call-and-response conversations about firing Cobb. "What should I do? I think I should fire Cobb. Do you think I should fire Cobb? I think I should."

He needed a killer lawyer. He asked this question of everyone: "Where's my killer lawyer?" Suddenly there was another push to find a major law firm with the resources to stand up to the United States government. But big firms have executive committees that carefully weigh the upside and downside of taking on difficult clients like Donald Trump. In this case, the downside—the likelihood of being publicly fired by Trump and then being stiffed for the bill—was just too great.

No matter. Trump didn't want a lawyer from a major law firm anyway. He wanted a killer lawyer. "You know," he would say, as though with precise specificity, "a killer."

In this, the law was not the law to him, but a battlefield, a theatrical one. And he knew just the type of killer-actor he wanted.

For several months now, Stormy Daniels, a porn star with whom he'd had a relationship, and whom Michael Cohen had theoretically handled with a payoff, had been in the news. Trump had little interest in Daniels, baldly lying to everyone, all of whom understood that he was lying to them, that his affair with Daniels had never happened.

But what he could not get enough of was Stormy Daniels's new lawyer, Michael Avenatti. The man was a killer. As important, he was terrific on television. Avenatti looked the part; he looked like he could play a lawyer on television. This was the kind of lawyer he wanted.

"He's a star," Trump said. That's what he needed if he was going to face this kind of pressure and these kinds of attacks. "Get me a star."

The corollary was that all of his little problems grew into big problems because he didn't have a lawyer like Avenatti—a lawyer who will do anything it takes. This line of thinking quickly turned into a dark self-pity: he became convinced that somehow all the killer lawyers were being kept from him.

* * *

"Dershowitz," Trump kept announcing, was "the most famous lawyer in the country." Then he would add, "Let's get Dershowitz."

Although Alan Dershowitz had long held a teaching position at Harvard Law School, retiring in 2014, he was regarded by many in his profession less as a legal scholar or practitioner than as a gadfly. He had inserted himself into a variety of public debates and high-profile cases, including those involving Patty Hearst, Mike Tyson, and O. J. Simpson. But if the books he wrote and the attention he garnered—from TV appearances and movie portrayals—did not enhance his reputation as a scholar, they created a type of celebrity that provided other value to him. His aggression, erudition, showmanship, and grandiosity had indeed turned him into one of the most famous lawyers in the nation. None of that necessarily made him a good lawyer, of course. "Whatever he advises, do the opposite," said one well-known, unsatisfied former Dershowitz client. But certainly Dershowitz was among the most brilliant and successful television lawyers in the country—and Trump, most of all, wanted someone who could play a lawyer on television. Acting, in his view, was the greater and more important legal skill.

Recently Dershowitz had gotten Trump's attention by arguing in a series of television appearances that the president of the United States was above the law, or anyway that he occupied a special, kingly sort of status. In early April, Dershowitz was invited to dinner at the White House to discuss representing the president. He was just the kind of lawyer the president thought he needed: an aggressive advocate who could argue his case on television.

Over dinner, Dershowitz asked for a retainer of a million dollars.

Trump, ever believing that part of the legal game was not paying your lawyers, told Dershowitz he would get back to him. But the conversation was over. Never in a million years would he pay a lawyer a million bucks up front!

* * *

Rudy Giuliani, the man once called "America's Mayor," had been out of office for seventeen years. In that time, he had been a failed presidential candidate, peripatetic speaker, toastmaster, rainmaker, consultant, and anything-for-a-six-figure-fee man. He was desperate, according to his client and longtime friend the former Fox News chief Roger Ailes, to get back to center stage.

Giuliani's first two marriages had been bad, but his third was far worse. To Giuliani's friends it was a topic that provoked constant incredulity and guffaws. Judy Giuliani relentlessly needled and belittled the former mayor.

"Poor Rudy, I never saw such a mess," said no less than his friend Donald Trump. Trump particularly disliked Judy Giuliani, ordering that she be kept away from him.

The desperation of the marriage had led, in Ailes's astounded view, to Giuliani's willingness to debase himself in hours of television appearances after the release of Trump's infamous grab-them-by-the-pussy tape.

"He will do anything to get out of the house," said Ailes.

But his loyalty to Trump was also real. Giuliani believed—with a sincerity that might not be felt by anyone else about Trump—that he owed Trump a debt of the heart. After Giuliani's second marriage imploded in 2000, a particularly awful public breakdown, Giuliani's children rejected him. His son Andrew's feud with him seemed unrelenting. But Andrew was a passionate teenage golfer; he even hoped to be a pro someday. Trump, hardly known for his empathy but nevertheless returning the many favors Giuliani had extended him as mayor of the city in which Trump was an active real estate developer, went out of his way to invite Andrew to play with him on Trump golf courses. Trump made the father's case to the son, with some positive results. Much later, Trump brought Andrew into the White House with the title of associate director for the Office of Public Liaison, granting him, along with a dozen or so other people, unescorted access to the Oval Office.

Giuliani's loyalty, together with his willingness to defy credulity and logic in the defense of Trump, incurred a debt that inclined Trump to give Giuliani a senior position in the new administration. During the transition, this inclination became an acute problem for everyone around the president-elect. Rudy was, in almost everyone's estimation—including, sometimes, Trump's—off. "Dementia," declared Bannon. "Plus he drinks too much," said Trump, who more than once during the campaign had told Giuliani to his face that he was "losing it."

This sense of Giuliani's offness was curiously ironic, since it bore an almost eerie similarity to Trump's own hysteria, grandiosity, and tendency to say almost anything that came into his head.

For many of the senior aides who worked on the transition team, excluding the seventy-four-year-old Giuliani from a top administration job was viewed as one of their singular accomplishments. "That was at least one bullet that we missed," said Trump's first chief of staff, Reince Priebus.

Giuliani—reportedly urged on by his wife, who had once imagined herself as the nation's First Lady—cooperated in the effort to deny him a role in the administration by insisting that the only job he would take was secretary of state. Even Trump appreciated the possibility that Giuliani might not be diplomatic enough for the position; instead, he urged him to take the attorney general spot. "I'm too old to go back to practicing law," a disappointed Giuliani told Bannon, who had brought him the news that the job of secretary of state was out.

But now a new opportunity had arisen, and on April 19, Giuliani, while far from the first choice, became, to the horror and astonishment of almost everyone around Trump, a cockeyed version of the killer lawyer the president had been searching for. This was a headline-grabbing entry in the you can't-make-this-stuff-up annals: Giuliani, the former boss of James Comey, would star in a comeback role in which he would take on both Comey and Mueller.

And the price was right: of course he would work for free, Giuliani told Trump.

In a series of rambling calls, Trump—whom Giuliani described to friends as "crying into the phone," while Trump described Giuliani as "begging for the job"—sought to persuade Giuliani that he needed to "get up there with Avenatti."

Once Giuliani arrived in the White House, the plan was for him to assemble a group of associates at his firm, Greenberg Traurig, which, together with his litigation partner Marc Mukasey (son of former Bush attorney general Michael Mukasey), would act as the president's legal team. Giuliani would be the public face of the president's defense, while the Greenberg Traurig group would be hard at work on the president's legal moves back at the office.

Greenberg Traurig, where Giuliani was less a working litigator than a procurer of business opportunities, thought otherwise. As with other law firms, the Greenberg Traurig management committee believed that defending Trump would be deeply unpopular in the firm, and, too, the firm's partners doubted that their bill would ever get paid.

Giuliani—determined if not desperate to take the job—decided to step down from his firm and defend the president on his own.

4

HOME ALONE

A raging and vengeful Trump might seem to be a constant presence in the White House, but in truth this Trump was often eclipsed by a lazy, disengaged, and even self-satisfied Trump—a seventy-one-year-old man fondly reviewing his own extraordinary performance and accomplishments.

"It might seem bad, really bad, but he can be as happy as a clam," said Ivanka Trump, describing her father's White House disposition to a friend.

This was the Trump bubble. Trump was incapable of admitting vulnerability—any at all. He could not acknowledge that his White House might be troubled or that he himself might be in peril. No one in a wide circle of acquaintances and colleagues had ever heard him express a regret, doubt, or wish to have acted any differently than the way he had acted. When Trump's bubble opened and anything less than adulation entered, someone needed to be blamed—and quite possibly fired.

But mostly the bubble stayed closed. One effect of Trump's mounting legal difficulties was that more and more people, fearful about their own exposure to these issues, avoided talking to him about his problems. Many of his late-night real estate buddies—Richard LeFrak, Steven Roth, and Tom Barrack, all of whom had served as voices of some measure of reality and practicality—were afraid of being called by Mueller. Trump's bubble was smaller and increasingly less penetrable: he was left, at night, in bed, eating his favorite candy bars—Three Musketeers—and talking to a slavish and reassuring Sean Hannity.

Trump could only be part of an organization that attended to him with unalloyed devotion; he could not really imagine another type. He insisted that the White House operate more like the Trump Organization, an enterprise dedicated to his satisfaction and committed to following and covering for his peripatetic and impulsive interests. Trump's management practices were entirely self-centered, not task-oriented or organizationally based. An outward focus, or focus of any sort, was not his concern or his method.

Barring a grievance that might strike him in the night, Trump arrived late to the office and then on most days enjoyed a lineup of staged meetings with a person or group in the Oval Office or Roosevelt Room, the purpose of which was to praise, congratulate, and distract him. And as his staff knew very well by now, a distracted Trump was a happy Trump.

When Trump was disengaged, the White House and greater executive branch were also happy. In this favorable environment, the political and bureaucratic professionals were able to move ahead with the work that Trump took no interest in—and Trump took no interest in a large majority of their work.

* * *

If Trump tended to be at his most cheerful when distracted, he was also liable to be in a good mood when in the midst of the personal crushes he regularly developed. Though they invariably passed, they were powerful in the moment. Michael Flynn had been a crush. Bannon had been one. Rob Porter and even Paul Ryan had had their day in the sun.

And then there was Rear Admiral Ronny Jackson, the White House doctor. Jackson would be nothing short of delirious when heaping flattery on the president. In his review of the president's health in January 2018, he professionally opined, "Some people have just great genes. I told the president that if he had a healthier diet over the last twenty years, he might live to be two hundred years old."

In late March, Trump had fired David Shulkin, the head of Veterans Affairs, and then nominated Jackson as his replacement. It was an odd choice—Jackson had no administrative experience, nor any professional engagement with veteran-related matters—but it was wholly in keeping with Trump's desire to reward friends and supporters. In the weeks that followed, Trump was only dimly aware that a cadre inside the White House had commenced a sophisticated campaign to undermine his nominee, a campaign that originated in the office of the vice president.

Trump had never warmed to his vice president—indeed, Mike Pence had annoyed him from the first weeks of his administration. (Pence was the governor of Indiana from 2013–17; for twelve years before that, he was a member of Congress.) Trump demanded subservience, but when he got it he was suspicious of the person providing it. The more Pence bowed, the more Trump tried to figure out his angle.

"Why does he look at me like that?" Trump asked about the way Pence seemed to stare at him near beatifically. "He's a religious nut," Trump concluded. "He was a sitting governor and was going to lose when we gave him the job. So I guess he's got a good reason to love me. But they say he was the stupidest man in Congress."

In June 2017, Bannon had helped install Nick Ayers—a young, disciplined, making-a-name-for-himself Republican political operative—as Pence's chief of staff. Pence, "our fallback guy," in Bannon's parlance, "who doesn't know where he is half the time," clearly needed help. The result was that Pence's office, led by Ayers, had become the most efficient operation in the West Wing.

This was not saying very much. By spring 2018, many of the individual fiefdoms around Trump were in a state of relative collapse. The chief of staff's office, given Trump's persistent animosity toward Kelly, was surely among the weakest in history. Kushner's various initiatives and power centers in the White House—notably the White House Office of American Innovation—had all flamed out. National Security Advisor H. R. McMaster, who had finally resigned in March, had for the better part of six months been nearly persona non grata in the West Wing, with Trump often performing McMaster imitations (a droning voice and heavy breathing). Marc Short and the congressional liaison office had been shunned by the president ever since the appropriations bill contretemps.

And the communications department was in ludicrous disarray. The three key figures—Mercedes Schlapp, the White House director of strategic communications; Sarah Huckabee Sanders, the press secretary (for Trump, the "Huckabee girl"); and Kellyanne Conway, with communications responsibilities largely unknown to everyone else—each tried to undermine the other on an hour to-hour basis, with Hope Hicks, an "on background" voice to the media, reliably zinging her former colleagues from outside the White House. "A catfight," Trump pronounced with some apparent satisfaction, as he handled a good part of the press outreach from his own cell phone.

The era of Reince Priebus, the chief of staff during the administration's first seven months, under whose reign the Trump White House seemed to have become a comedy of mismanagement, now rather looked like IBM in the 1950s compared to the current dysfunction. Amidst the breakdown, Pence's office could be depended on to execute White House business because of two people: Nick Ayers and Pence's wife, Karen.

Early in the administration, an article in *Rolling Stone* had quoted Pence referring to his wife as "Mother." The moniker stuck. Since then, Mrs. Pence has been known throughout the West Wing as Mother, and not with affection. She was seen as the power behind the vice presidential throne—the canny, indefatigable, iron-willed strategist who propped up her hapless husband.

"She really gives me the creeps," said Trump, who avoided Mrs. Pence.

Along with George Conway, Kellyanne Conway's husband, a top Wall Street litigator who tweeted derisively about the president, and John Kelly's wife, Karen Hernest, who had taken to buttonholing near strangers to express how much her husband hated the president, and Steve Mnuchin's wife, the former actress Louise Linton, who regularly offered the gag gesture, Mother was one more spouse who regarded the president with disbelief.

While Pence performed daily acts of obeisance to Trump and demonstrated an abject and almost excruciating loyalty, Ayers and Mother were anticipating the worst for the Trump presidency and positioning Pence as the soft landing if impeachment and expulsion or resignation came, an eventuality that Mother variously rated to friends as 60/40 either way. By April 2018, both Ayers and Mother believed the House would be swamped in November and that even the Senate majority was imperiled, giving rise to a new and vaunting ambition in the Pence orbit.

Trump, however, appeared to remain unaware of the Pence—or Pence family—perfidiousness. He had no inkling that the nomination of Admiral Jackson was about to become a test of the Mother–Ayers (and thus Pence) strength, and of the president's weakness.

Jackson—physician to the president in the Obama administration and now in the Trump White House—was the go-to doctor for the president, cabinet members, and senior staff, supervising the White House's on-site medical unit. Jackson was a popular get-along figure, not least because he was casual about prescribing medication. He kept the president stocked with Provigil, an upper, which Trump's New York doctor had long prescribed for him. For others, Jackson was regarded as a particularly easy Ambien touch. He got along especially well with the men—an "old-fashioned sort of drinker," in one description. He got along much less well with the women, accruing several complaints.

One woman he crossed was Mother.

During the first year of the Trump presidency, she had consulted Jackson about a gynecological problem. Jackson, participating in the general ridicule of the vice president's wife, was indiscreet about her issue. Mother soon learned about this breach, and her mortification and anger quickly turned into a determination for revenge.

Many of the leaks about Jackson's drinking, free hand with pills, and the harassment claims against him—which Trump began to blame on Democrats and other enemies, and which, by mid-April, were part of the daily Trump news cycle—came from Mother and Ayers. Before long, the nomination was strangled. Jackson withdrew his name from consideration on April 26.

"This was one of the most impressive things I've seen the West Wing do, lay the hit on the admiral," said Bannon. "They whacked that son of a bitch."

* * *

The Jackson affair could be read as an instance not so much of opposing Trump, or of being disloyal to him, but of getting on with the business at hand in spite of him. It often seemed as though Trump, remote from the technical operations of governing, glued to the television and obsessed by its moment-by-moment challenges and insults, did not really intersect with his own White House. Mother and Ayers took political revenge because they could. And while Ronny Jackson may have been Trump's pick, it was an idle pick. Jackson was certainly not part of any grand Trump plan, and, to boot, he had offended Mother, so why not whack him?

Still, despite Trump's inattention, the Jackson debacle inflamed his conviction that he should be able to appoint whomever he pleased. Appointments were a reliable hot button; opposition to his personnel choices seemed like a direct challenge. Confused to find that the power of the presidency had limitations, he came to see the limitations as his own—a sign of his own weakness. Veterans Affairs was a no-account little job, so why couldn't he appoint whomever he wanted? It was the White House standing in his way. It was Washington standing in his way. It was the whole gargantuan bureaucracy failing to support him.

Despite such feelings, many around Trump were surprised to record an unexpected character note: he wasn't paranoid. He was self-pitying and melodramatic, but not on guard. Negativity and betrayal always startled him. Narcissism, really, is the opposite of paranoia: Trump thought people were and should be protecting him. He was surprised, and all the more deeply wounded, to realize that he had to look after himself.

Here again, as with the spending bill, was a moment that delivered bitter instruction. Even Mike Pence, suck-up, did not have his back. When Ivanka explained the precise issue to him—Jackson's disrespect of Mrs. Pence—Trump chose to avoid that uncomfortable matter. Instead, he continued to dwell on the issue of his limited power. He was the president of the United States. Why couldn't he get what he wanted?

* * *

The problem was the White House itself. Its many personalities and power centers demanded a savvy and politesse and diplomacy and adroitness—indeed, a willingness to work with others—that, counter to everything in Trump's life, he was not now going to summon. The many empty billets at the White House were in part unfilled because of a lack of candidates; equally, however, Trump was unmoved to hire anybody.

The story of the past fifteen months had not been about a president strengthening his White House team, but about the attrition of the relatively weak team that Trump had been rushed into accepting. Almost the entire top tier of White House management had been washed out in little more than a year. Flynn, Priebus, Bannon, Cohn, Hicks, McMaster—all of these and so many others, gone. In some sense he had no chief of staff, no communications department, no National Security Council, no political operation, no congressional liaison office, and only a sputtering office of the White House counsel.

Those who remained or joined up seemed to better understand the rules: they worked for Donald Trump, not for the president of the United States. If you wanted to survive, you could not see this as an institutional relationship; instead, you needed to accept that you were serving at the pleasure of a wholly idiosyncratic boss who personalized everything. Mike Pompeo was so far succeeding because he seemed to have put down a big wager that his future lay in being subservient to Trump. Indeed, it was his guess that stoicism and holding his tongue might someday make him president. Meanwhile, Larry Kudlow, replacing Gary Cohn on the National Economic Council, and John Bolton, replacing H. R. McMaster, were perfect substitutes because they both desperately needed the job—Kudlow had lost his show on CNBC and Bolton had long been consigned to the foreign policy wilderness with little hope of escape.

These replacements aside, more than a year into the Trump administration, many White House jobs remained unfilled. The risks of legal costs were too high, the pain of working for Donald Trump too great, and the stain on one's career too evident.

Sometimes the West Wing could seem almost empty. Trump was as alone as he had ever been.

* * *

But really, did it matter? The only show that had ever worked for Donald Trump was a one-man show.

The White House Correspondents' Dinner, an annual celebrity event during which presidents traditionally roast a wide range of politicians and media people, and in turn find themselves roasted by a popular comedian, was set for April 28. The dinner was for Trump perhaps the singular example of not just the media's unending effort to gang up on him but, as he saw it, the media's insistent demand that he be deferential to them.

"I'm not a suck-up. Trump doesn't suck up. I wouldn't be Trump if I sucked up," he told a friend who argued that he would benefit from attending the dinner and telling some jokes about himself. He refused to go, saying, "Nobody even shows up anymore. It's dead."

As the event approached, he looked for ways to try to upstage it with a Trump rally, or at least try to compete with it, as he had done in 2017. He settled on a plan to travel to Washington, Michigan. Once the event was scheduled, the president's aides quickly realized that the rally would become a major political event: it would serve as the unofficial kickoff of the 2018 midterm campaign. So far largely inattentive to the looming midterms, Trump now cast himself as the central figure in the race.

On the evening of April 28, the comedienne Michelle Wolf heaped scorn, bile, and ad hominem cruelties on the president in front of a large and mostly appreciative crowd at the Washington Hilton Hotel. Meanwhile, in Michigan, Trump spoke for over an hour to a raucous rally at the Total Sports Park arena in Washington Township. His specific intent was to support Bill Schuette, Michigan's attorney general, a candidate running against Lieutenant Governor Brian Calley, who had committed the unpardonable sin of withdrawing his endorsement of Trump just before the 2016 election. The president offered a bare mention of Schuette near the beginning of his speech, then digressed into a long account, as vivid as it was demented, of all that he alone was up against.

After riffing for a while on several of his favorite topics—the American flag, the Wall, China, the stock market, North Korea—Trump took aim at Jon Tester, the senator from Montana who he believed was to blame for sabotaging Ronny Jackson's nomination for head of Veterans Affairs.

"I'll tell you, what Jon Tester did to this man is a disgrace. Admiral

Jackson started studying, and he was working so hard. I suggested it to him. You know, he's a war hero, a leader, a great, you know, he's a, admiral, a great, great guy, fifty years old, and he started studying, and then he started getting hit with vicious rumors, vicious, and the Secret Service told me, 'Just coming in, sir. We checked out all of those things, sir, they're not true.' They're not true, so they try and destroy a man.

"Well, they're doing it with us, they're trying their damnedest, but that, but a little—I want to thank, by the way, the House Intelligence Committee, okay? They do it with us, too. Russian collusion. You know, I guarantee you, I'm tougher on Russia, nobody ever thought. In fact, do you, have you heard about the lawyer for a year, a woman lawyer, she was like, 'Oh, I know nothing.' Now, all of a sudden, she supposedly is involved with government. You know why? If she did that, because Putin and the group said, 'You know, this Trump is killing us. Why don't you say that you're involved with government so that we can go and make their life in the United States even more chaotic?' Look at what's happened! Look at how these politicians have fallen for this junk. Russian collusion—give me a break!

"I'll tell you, the only collusion is the Democrats colluded with the Russians, and the Democrats colluded with lots of other people. Take a look at the intelligence agencies, and what about, hey, and what about Comey? You watch him on the interviews? 'Ah, ah, ah . . .' What about Comey? What about Comey? How about that? So Comey, how about this guy Comey? He said the other night—the fake, dirty dossier—he said the other night on Fox, he said, very strongly, 'No, I didn't know that it was paid for by the Democrats and Hillary Clinton.' He didn't know, he didn't know—how about that? They start something based on a document that was paid for by the DNC and Hillary Clinton. Honestly, folks, let me tell you, let me tell you, it's a disgrace. We got to get back down to business. It's a disgrace what's going on in our country, and they did that, they did that to Admiral Jackson. They are doing it to a lot of people.

"Innuendo. You know, in the old days, when the newspapers used to write, they put names down. Today they say, 'Sources have said that President Trump . . .' Sources! They never say who the sources are, they don't have sources. The sources don't exist, in many cases. They don't have sources and the sources in many cases don't exist. These are very dishonest people, many of them. They are very, very dishonest people. Fake news, very dishonest. But you watch Comey, and you watch the way he lies, and then he's got the memos. I wonder when he wrote the memos, right? Then he's got the memos and he puts them up. Watch the way he lies, it's the most incredible thing . . .

"By the way, by the way, by the way, is this better than that phony Washington White House Correspondents' Dinner? Is this more fun? I could be up there tonight smiling, like I love where they are hitting you, shot after shot. These people, they hate your guts, shot, and then I'm supposed to . . . [he smiles]. And you know, you have got to smile. And if you don't smile, they'll say, 'He was terrible, he couldn't take it.' And if you do smile, they'll say, 'What was he smiling about?' You know, there's no win . . ."

Trump, unbound and in his element, went on in this way for eighty minutes.

5

ROBERT MUELLER

Trump might often come to the brink of firing Mueller, but he kept stepping back from it, too. This was not so much restraint as a cat-and-mouse game: threatening to fire him and then not firing him was Trump's legal strategy. You were intimidated or you intimidated was Trump's legal theory. Several rounds of imminent Mueller-to-be-fired stories came from Trump's own direct leaks. "You've got to mess with them," he explained.

As the leak-free investigation continued—its silence among the most aberrant things in Trump's aberrant Washington—the special counsel came to be a sort of hologram in the West Wing, always there, but yet not there. Though the constant presence of Mueller's investigation often annoyed Donald Trump, its ghostly, amorphous quality also seemed to encourage him. He believed that if they had something, well, of course they would be leaking it.

"It's all chicken shit, what they have," said Trump shortly after the end of his first year in office to a friendly caller. "Chicken shit, chicken shit, chicken shit. When I say witch hunt"—the sobriquet he applied, often on a daily basis, to the Mueller investigation—"I mean chicken shit."

Trump believed he knew what he was doing. After all, he had been in litigation virtually nonstop for all of his professional life. His was a career of legal conflict. He believed he could spook the other side. Mueller was the kind of opponent he had always felt contempt for—a guy who played everything straight down the middle—and he knew just how to handle him. Everyone else might see Mueller's rectitude as his strength, but Trump saw it as his weakness.

"Remember," he told McGahn, "Mueller does not want to be fired. What happened to that guy Nixon fired? Saturday Night Massacre, sure. But do you remember the guy who got fired? No."

Mueller was a "phony," Trump said, a "joke," a guy who "thinks he's smart, but is not smart"—by which Trump meant not street-smart, not willing to do whatever it takes. "I know this kind of guy—acts tough but isn't."

* * *

Trump and Mueller had, curiously, parallel biographies. Parallel but, at the same time, mirror images of each other.

Trump was born in 1946 in New York; Mueller was born in 1944 in New York. Both descended from German immigrants who arrived in New York in the nineteenth century. Both grew up in the postwar years, their parents members of the exclusive and salubrious upper-upper-middle class.

But here the similarities ended. Trump was the son of one sort of American archetype: his father, Fred, who, with animal instincts, operated in what he viewed as a cutthroat and zero-sum world, believed in winning at all costs. Trump, from a very young age, meant to outdo him. Mueller was the son of another type: his father, a buttoned-down white-collar executive at DuPont, who, with 1950s sublimation, operated in a world in which success was inextricably bound up with not rocking the boat. And Mueller, from a very young age, meant to follow his father's example.

Robert S. Mueller III, Princeton class of '66, was a member of the last generation of Ivy League Republicans—moderate, establishment, upper-class Republicans. Since the 1960s, the Ivy League had inexorably transformed into a left-wing cultural club, but within modern memory its true self was better represented by the Bush family and other country club sorts. Its higher version was the Mueller family: unemotive WASPs, they eschewed personal vanity and were absent any feeling of entitlement. Bob Mueller was a scholar-athlete—an old-fashioned ideal combining brains

and muscle—at St. Paul's School in Concord, New Hampshire, he cap-
tained a sport every season. He was a figure to be found in certain novels
and stories of the 1940s, '50s, and '60s: John Knowles's *A Separate Peace*,
published in 1959, wherein the sense of class and propriety is already
passing; Louis Auchincloss's novels, about the pain and disappointments
of the American aristocrat; and short stories from the *New Yorker* of the
period that depicted a preppie stoicism and a constricted emotional life.
These were figures quite roundly mocked in later fiction.

Like his St. Paul's classmate John Kerry—future senator, presidential
candidate, and secretary of state—Mueller went to Vietnam after college
in 1968. The antiwar movement was shortly to sever any tradition of Ivy
League soldiers, and Kerry would rise to political prominence as an antiwar spokesman and build a career in liberal politics. But Mueller, with a
parallel career in government, managed somehow to remain at a remove
from the next forty years of cultural and political turmoil. "He was above
it or out of it—you couldn't necessarily tell which," said one DOJ colleague.

With only a tight circle of intimates, few people would learn much
about what he felt, what he believed, or what, if anything, he might want
to truly express. While some found him cryptic in a way that could be
construed as wise or brilliant, others often suspected he merely had nothing to say. He was arguably the most important modern FBI director:
stepping into the job just days before 9/11, he converted the FBI from
an organization focused on prosecuting U.S. crime to one focused on
fighting worldwide terror. And yet, Garrett Graff, whose book *The Threat
Matrix* chronicles the War on Terror and the making of a new FBI, finds
Mueller's public profile so modest that he appears to be little more than
"a sideline character."

Mueller's keen suspicion of personality became his personality. He
was a prosecutor in the old sense of representing the bureaucracy; he
operated by the book and never promoted his own independence, a kind
of anti-Giuliani. He had no press aptitude or interest and found it nearly
incomprehensible and morally troubling that anyone did. He was, in
the old nomenclature, a decent family man, married to his high school
sweetheart, the father of two children. In short, he was a hopeless square,

and he remained that way even as American culture sent squares to the dustbin of history—which, curiously, now made him a hero to left-wing, culturally hip, anti-Trump America.

In a notable change of practice, his ten-year term as FBI director was renewed in 2011 for an additional two years by Barack Obama. The two men, Obama aides report, neatly bonded, alike in their code of government service and personal virtue, their analytic approach to all problem solving, and their dislike of personal and professional drama.

It is difficult to imagine a greater opposite to Robert Mueller than Donald Trump. Possibly no two men of the same age and general milieu could be more different in outlook, temperament, personal behavior, and moral understanding. Possibly no two men better illustrated the difference between institutional weight and rules, and individual savvy, risk taking, and presumption. But it may not have so much been a clash of cultures as much as a simple mismatch: symmetrical against asymmetrical, earnest versus disruptive, restraint against all-in.

"He's got no game," Trump characterized Mueller to a friend.

When Steve Bannon appeared before the special counsel in January 2018—fifteen FBI agents and eight prosecutors crowding into the room to see Darth Vader—Mueller came in just before the deposition began. He walked directly to Bannon, greeted him in a gentlemanly way, and then said, wholly catching Bannon off guard, "I really think Maureen is going to enjoy West Point."

Bannon's daughter, Maureen, an army captain, had, unbeknownst even to her closest friends, just accepted a post at West Point. Recalled Bannon, "I'm thinking, 'Damn, what the fuck?'"

During the break, Bannon queried his lawyer Bill Burck: "What do you think that was about?"

"I know what it's about," said Burck. "He's saying, Don't ever forget that your daughter is one of us. He's telling you that *you're* one of us."

* * *

Almost immediately after his appointment in May 2017, Bob Mueller had recruited Andrew Weissmann, the Justice Department's chief of the criminal fraud division and its most experienced white-collar prosecutor.

Many believed Weissmann was the most aggressive white-collar prosecutor in the nation.

Donald Trump thought he knew all about Weissmann. He was a screw-up and a loser, said Trump. Weissmann had prosecuted Arthur Andersen, the Big Five accounting firm, in the Enron case. Weissmann had gotten a conviction and put one of the world's largest companies, with eighty-five thousand employees, out of business. And then the conviction had been overturned. That, Trump said, was a business tragedy, and Weissmann should have been disbarred. The president called him "Arthur Weissmann."

To the degree that the Andersen case might have tainted Weissmann, it also reinforced his reputation for waging total war. For Weissmann, overreach was something of a philosophical belief: in his view, white-collar criminals were trying to beat the system, so the system had to beat them. And Donald Trump's entire life and career were about beating the system.

By March 2018, Mueller's team was contemplating an audacious move. In an initiative led by Weissmann, the special counsel's office laid out an indictment of the president. The proposed indictment provided a virtual road map of the first year of Trump's presidency.

There were three counts in "UNITED STATES OF AMERICA - against - DONALD J. TRUMP, Defendant." The first count, under Title 18, United States code, Section 1505, charged the president with corruptly—or by threats of force or threatening communication—influencing, obstructing, or impeding a pending proceeding before a department or agency of the United States. The second count, under section 1512, charged the president with tampering with a witness, victim or informant. The third count, under section 1513, charged the president with retaliating against a witness, victim or informant.

According to the draft indictment, Donald Trump's scheme to obstruct justice began on the seventh day of his administration. It traced the line of obstruction from National Security Advisor Michael Flynn's lies to the FBI about his contacts with Russian representative, to the president's efforts to have James Comey protect Flynn, to Comey's firing, to the president's efforts to interfere with the special counsel's investigation, to his attempt to cover up his son and son-in-law's meeting with Russian governmental agents, to his moves to interfere with Deputy Director of the FBI Andrew McCabe's testimony and, as well, to retaliate against him. The indictment also spelled out what the special counsel considered the overriding theme of Trump's presidency: since the beginning of his tenure, Trump had gone to extraordinary lengths to protect himself from legal scrutiny and accountability, and to undermine the official panels investigating his actions.

Since Watergate, now forty-five years ago, the question of whether prosecutors could haul a sitting president into court and try him for breaking the law like an ordinary citizen had hovered around the edges of constitutional theory and White House scandals. The Office of Legal Counsel, a little-known adjunct to the Justice Department that supplies legal advice to the attorney general, had, during Watergate, and after the Clinton-Lewinsky scandal, offered an opinion that a sitting president could not be indicted. Although this was far from a legal prohibition or a court ruling against the indictment of a president, it had become the default position, not least because no one had ever tried to indict a president.

In some constitutional circles, the question of whether a president could be indicted provoked quite a raging debate. Over the objections of many liberals, Ken Starr, the independent counsel investigating Bill Clinton, argued that the Constitution did not immunize a sitting president from indictment, and that like any other citizen or federal official, he or she was subject to indictment and criminal prosecution. Some had called Starr's position overreach.

* * *

By the end of March, the Mueller team had not only the particulars of the proposed indictment but a draft of a memorandum of law opposing the "defendant's"—that is Donald Trump's—anticipated motion to dismiss his indictment.

The memorandum explicitly contradicted the standing opinion issued by the Office of Legal Counsel. Nowhere, it argued, does the law say the president cannot be indicted; nowhere is the president accorded a different status under the law than other federal officials, all of whom can be indicted and convicted as well as impeached. The Constitution is precise in the immunity it grants—and there is none provided for the president.

"The Impeachment Judgment Clause, which applies equally to all civil officers, including the President," argued the brief, "provides that a civil officer may be impeached and removed from office but that the Party convicted shall nevertheless be liable and subject to Indictment, Trial, Judgment, and Punishment, according to law.

"The Impeachment Judgment Clause takes for granted . . . that an officer may be subject to indictment and prosecution before impeachment. If it did not, the clause would be creating, for civil officers, precisely the immunity the Framers rejected."

The argument was clear and basic. There was no statutory exception from the law for the president; quite the opposite, in fact, since the entire Constitutional framework made clear that the president was not above the law in any respect. Impeachment was a remedy that could be used against all civil officers of the United States, but it did not protect them from indictment; hence, the impeachment clause should not protect the president from indictment. The so-called balancing argument—that the burden of a criminal process on the president would interfere with his ability to carry out his elective duties—was specious because the weight would be no greater than the significant burden involved with an impeachment proceeding.

* * *

But Bob Mueller had not risen to the highest levels of the federal government by misconstruing the limits of bureaucratic power. Indeed, he was among the government's most accomplished players.

On an almost daily basis, Mueller and his staff continually weighed the odds that the president would fire them. The very existence of the special counsel's investigation had in a sense become the paramount issue of the investigation itself. Shutting it down, or delaying it, or damaging it was, in an underappreciated irony, the natural next step by the president or his chosen surrogate, given the obstruction case that the Mueller team was building against him.

Throughout the winter and spring of 2018, while piecing together an obstruction case against the president, the special counsel's office was trying to get up to speed on this potential ultimate act of obstruction. What it learned was not reassuring.

"Can President Trump order Sessions to withdraw the special counsel regulations (and fire him if he doesn't)?" asked one of the memos circulated internally.

"The short answer is yes," concluded the team's research. Even though he had recused himself from the investigation, Attorney General Sessions could repeal the special counsel regulations and open the way for Trump to fire Mueller directly.

The only thing that seemed to stand in the way of such a drastic move was fear of a repeat of Nixon's Saturday Night Massacre; firing the special counsel could cause a domino drama of resignations and firings that might backfire despite a Republican Congress, and, in turn, damage Republican chances in the midterms. Indeed, Mitch McConnell, willing to do nearly anything to protect his Senate majority, sent dark warnings to the White House that the Senate could not be counted on to stand with the president if he acted recklessly toward Mueller.

But a fear of drama, or of unintended consequences, or of McConnell's nervousness, could obviously not be considered among the overarching concerns of this president. What's more, the drama might be limited if Trump could avoid everybody else's fears and dithering and just fire Mueller directly. Was that possible?

It was in fact possible, the Mueller research concluded: "The president could fire the special counsel directly and justify that action by arguing that the special counsel regulations are unconstitutional insofar as they limit his ability to fire the special counsel." That, the research argued, would likely be found to exceed presidential authority. But "there is at least some chance the president's actions could be upheld if reviewed in court—especially because the relevant regulations [governing the office of the special counsel] were never enacted by Congress into the U.S. code."

The special counsel, as it turned out, was a weirdly fragile and iffy construct.

Asked another of the Mueller team's existential memos: "What happens to the special counsel's office, staff, records, pending investigations, and grand juries reviewing the evidence presented if the special counsel is fired, or, alternatively, if his investigation is discontinued?"

The short answer: "The question does not lend itself to a conclusive answer grounded in statute or case law." And then the research hammered the point: "For better or worse, there is no statute or authoritative case law that neatly delineates the effect that . . . termination would have on this office, staff, pending investigations, and investigative materials." Overnight, the entire operation might be dismantled and its work shredded.

Still, there could be a window of time during which the special counsel might be able "to share grand jury materials with fellow prosecutors for the purpose of enforcing federal criminal law." In fact, that process—moving part of the investigation, such as the Michael Cohen case, to the Southern District of New York—had already begun, both to protect the case if Mueller was fired and to anticipate any criticism of overreach by the special counsel.

And then there was the looming July 1 deadline. That's when Mueller's budget request was due—ninety days before the beginning of fiscal year 2019. The attorney general—or, with his recusal, the deputy attorney general—had the unilateral right to refuse this budget request and shut down the special counsel's investigations as of September 30, 2018.

True, Deputy AG Rod Rosenstein, who had told Congress that he would not carry out a presidential order to remove Special Counsel Mueller absent "good cause," would, according to this hopeful perspective, "be concerned about the political fallout that would accompany" a decision to defund the office. On the other hand, the president was regularly threatening to fire Rosenstein.

But what if the budget request *was* refused and the investigation shut down? "If the special counsel's office is shuttered it is possible, and perhaps likely, that the mandate of any special grand jury impaneled by Special Counsel Mueller would expire and prompt the court to discharge it."

And, just as possible, the work product would be headed, via shredder, to the dustbin.

Still, the research went on to describe a more hopeful scenario: "It is also possible that another 'authorized attorney for the government,' most likely a U.S. attorney's office, would continue the grand jury investigation, in which case the court would not necessarily discharge the grand jury."

And what if the worst did happen? What if the president fired the special counsel? Or if there was a systematic massacre of the chain of command responsible for the investigation? Could anybody fight back? Alas, neither an attorney general nor a deputy attorney general could fight their own removal, because they are both appointed by the president, the special counsel's research concluded.

The questions kept coming. Could the special counsel, because he was not a presidential appointee, challenge his own firing? Almost certainly not, because there is "no private right of action" under the special counsel regulation. Reaching, he might claim a constitutional violation—that his firing was, itself, an instance of obstruction of justice. Furthermore, members of Congress might have standing to sue, the special counsel's research theorized. Maybe even individual members of the special counsel's staff could sue. Or perhaps there might be "third-party standing"—such as the American Bar Association or Judicial Watch—that is, grounds for an exception to be made to the rule that a plaintiff cannot bring suit to assert the rights of others. But by this point there was a dwindling set of possibilities, the research suggested, and mostly only tortured scenarios.

Pages and pages of research explored many different scenarios involving any attempt to shut down the special counsel and his operation. But the truth of the matter was straightforward: as long as the president had the continued support of the majority party in Congress, he held a very strong, and likely winning, hand.

* * *

On May 2, after drinks at a midtown restaurant, Rudy Giuliani went on *Hannity* for one of the most peculiar television appearances in modern politics, combining, in an eighteen-minute interview, the nonsensical and incoherent. Here was a bar-stool lawyer delivering the president's legal strategy.

"I know James Comey. I know the president. Sorry, Jim, you're a liar—a disgraceful liar," said Giuliani to Hannity. "It would have been good for God if God had kept you out of being head of the FBI."

He rambled on: "Look at what's going on with North Korea. I told the president, you're going to get the Nobel Peace Prize."

And: "I believe, I believe that Attorney General Sessions, my good friend, and Rosenstein, who I don't know, I believe they should come in the interest of justice, end this investigation."

And: "I'm not going to have my client, my president, my friend, and a president that's achieved more in a year and a half against all odds than anyone had a right to expect—I'm not going to let him be treated worse than Bill Clinton, who definitely was a liar under oath . . . I mean, he's being treated much worse than Hillary Clinton . . . I'm not going to let him be treated worse than Hillary Clinton."

And: "I'm sorry, Hillary, I know you're very disappointed you didn't win, but you're a criminal."

Bannon was horrified by Giuliani's performance. "Dude, you can't do this," Bannon told Hannity afterward. "You can't let him out there like that."

"I'm not the babysitter," Hannity replied.

"It's Rudy. You've got to be."

But Giuliani wasn't done. A few days after the *Hannity* appearance, Giuliani was interviewed by ABC's George Stephanopoulos. Giuliani denied Trump's relationship with Stormy Daniels and, at the same time, acknowledged that Trump had paid her.

"What matters to me are two things," Giuliani told Stephanopoulos. "There are two relevant legal things, which is what my job is. Number one, it was not a campaign contribution because it would have been done anyway. This is the kind of thing that I've settled for celebrities and famous people. Every lawyer that does that kind of work has. And number two, even if it was considered a campaign contribution, it was entirely reimbursed out of personal funds, which I don't think we'll even get to, because the first one's enough. So . . . case closed—case closed for Donald Trump."

Watching the show, Bannon remarked that Stephanopoulos had been almost gentle with Giuliani. "Stephanopoulos could have destroyed him, but you realize he's a cripple. How can you kick the guy?"

Bannon shook his head in wonder. "Drinking aside, guys'll tell you that Rudy can't engage in a real conversation. You see that by the facial tics, the big eyes, and the asides like he's speaking to himself while he's telling you some bombshell information. Come on: Rudy's wife, future First Lady or at least, she imagined, Queen of Foggy Bottom, ain't walking away from this unless she knows there's no more squeeze in the lemon. It's mind-boggling."

* * *

Even Trump was bewildered by Rudy.

He was glad to see that Giuliani had embraced the nullifying legal theories with which Alan Dershowitz had so impressed the president in his many cable interviews: *There could be no criminal liability for a president exercising his constitutional powers, no matter the reason he was exercising them. If the president chose to fire someone, the Constitution gave him the authority to fire, period. Even if the president was firing this person as part of, say, a cover-up scheme, there was no issue. Absolute presidential powers were absolute.*

But Dershowitz's theory about presidential impunity seemed peculiar in Giuliani's mouth. As the U.S. attorney for the Southern District of New York, he had made his reputation—and later his political career—on law-and-order cases and prosecutions that took down the powerful. Famous for his take-no-prisoners approach, he was quite the opposite of a wily, intellectually deft, morally relativist defense attorney. But now, suddenly, he seemed desperate to play this part.

Trump, ever fixated on physical details, kept rerunning Giuliani's television performances and pointing out his "crazy, crazy eyes." Trump also commented on his weight, which was climbing toward three hundred pounds, and his unsteady gait. "He looks like a mental patient," said Trump.

To almost everyone in the White House—and especially to Don McGahn—Giuliani's defense of the president was as wacky as it was alarming. Trump found himself in the unlikely role of trying to calm Giuliani down and, as well, to get him to stop drinking so much.

And yet, somehow, the more Giuliani seemed to come unhinged, the further he volubly traveled from conventional legal strategy, the more he seemed to be moving the needle away from the special counsel and in Trump's favor. The sheer force of his assertions, together with an almost madcap confusion created by Giuliani's off-the-cuff utterances, opened a new front. It was not a legal front but a television front. On the one hand was the special counsel—mum, plodding, buttoned-down, prosaic, utterly establishment. On the other was Rudy and Trump—improvisational, unpredictable, audacious, always a spectacle. How to predict what crazy men will do?

Abruptly there was a new sense in the White House of Giuliani's quite inexplicable genius. Rudy was crazy, but crazy was working. Rudy was executing pitch-perfect Trump. He manically put up a defense that was nonsensical, outlandish, fatuous, and hyperbolic. But in terms of pure theatricality, it bested and belittled the small-bore technical points of law. In Trump's long career as a litigant, bravado and confusion had always paid a substantial dividend. Now Rudy was gleefully executing exactly that strategy.

The silent prosecutor, toiling in anonymity, was on the defensive. Maybe the special counsel would be fired—maybe at any moment. As Trump liked to say, ever building suspense, Who knows what will happen? In Giuliani's new interpretation of the law, whatever happened would be precisely what the president wanted to happen. The president, according to a brazen, dismissive, garrulous Giuliani, held all the cards, and he would decide when and how to play them.

As it happened, Mueller saw the situation much the same way.

* * *

In a world where no one knew the rules—or, for that matter, who might have the power, after the midterm elections, to set them—almost any claim was potentially valid.

Giuliani's former partner and sidekick Marc Mukasey heard a rumor about the plan to indict the president. It would take Rod Rosenstein, in his role as the person overseeing the investigation, to approve the plan. To do so, the deputy attorney general would have to overrule the DOJ's office of legal counsel's opinion that a president could not be indicted.

Then again, you could hardly overstate how much Rosenstein abominated Trump. Trump was a con man, the prosecutor told friends. Trump was a liar. Trump was unfit.

Yet on May 16, relying on what reasoning nobody seemed quite able to imagine, or a direct line to God that no one knew he had, Giuliani declared that there would be no indictment of the president. And he went further, saying that the special counsel's office—pay no attention to the indictment papers it had already drawn up—had told him that it agreed with the Justice Department's standing opinion that a president could not be indicted.

This was a half-cocked, perhaps drunken Giuliani. Or a canny, asymmetric one. Or both.

Giuliani's gambit—to publicly announce a legal position held by the special counsel—served as a kind of taunt. Now Mueller faced a choice. He could either publicly disagree with the president's lawyer and, thereby, open the door and step into the political debate. Or he could remain quiet, continuing to keep his own counsel, and let everyone tacitly assume that what Giuliani said was true. Indeed, in the coming months almost every expert and media outlet blandly accepted that the president was not in danger of indictment.

* * *

As much as Andrew Weissmann wanted to indict the president, Bob Mueller wanted to stay in business. And as much as the Trump lawyers wanted to believe that a president could not be indicted, they appreciated that their client could be the exception.

Delay became the tool of both sides.

From Trump's point of view, if the administration reached the midterms—which Trump still blithely assumed he and the Republicans would win—without Mueller having moved against the president, then he could fire Mueller, no problem. The Mueller team believed that if they reached the midterms without being fired and the Democrats won the House, then their investigation was home free.

In a conference call with Trump's lawyers toward the end of April, members of the Mueller team had outlined the areas of interest in which they sought to question the president. Jay Sekulow then turned the points raised by the special counsel into a list of specific questions—and then leaked them, as though these were in fact the special counsel's questions.

While this appeared to indicate that a showdown was coming, in some sense it was designed, on the part of both the prosecutors and Trump's lawyers, to have the opposite effect: to caution Trump and stop him from going full speed ahead. For both sides, raising the prospect of the president testifying—and the absolute certainty on the part of everybody other than the president that unrestricted testimony would sink him—was a delaying tactic.

If the list of questions did not entirely dissuade Trump, they at least gave him pause. Even so, the determined, loquacious, ever confident president believed there was no room anywhere that his presence and persuasive powers could not sway. Nor, certainly, would he admit to any measure of fear. His lawyers might be afraid, but never him. He was, in his mind, a master salesman, an artful seducer, the most charming man on earth. When necessary, he wouldn't hesitate to employ boot-licking flattery to achieve his ends. He could convince anyone of anything.

This approach may have worked well for Trump in New York, where the currency was salesmanship. But in Washington it had in the thousand instances when Trump had tried to apply his irresistible Trump charm succeeded, by Bannon's count, exactly never.

Here were the terms of the de facto truce: as long as the special counsel and his people did not press him too far, the president would not yet confront them. And as long as Trump still had the power to carry out his threats to annihilate Mueller's team, they would not yet confront him. Limbo held—for now.

6

MICHAEL COHEN

B annon often recounted, with continuing astonishment, the many times the president "looked me in the eye and lied," and how he invariably did this with maximal sangfroid and aplomb.

The pee-tape episode was a formative lesson.

The U.S. intelligence chiefs, on January 6, 2017, two weeks before the inaugural, had come to Trump Tower to brief the president-elect on some of the nation's key secrets. James Comey, the director of the FBI, then stayed behind and informed Trump about the existence of the Steele dossier, a report prepared by Christopher Steele, a British intelligence operative, and largely funded by the Democrats. The report—a raw file of rumors and speculation that was already circulating among various U.S. press outlets, one or more of which would likely publish it soon—said the Russians had information that could compromise Trump. This purportedly included video and audio recordings of scenes that took place in the room where Trump was staying at the Moscow Ritz-Carlton hotel in 2013 during the Miss Universe Pageant—most especially images of prostitutes urinating on the king-size bed, the same bed that Barack and Michelle Obama had slept in when they had visited Moscow.

Not long after the briefing, an angry and resolute Trump sat Bannon down. With powerful, forthright assurance and dead-on eye contact,

Trump declared that this was preposterous—and in fact impossible. The reason was simple: he hadn't stayed overnight in the hotel. After his plane had landed that day, he—along with Keith Schiller, his security aide—had gone from the airport to the Ritz Carlton to change his clothes, then to the pageant and dinner, and then back to the plane.

"That story was told to me a dozen times, maybe more, verbatim, and the details never changed," Bannon recalled. "It was only later that I found out that story is correct except for one small difference: they came over a day earlier. They arrived on Friday morning, not Saturday morning, they were there for an entire day—and that's when the girls got sent over and Keith, now in the revised telling, sent them away."

Also on Bannon's list of whoppers was Trump's assertion that he had never spent a night with the porn star Stormy Daniels. "Never happened," he told Bannon. He also lied about the payoff to Daniels: he had no idea. Both denials would, in short order, implode.

His lies, Bannon came to understand, were compulsive, persistent, and without even a minimal grounding in reality. Once, imperturbably denying the undeniable, Trump told the Fox News anchor Tucker Carlson that it was in fact not him on the grab-them-by-the-pussy tape—just trickery to make him look bad.

Understanding that the president was a barefaced liar left his aides with a nearly continuous sense of alarm and foreboding. But the trait also helped define Trump's strength: lying was a powerful tool in his arsenal. Politicians and businesspeople dissemble and misrepresent and spin and prevaricate and mask the truth, but they prefer to avoid out-and-out lying. They have some shame, or at least a fear of getting caught. But lying willfully, adamantly, without distress or regret, and with absolute disregard of consequences can be a bulwark if not a fail-safe defense. It turns out that somebody always believes you. Fooling some of the people all of the time defined Trump's hard-core base.

Trump's constant lies forced the people around him to become complicit in those lies, or, at the very least, sheepish bystanders to them. Sarah Huckabee Sanders, the White House press secretary, had developed a particular pained and immovable expression when called on to repeat and defend the president's lies.

Kellyanne Conway, for her part, took a literal, almost moralistic position. If the president said something, the mere fact that he had said it meant that the statement deserved to be defended. In this, like a lawyer (and she was a lawyer), she could defend the statement because her client had not told her it was untrue.

Conway, in fact, had perfected the art of satisfying Trump while running from him. She had come into the White House professing her desire "to be in the room," but she survived by never being in the room, understanding that the room is where Stalin kills you.

Kellyanne Conway's defense of the president's lies had additionally seemed to bring her into a public confrontation with her husband, George Conway, a partner at the Wall Street firm Wachtell, Lipton, Rosen & Katz, one of the wealthiest and most prestigious in the country. Conway found himself under enormous pressure from his firm to distance himself from Trump and his lies; he accomplished this, apparently at his wife's expense, through Twitter, offering a running commentary on the president's falsehoods and misrepresentations regarding his legal position. Conway's stream of tweets became something of a new political genre, the spouse commentary.

In fact, the Conways' public disagreement was, some acquaintances and colleagues believed, itself a lie, one in which the couple conspired to distance themselves from Trump's lies. "They are of one mind about Trump," said a friend of the couple's. "They hate him." The husband would take a moral stand, protecting his own reputation and law firm partnership, while the wife, who privately professed to be aghast at Trump, continued to defend her client. The Conways had an $8 million hotel-size house near the Kalorama neighborhood in Washington, not far from Jared and Ivanka's house, a manse that the couple very much liked. The neighborhood, reliably anti-Trump, gave the cold shoulder to Jared and Ivanka. George Conway's public objections to the president helped keep the neighbors happy.

Still, while Trump's adamant falsehoods unnerved his aides, they also reassured. Neither evidence nor logic would force the president into an admission. He would hold like the toughest barnacle to his lies.

On the part of many in the White House, there was a constant fear, if not assumption, that some piece of irrefutable evidence would eventually surface and cause severe, perhaps fatal, damage. What if, for instance, someone actually produced a copy of the pee tape? Not to worry, said those who knew him best: even in such a predicament, Trump would not only deny it but convince a good part of the electorate to embrace his denial. It would be his word against a fake video.

The truth would not be shaken loose from him. You could count on him: no matter what the circumstances, Trump would never be beaten into submission. It was his word against, sometimes, everybody else's, but it was his word and he would never waver from it.

One could argue that Trump's métier—indeed, his primary business strategy—was lying. Trump Tower, Trump Shuttle, Trump Soho, Trump University, the Trump Casinos, Mar-a-Lago—all these enterprises were followed by a trail of claims and litigation that told a consistent story of borderline and often outright fraud. Broke in the 1990s, he somehow returned a few years later to billionaire status—hell, a billionaire ten times over!—at least in his telling. He *was* a con man, but that was not the surprising part. The surprising part was that Trump, in the face of the obvious, could so steadfastly deny the drumbeat of particulars regarding his dubious dealings and malfeasance. Very little about him was real, and yet he managed to be at least halfway believed by enough people so that he could continue the con.

This was where he really shone: he always stayed in character. When a person who is the target of multiple investigations remains outwardly untroubled, the effect is quite extraordinary. Such apparent coolness under fire fully exploits, to an almost unimaginable degree, the concept of innocent until proven guilty. Trump believed he would never be proven guilty; therefore, he was innocent. And he carried the total confidence and even serenity of the innocent—or at least of someone who knows how difficult it is to establish the guilt of a person capable of admitting nothing, of never wavering. The fact that he had stayed out of jail showed, impressively for many, how easily the system could be played. Seen from this point of view, he really might be a genius.

Through it all, Trump remained indomitable. He might complain that the accusations against him were outrageous, but he never seemed less than sanguine about the eventual outcome.

"I always win," he frequently declared. "I know how to handle it." Or, another favorite: "I never blink."

* * *

Trump modeled his business organization on a criminal enterprise: the truth needed to be contained in a tight circle—that was the secret sauce. Trump measured loyalty, that significant currency of his business and walk-on-the-wild-side lifestyle, by who was so dependent on him, and as clearly exposed as he was, that they would of course lie for him.

The inspiration here was mobster life. Trump not only knew mobsters, and did business with them, he romanticized them. Mobsters had more fun. He would not conform to behavior that respectability demanded; he would go out of his way *not* to be respectable. Trump was the Dapper Don; it was a joke he embraced. His New York, his era of nightlife and prizefights—with Roy Cohn, the gold standard of Mob lawyers, by his side—was a Mob heyday.

Hence the special nature of his inner circle at the Trump Organization. They were all truly *his*: his executive assistant (holding the title of senior vice president), Rhona Graff; his accountant, Trump Organization CFO Allen Weisselberg; his lawyers, Michael Cohen and Marc Kasowitz; his security man, Keith Schiller; his bodyguard, Matt Calamari, eventually elevated to Trump Organization COO; his children. Later, in the White House, Hope Hicks would join this trusted circle, as would Corey Lewandowski.

This was extreme codependence. You became an extension of DJT, a part of the strange organism that, daily, demonstrated an uncanny ability to survive every threat.

* * *

One person who became a part of this organism a dozen years before Trump became president was Erik Whitestone, a young sound engineer in New York City. Whitestone worked for Mark Burnett, the TV producer who in 2004 launched *The Apprentice*, the reality show that presented the virtually bankrupt Trump as a supremely successful businessman—and made him world famous. In the first week of production, Whitestone was assigned the job of putting the microphone up Trump's shirt. Given the physical proximity this task required—you had to reach under the jacket and shirt—everyone else on the production team had resisted it. Trump, with his size, height, and glowering demeanor, was not only off-putting; for no clear reason, he would unzip his pants and pull them down partway, exposing tighty-whities. "It was like sticking your head in the lion's mouth," said Whitestone, who found himself stuck with the job.

Not long after the show's production got under way, Whitestone, now on permanent Trump-mic duty, took a day off and someone else, an African American sound technician, was given the assignment. Trump flipped out.

A frantic Burnett found Whitestone at home. Trump had barricaded himself in the bathroom. "Donald won't go on until you get here," said Burnett. "So get here immediately!"

An hour later, Whitestone came rushing in to find Trump screaming from behind the bathroom door. "Erik, what the fuck, they tried to fuck me up . . . They put dirty fingerprints on my collars, they tried to fuck up my tie."

Once the day's filming was over, Burnett took Whitestone aside. "Dude, from now on, all you do is deal with Donald," said Burnett, turning Whitestone into *The Apprentice*'s official Trump whisperer.

After that, every single morning of the shooting season, for the next fourteen years, Whitestone would show up at Trump's apartment and meet Keith Schiller, becoming a constant shadow presence in Trump's life—"countless hours sitting in his apartment," as he put it.

Reflecting on the experience, Whitestone said, "I was with him so intimately for such a long period of time he'd get kind of sentimental: 'Erik, you're like a son to me and I have a son named Eric, isn't that weird?'"

It was a no-intimacy intimacy. Trump would offer Whitestone gifts of things that he had gotten for free, such as products from the Art of Shaving, a kitschy men's line. Trump turned everyone into a family member, at the same time offering a running commentary on his family's flaws. "He kept saying how much he wished he'd never given Don Jr. his name and wished he could take it back," recalled Whitestone.

Once, riding in his limo, Trump had a sudden inspiration. "'Erik, I'm going to write your father a letter about what a wonderful guy you are.' And a week later, Rhona called and asked for my parents' address. And two weeks later my dad calls and says, 'I got a great letter from Mr. Trump about what a wonderful guy you are. I think I'll write him back.' The show wrapped and I didn't see Trump for about four months. And then I walk into his office and he's like, 'Erik, I got a letter from your dad.' And he recited verbatim from a letter he got four months ago. 'Your father agreed with me that you're a great guy.'"

Trump did favors for Whitestone—or, anyway, got other people to do them. Michael Cohen, for instance, got Whitestone's child into private school in New York.

Whitestone became what everyone around Trump had to become— long-suffering—because Trump was always ready to explode with anger. "It's not your fault," said Whitestone. "It's just your turn, was how we put it."

"How's the weather?" was the code for the boss's mood.

But Trump was a simple machine. Whitestone understood his singular interests—sports and girls—and learned they could be used as reliable distractions.

"If he was in a bad mood and we were going from office to boardroom—we had to go through the Trump Tower lobby—with these eastern European tourists looking at the waterfall—'God's urinal,' he called it—I would scan for an attractive woman. 'Hey,' I'd say, 'at six o'clock.'"

Girls were the constant. "'Erik, go get her, and bring her up.' And so, me: 'Mr. Trump wants to know if you want to come up and see the boardroom.' He'd hug them and grope them and send them on their way."

Riding in the limo, "He'd just roll down the window and say 'What's up?' to the ladies. 'Hello, ladies . . .' to two hot girls. 'That was fun,' he'd say, 'remind me to do that again.'"

Once, coming back from Chicago, a young woman, an attractive interior designer who was pitching Trump on a project, hitched a ride on

Trump's plane. "He led her into the bedroom with a mirrored ceiling . . . She comes out, half an hour later, dress ripped off, staggering out, she sits in the seat . . . and then he comes out with his tie off, shirt untucked, and says, 'Fellas . . . just got laid.'"

There was always one or another of Trump's assistants in the car with him. "All his executive assistants were superhot. 'Come with us,' he'd order one of them on the way out to the limo. He and she sitting next to each other as he tries to grope her, with her blocking him like she's done it a hundred times before."

In some sense, everybody around Trump, everybody in the intimate Trump circle, became a Trump body man. "We're flying to Chicago, and the Trump plane wasn't working so we had to use another little plane and I had to sit facing him—knees almost touching—and he's all pissed off because his plane's broken down. I pull out a book to avoid eye contact. It was the book *DisneyWar*. But he can't be ignored. He needs to talk. 'What book is that . . . What's it about . . . Am I in it? Read it to me.' I tell him it's got Mark Burnett pitching *The Apprentice*. 'How does it make me look?'"

You had to adapt yourself to an idiosyncratic and quite alarming creature, Whitestone observed. "He can't walk down steps . . . can't walk down hills. [He's got] mental blocks . . . [He] can't handle numbers . . . they have no meaning to him."

His transparency was as appalling as it was mesmerizing. "Once, we were with a bunch of people and Don Jr. suggested that Trump had been to two Yankees games in a row where they had lost, so maybe his father was bad luck. And he went ape-shit. 'Why the fuck would you say that in front of these people? These fucking people are going to go out into the world and tell everyone, "Trump is bad luck."' Don Jr. was practically crying. 'Dad, I'm sorry. I'm so sorry, Dad.'

"And at the hospital, when his grandchild was born, Don Jr.'s kid, [Trump said], 'Why the fuck do I have to go see this kid? Don Jr. has too many fucking kids.'"

Everybody around Trump got drafted into his schemes. In the early days of the presidential campaign, Whitestone, not least because he was inexpensive, became part of the media team. "He's got a plan. I'm going to do his campaign commercials: 'I want you to use our boardroom set and get a bunch of Arabs and all their Arab gear and we'll put a sign on the table that says "OPEC" and we'll have them going, "Hoooluuuuluuuhooo, hoooluuulyyhoood," and we'll have this subtitle, "Death to the Americans," or "We'll Screw the Americans," and then I'll walk in and I'll say a bunch of presidential bullshit . . . and then we'll make it go viral. Call Corey Lewandowski—here's his number—and set it up.'"

As Whitestone knew, the unbound Trump, to which the insiders at *The Apprentice* were regularly exposed, was captured on thousands of hours of outtakes. Those fabled tapes still exist, but they are now controlled by Burnett and MGM. "Like the ark of the covenant in *Raiders of the Lost Ark*, [they are] somewhere on a pallet, wrapped in tape, in a desert outside of Los Angeles. Eighteen cameras shooting almost twenty-four hours a day are saved on DVDs . . . We didn't have hard drives."

It is probably the richest historical record ever made of a man in his pre-presidential professional capacity—fourteen years of *The Apprentice* preserved. Whitestone remembered certain moments with particular clarity.

"Someone said 'cunt' and someone else said, 'You can't say "cunt" on TV,' and Donald said, 'Why can't you say "cunt"?' and said 'Cunt, cunt, cunt, cunt. There, I've said it on TV. Now you can say it.'"

And: "'You're very pretty, stand up, walk over here, turn around.' [There was] constant dialogue about who has better tits and then bitter fights with producers about not using this. 'Why can't we?' he'd say. 'This is great. This is great television.'"

Speaking about Trump more generally, Whitestone said: "A twelve-year-old in a man's body, all he does is takedowns of people based on their physical appearance—short, fat, bald, whatever it is. There weren't producers who could say, Don't say that . . . We would just send him through the doors and hit Record . . . It's like being in the backseat of a car being driven by a really drunk driver . . . holy shit. He was as incoherent then . . . no more, no less . . . as he is now, repeating thoughts and weird phrases . . . His weird sniffing thing ('I have hay fever') . . . [He was] always eating Oscar Mayer baloney . . . [Once he] pulled a slice of baloney out and shoved it in my mouth . . ."

* * *

Michael Cohen stepped into the Trump circle in 2006. Cohen was an upper-middle-class, son-of-a-surgeon Long Island Jewish kid. Impressed by an uncle who owned a Brooklyn restaurant, a popular Mob hangout, Cohen recast himself as a would-be tough. He married a girl from Ukraine whose family had immigrated to Brooklyn, then got a degree from Western Michigan University Thomas M. Cooley Law School (the nation's lowest-ranked law school, according to the legal website Above the Law), became a lawyer, and amassed a fleet of taxis. His wife's father helped introduce Cohen to Trump, and for Cohen, Trump stood out: he was a dazzling model of fast-and-loose business practices and lifestyles-of-the-rich-and-famous glamour.

A successful career at the Trump Organization depended on getting Trump's attention and favor. Cohen, like Trump, played at being a mobster to the point of becoming one. The coarser, grosser, and blunter you could be, the better; such behavior affirmed your standing with the boss. Trump's oft-used injunction—"Don't bring me problems, bring me solutions"—was taken as both license and direction to do whatever it took to advance the Trump cause.

Sam Nunberg, testifying before the Mueller grand jury, said that when he worked at Trump Tower in the years before the campaign, he saw Cohen with bags of cash. Cohen was, for Trump, literally a bag man, dealing with women and other off-the-books issues.

In the world of the Trump Organization, Trump lieutenants received a lot of their compensation in side deals. Michael Cohen styled himself as speaking for Trump around the globe; he tried to negotiate lucrative deals and seize "branding opportunities." These efforts soon earned Cohen the hostility of Ivanka and her brothers, since this was exactly what they were supposed to be doing. In their eyes, the lawyer was one more competitor for Trump's attention.

During the 2016 campaign, Cohen continually tried to impose himself on the operation, ever shuttling from the Trump Organization offices in Trump Tower to the floor housing the campaign. Finally, in August 2016, Bannon banned him from the political offices. At one point, Cohen tried to "fix" the election by himself, conducting his own negotiation with one of the myriad people who claimed to have Hillary Clinton's thirty-three thousand missing emails. He was shocked when he did not get the call to replace Corey Lewandowski as campaign manager; Cohen thought he had set up this move with Don Jr., but Paul Manafort got the job instead. And he was shocked again when he wasn't tapped to replace Manafort—the job Bannon got.

For the media, Cohen was a reliable leaker about Trump and the campaign. Among senior campaign aides, he was later regarded as a central voice in NBC correspondent Katy Tur's book about the campaign, despite Trump's antipathy toward her.

After Trump's unexpected victory, Cohen still aimed high: he expected to be chief of staff. Keeping Cohen out of the White House involved a dedicated effort by the Trump presidential circle. His exclusion came as a bitter disappointment.

Cohen effectively had no supporters other than Trump himself, whose support for him, as with almost everyone, was shallow and fleeting. "He's supposed to be a fixer," said Trump about Cohen, "but he breaks a lot of stuff."

All of Trump's people saw Cohen as a flashing danger signal. In Bannon's head-shaking view, you had to carefully circumscribe your suspicions about "what kind of crazy shit he's done with Trump over the years. You have no earthly idea what kind of stuff—none."

After the raid on Cohen's office, Trump was yet unconcerned about Cohen's loyalty. Many in the Trump circle had a different view: they knew that Cohen felt not just slighted by Trump but frequently cheated by him. Cohen secretly taped some of his meetings with Trump, at least in part to have a record of their loosey-goosey financial arrangements. But, at the same time, Cohen was as likely to be cheating Trump as trying to please him. Either way, they were both in it together.

The Stormy Daniels payoff was a characteristic Cohen operation, designed as much to please Trump as to solve a particular problem. Marc Kasowitz, Trump's outside lawyer, had spurned the idea of making any sort of payment. After all, Daniels's story was already out: the *Wall Street Journal*, citing reports of another affair in 2006 and 2007 with Karen McDougal, had mentioned this one as well. Bannon, too, shrugged it off, saying that, following the grab-them-by-the-pussy tape, an article about another Trump affair would change no votes. But Trump, as he often did, ignored the counsel of his advisers and encouraged his most loyal fixer to fix it.

* * *

Trump was personally offended by the FBI's behavior during the raid of Cohen's home and office, citing the "Gestapo tactics" used on his lawyer, in which he saw the heavy hand of the Justice Department. But he was also oddly sanguine. "I have deniability," he repeated, reassuring nobody.

The truth was, nobody knew what Michael Cohen knew. The Trump Organization was a freelance affair, with everyone acting on the whim of Donald Trump or in the name of Donald Trump or trying to satisfy the anticipated urges of Donald Trump.

And anyway, Trump believed, whatever Cohen knew, he wouldn't talk about it, because Trump could always pardon him—that, for both Trump and Cohen, was money in the bank. Indeed, Trump felt uniquely protected by his pardon power, and uniquely powerful because of it. But, in a progression of Trump thinking, he went from seeing his pardon power as a tool for his own protection to seeing it as a gift he could bestow. Or, as powerfully, he could threaten not to use it.

To Trump's mounting displeasure, not long after the FBI raid, Cohen began to regularly appear at the outdoor café around the corner from the Regency, on Sixty-First and Park Avenue in Manhattan. Here again, he seemed eager to style himself as a mafioso, using the Upper East Side café as his version of a Brooklyn social club. He smoked cigars for the paparazzi and appeared not to have a care in the world.

Cohen's visibility was his way of sending his pointed and threatening message to the president—I'm out here, for everyone to see. And as important as the pardon he expected to come was the expectation that Trump would foot his legal bills. Because if he didn't . . .

But the message received by Trump was not so much a threat, something he might have understood. Instead, he saw a man stealing the limelight. The factotum, the toady, was trying to claim attention for himself. And, what's more, he wanted Trump's money!

Ivanka, too, was focused on and personally offended by Cohen's showboating, prompting her to bring Cohen's daughter's Instagram feed to her father's notice. Trump became inordinately interested in following Samantha Cohen, whose posts provided a travelogue of the nineteen-year-old's expensive trips, unabated since her father's travails had begun. The teenager seemed to particularly enjoy posing in an almost unending array of bikinis and resort wear.

As April wore on, Trump became obsessed with what Cohen was likely to get out of all this attention. He was trying to be a star, said Trump. "He has a media strategy," declared Trump with evident surprise. He began to compare Cohen unfavorably to Manafort, who was "keeping his head down."

It was a weird and potentially dangerous break in the Mob ethic. While a more conventional approach might sensibly have focused on the care and feeding of Michael Cohen, understanding the intersection of the Trump and Cohen interests, Trump, as in so many situations, seemed not to be able to align cause and effect. Instead, he appeared to go out of his way to antagonize his former lawyer, publicly belittling and insulting him.

He turned on Cohen's daughter, too, and her Instagram travelogue. "She just waves her tits around," he told a friend. "No respect for the situation."

Trump, by insisting on Cohen's utter lack of importance, created exactly the opposite situation: after years of toadying and bag carrying for the Trump Organization, after the ceaseless tending to and caring for Donald Trump, after worshipping a man who returned no consideration at all, Michael Cohen had arrived. Suddenly, he and Trump were united with equal weight and equal power, their names appearing nearly every day in news accounts in the same paragraph. Their fates were joined—just as Michael Cohen had always dreamed.

7

THE WOMEN

On May 7, the president came lumbering out into the Rose Garden. After greeting the vice president, already sitting in the front row of a gathering on the lawn, Trump took his seat on a folding chair.

A big outdoor television monitor began showing a video. The president's wife, in a voice-over, speaking in her carefully enunciated, accented English, introduced the themes she would focus on as First Lady. For seventeen months the White House had been uncertain about what Melania Trump's message or purpose should be. So here it was: she would advance the interests of children, alert people to the dangers of social media, and help bring attention to the opioid epidemic. The First Lady's initiative was called, oddly emphasizing her constricted English, "Be Best."

A week later, Melania entered Walter Reed National Military Medical Center. The White House was almost wholly unprepared for this event. No one seemed to have a plan for how to announce or characterize her hospitalization; no one appeared to know how to deal with the natural questions that might arise for what was described as a "benign kidney condition," a designation that satisfied no one.

First Ladies are good copy. A hospital stay for a First Lady is flood-the-zone media stuff. The standard White House playbook is straightforward: have answers for all inquiries. Mystery or secrecy opens the door to speculation, which is, inevitably, the White House's enemy. But with few credible answers forthcoming, speculation about Melania's health quickly became breathless. Why was the First Lady in the hospital for the better part of a week—and at Walter Reed, where no one chose to linger—for a condition that, as described, should have required no more than a single night's stay, or even should have been an outpatient procedure? Soon a hundred theories blossomed, from the conspiratorial to the macabre.

In the end, blame for the communications failure seemed to logically fall on one of two targets: the hopeless dysfunction of the White House comms team or the apparent dysfunction of the president's marriage. The president chose the former. It was a frequent rant: the idiots on his comms staff. But almost everyone else in the White House chose to blame his marriage.

All presidential marriages are a mystery. How do you justify, and compensate for, the loss of the very point of marriage, a private life? In this case, however—at least in the opinion of nearly all those who had an up-close view of their relationship—the situation was more clear-cut. A deal had seemingly been struck. "It's a Katie Holmes–Tom Cruise deal" was the general understanding. The mystery here was about whether the deal would hold.

* * *

As the Trump campaign gained altitude in 2016, the questions surrounding the marriage became more serious. Ivanka, hardly a fan of her step-mother, kept posting red flags. Of much concern were the issues related to Melania's background as an eastern European model, as well as questions about how the couple had met. Who was Melania Knavs (or, as the president preferred, in its German variation, Knauss)? More problematic, at least in traditional political terms, was the fact that for quite some time the Trumps had seemed to live openly parallel lives.

Other intimates, worried about the questions that would invariably be asked and the lack of ready answers, tried to raise the subject with Trump. Among them were Keith Schiller, Trump's security man, and Tom Barrack, Trump's closest businessman friend. Trump's response was dismissive: he wasn't any different from Kennedy. The counsel that at this point in time JFK would hardly offer cover for a disorderly personal life was met by a particularly sour Trump face: *Don't be a pussy*.

After the *Daily Mail* implied in August 2016 that Melania's career as a model had at times crossed the line to being an escort, Trump's solution was to hire a lawyer. Charles Harder, who had won Hulk Hogan's suit against the gossip site Gawker for posting a privately made Hogan sex tape and thereafter become the go-to lawyer for celebrity libel complaints, sued the *Mail* on Melania's behalf. The suit was filed in the UK. Harder was suing under the more favorable libel laws in Britain. In the United States, a president and his family, as public figures, face insuperable hurdles to a defamation or invasion of privacy claim. Eventually, the suit was settled: the *Mail* agreed to retract the article and apologize to Melania for it, and paid her unspecified damages. Trump's willingness to sue, and doing so successfully, together with Harder's post-Gawker reputation, helped limit campaign speculation of Melania's past and the Trump marriage.

Melania did not really become a political wife until the moment, on November 8, 2016, at approximately 8:45 p.m. EST, when it became clear that, almost miraculously, her husband—or, in the interpretation of some, her estranged husband—would become president of the United States. Over time, a political wife develops habits and rationalizations and personal armor to deal with the loss of privacy and self, as well as the sometimes alarming public face of the man she has married; Melania had none of these defenses.

To the extent that the Trumps had lived separate lives—helped by the considerable distance between them allowed by their ample real estate, including at least one house near his golf club in the New York suburbs that Trump kept carefully hidden from his wife—this now became impossible. Whatever polite arrangement they had had prior to the campaign had certainly come crashing down in October with the grab-them-by-the-pussy tape. There was not only this terrible public coarseness, but the ensuing public testimony of multiple women claiming abuse at Trump's hands. But now, with her husband's election, Melania was exposed beyond anything she could have possibly imagined.

* * *

"Exogenous events" was the term Steve Bannon used for the unexpected disruptions that seemed to constantly accompany Trump. High on quite a long list of exogenous events that Bannon believed could end the Trump presidency were these two: if someone came forward with proof that Trump had ever paid for an abortion or if his wife publicly left him.

Perhaps a Trump-style denial could deal with even an abortion. But however much Trump could flat-out lie, he could hardly deny a public meltdown with an unforgiving and pitiless wife. And Bannon believed that it was not so much the scandal of a public breakup that would bring him down, but the pain of his own public embarrassment.

In 1996, his second wife, Marla Maples, was caught one night with a Trump bodyguard on the beach near Mar-a-Lago under the lifeguard stand. This, Bannon was aware, had been a primal blow for Trump.

"Almost everything he does is about trying to avoid humiliation," said Bannon. "And he's close to it all of the time. He's drawn to it. Caught red-handed, he'll stare you down. He's psychologically gifted. His father humiliated him. That humiliation broke Trump's brother. But he learned to withstand it. But that's the Russian roulette he's playing, waiting for the humiliation that will break him."

Trump seemed entirely incapable of acknowledging that he even had a personal life, much less that it necessitated any kind of emotional allowance or understanding. Indeed, his personal life merely demanded the same kind of "fixing" as his business life. When Marla Maples became pregnant in the early 1990s, before their marriage, he debated with one friend how he could avoid both the marriage and the baby.

Marriage, for Trump, was at best a fitful complication. For his advisers, this became a serious political challenge, because Trump, in one more instance of being unprepared for the presidency, would not—or could not—allow for a discussion of how his personal life should be figured into the administration's basic messaging or the look and feel of the White House. "I never saw any evidence of a marriage," said Bannon of his time in the White House. Most mentions of Melania drew a puzzled look from Trump, as if to say, "How is she relevant?"

* * *

Trump came into the White House with a ten-year-old son. Having young children is usually a humanizing and uplifting part of a presidential biography, but Trump had scant relationship with Barron.

Early in the administration, one aide, new to the Trump circle, suggested to Trump that he be photographed playing golf with his son. The aide went on giddily talking about the special bond golfing dads have with their sons until it was clear that he was getting the Trump freeze—an ability to pretend you didn't exist while at the same time intimating that he might kill you if you did.

By contrast, Melania's singular focus was her son. Together, mother and son occupied a bubble inside the Trump bubble. She assiduously protected Barron from his father's remoteness. Ever cold-shouldered by Trump's adult children, Melania and Barron were the non-Trump family inside the Trump family.

Melania sometimes spoke Slovenian with Barron, particularly when her parents were around—and they were frequently around—infuriating Trump and causing him to bolt from any room they were in. But the private living quarters in the White House were much smaller than their home in Trump Tower, making it more difficult for Trump and his wife to escape each other.

"We don't belong here," she widely repeated to friends.

Indeed, a distraught Melania, repeatedly assured by her husband during the campaign that there was no possibility he would win, had originally refused to move to Washington.

And, in fact, the First Lady was not really in the White House. It had taken Melania almost six months to officially relocate from New York to Washington, but that was largely in name only. Even beyond their separate bedrooms in the White House—they were the first presidential couple since JFK and Jackie to room apart—much of Melania's time was spent in a house in Maryland where she had installed her parents and established what was effectively a separate life for herself.

This was the arrangement. For Trump, it was workable; for Melania, quite a bit less so. Maryland was fine—she had become quite involved with Barron's school there, St. Andrews Episcopal School in Potomac—but what duties she had in the White House became more and more onerous as Trump's relationship with his son became increasingly difficult.

Over the previous year, Barron, who turned twelve in March 2018, had become more distant toward his father. This might not be unusual behavior for a boy his age, but Trump responded with hostility. This took the form of ignoring his son when they had to be together; Trump also went out of his way to avoid any situation where he might have to encounter him. When he did appear with his son in public, he would talk about him in the third person—seldom to him, but casually about him.

Trump had a fetish about being the tallest person in the room; by 2018 Barron, after a sudden growth spurt, was already approaching six feet. "How do I stunt his growth?" became a chronic mean joke made by Trump about his son's height.

Trump's friends, including Keith Schiller, advised Melania that this was the way Trump had always treated his children, especially his sons. He often failed to acknowledge his son Eric when they found themselves together. He seemed to single out Don Jr. just for ridicule—and at the same time praise Don Jr.'s rival in the Trump political circle Corey Lewandowski. Tiffany, his daughter by his second wife, Marla Maples, largely went unmentioned, whereas he treated his official favorite child, Ivanka, with heightened, rat-pack-like solicitude. "Hey, baby," he would say when greeting her.

Trump saw the world through the filter of other people's weaknesses. He saw people through their physical and intellectual shortcomings, or through oddities in the way they talked or dressed. He defended himself by ridiculing others. It sometimes seemed that his only option, other than outright scorn, was to make Barron invisible to him.

Melania, meanwhile, appeared to make every effort to live her separate life and protect her son from the ill wind of his father.

* * *

In the fall of 2017, as the *New York Times* and the *New Yorker* focused to devastating effect on Harvey Weinstein's long history of sexual predation,

Trump was busily defending him. "Good guy," he would say about Weinstein, "good guy." He was sure that like the Russia investigation this, too, was a witch hunt. What's more, he knew Harvey, and Harvey would get away with it. That was the thing with Harvey, said Trump—he always got away with it. It was the casting couch, the casting couch! For every girl who now had her panties in a twist, Trump claimed, there were fifty others, a hundred others, eager and willing. In Trumpland, there were few good ways to respond to such statements, perhaps none in the moment, so most people simply pretended they hadn't heard what he'd said.

#MeToo as a cultural phenomenon and political variable occupied a place of nervous denial in the Trump White House. It was of course never mentioned in the context of Donald Trump's behavior with women. That Trump might be the direct cause of this media, cultural, legal, and corporate uprising, one that would ultimately bring down scores of powerful and prominent men, was certainly never discussed.

Trump himself had not even an inkling of the new sensitivity regarding women and sex. "I don't need Viagra," he declared to everyone else's general mortification at a dinner party in New York during the campaign. "I need a pill to make my erection go down."

Since it could not be discussed, nobody in the White House could address the political what-ifs of renewed scandal.

And yet: What if the uprising *were* to finally reach him? Bannon—who had played the central political role during the pussy-tape scandal and was still incredulous that they had survived it—likened #MeToo to an episode of the old detective show *Columbo*, wherein the unrelenting, methodical, ever probing detective finally and invariably finds his way to the perpetrator's door. In Bannon's view, #MeToo would not be satisfied until it reached the White House.

Nobody knew the number of women who might have cause to come forward and accuse Trump of harassment or abuse. Bannon sometimes used the figure of a hundred girls, but sometimes, too, a thousand. Trump's lawyer Marc Kasowitz kept the books on this, but sometimes Trump diverted issues involving women to Michael Cohen. Or perhaps it was the other way around, and Cohen was the true bagman for dealing with his affairs and for what would now be understood as sexual assault, with Kasowitz handling the runoff. Either way, nobody knew what was out there.

A year before Weinstein, when the pussy-grabbing video had broken, Trump was faced with numbers of women suddenly making assorted cases—in Bannon's accounting, there were "twenty-five women, locked and loaded." At the time, all the cases had somehow conflated to a confused, almost undifferentiated, claim. But since then, the very nature of sexual harassment and assault accusations had changed. Each had an emotional narrative attached, each represented a singular attack and wound. Each accuser had a name and face. What's more, Trump's own denials regarding Stormy Daniels and Karen McDougal had, detail by detail, been stripped back to no basis in fact at all. He had dismissed and disputed everything, and everything had turned out to be true. He had become not just the ultimate, archetypal sexual predator, he had become the model denier—the main exhibit for why women ought to be believed.

After #MeToo broke, a haunting question in the White House became: What happened to those women whose accusations in 2016 Trump had dismissed and disputed? When might they come back? And not just those women—others, too.

"We compressed all these women," said Bannon of the campaign-period accusers. "People couldn't parse it. We just denied it all. Lumped it all together and denied it all. I ask everybody about the women, but nobody remembers. But I remember—I kept track of them all. They're in my dreams. Remember the girl at the China Club? I do. Kristin Anderson. She says he put two digits in her vagina at the bar. She's forty-three, forty-four now, and one of these days she's gonna look right in the camera on *Good Morning America* and she's going to say, 'He came in the back of the bar when I was eighteen years old and put two fingers in my vagina . . . my vagina . . . my vagina.' And you're going to hear that at 8:03 in the morning and she's going to start crying. And then two days later there is going to be the next girl . . . and the next girl. It will be siege warfare. This one today, then let it cook, then take out another and put it on. We got twenty-five or thirty or a hundred. Or a thousand. We'll take them one at a time, and every woman in the country is going to say, 'Wait, what did he do, why is she crying?'"

In front of the grand jury, prosecutors from the special counsel's office drilled down into the details of Trump's sexual behavior—where, how often, with whom, and of what nature. This was, speculated one witness who described Trump's "nefarious activities" in testimony, as much a way to bias the grand jury against Trump the lowlife as it was to help chart the relationships—such as those with Daniels and McDougal—that resulted in payoffs, and to look further at the allegations in the Steele dossier. Likewise, the Senate Select Committee on Intelligence, also looking to corroborate the Steele dossier and to ascertain how much the Russians might have on Trump, had taken, under seal, testimony from an individual who accompanied Trump to Moscow in 1996. This individual also introduced as exhibits in the confidential record photos of Trump with escorts on the trip.

* * *

If there were new or renewed accusations, no one could predict how well the blanket Trump denials would continue to hold up, especially with the base. But as bad as these potential situations might be, the ultimate bad-news scenario was that new accusations would cause Melania to leave him.

It did not help that, led by Michael Avenatti, Trump's relationship with the porn star Stormy Daniels became a daily saga by spring 2018. That was bad enough, with the First Lady doing her best to keep her son from the constant accounts. The unfathomable offense to Melania, however, was the unprotected sex. And Michael Avenatti repeated this almost as a personal taunt. In Avenatti's description, Trump and his client had not just had sex, they had engaged in a specific category of sex, "unprotected sex."

Trump's people had developed a heightened respect for Melania: she kept her cards close and played them well. She might, in the end, be the better Trump family negotiator. She made her leverage clear and settled for what she could get. But the constant patch-ups and new arrangements masked volatility on both sides. Nobody discounted the possibility, as a whole genre of stories and theories had it, that the rumored elevator video of Trump striking Melania might in fact exist. Inside the White House, the view was doubtful: if, however, such a video did exist, the incident had happened in Los Angeles, probably in 2014 after a meeting with lawyers that had been arranged precisely to negotiate a revision in their marital agreement.

The deal was always about letting Donald Trump be Donald Trump. "I only fuck beautiful girls—*you* can attest to that," he said to a Hollywood friend who visited the White House. (He had once left a voice-mail message for Tucker Carlson, who had criticized Trump's hair: "It's true you have better hair than I do, but I get more pussy than you do.") Being Donald Trump—*the* Donald Trump, unfettered Donald Trump—was the most important thing to him. And he would compensate Melania handsomely for that.

But the stakes, and Melania's leverage, had risen astronomically since Trump entered the White House.

* * *

Nobody in the West Wing believed the explanation for the First Lady's hospital stay. Melania entered Walter Reed on Monday, May 14, and for twenty-four hours there was hardly even an attempt to provide a coherent story. It was pure avoidance. *I see nothing. I know nothing.* And then, credulity pushed to its end point, the excited speculation inside the White House mirrored, or perhaps led, the speculation outside. Plastic surgery? A physical fight? An overdose? Mental breakdown? A standoff in a financial negotiation?

It was the East Wing—where Melania's aide Stephanie Grisham was seen as especially protective of the First Lady—against the West Wing, which, taking the president's lead, behaved as if Melania was of little concern. And as the week went on nobody could say when exactly Melania was coming back.

What was as notable as her absence was Trump's imperturbability. With questions mounting, John Kelly requested a far more detailed briefing. *What exactly is wrong with her?* Kelly asked. The president countermanded: "Nobody cares except the media. She's the First Lady, not the president." As with all his existential crises, arguably coming as fast as any in political history, he flipped it. He was fine. Melania was fine. Their marriage was fine. Totally fine. It was the world around him that was toxic, cruel, evil, obsessed, full of lies.

Indeed, the consensus was that Trump did not recognize that anything here was beyond the normal course of business, either in his marriage or, more generally, in his personal life. His marriage might be thought by some to be a Potemkin village, but that's what it was supposed to be. That was the arrangement!

This was a perverse sort of logic. There *was* no marriage—not, at least, that anyone had ever seen. So how could there be a problem with the marriage?

Here, to various onlookers, was the distinction upon which many of their own careers and futures depended. Was Donald Trump the what-me-worry cynical master of having it all? Or was Donald Trump simply oblivious to the terrifying fragility of his world, wholly unaware of the very real possibility that, at any moment, it could fall in on him?

On Saturday, May 19, the First Lady returned to the White House—or, in fact, she shortly returned to her home with her parents in Maryland. Nine days later, she missed the annual Memorial Day wreath-laying ceremony at Arlington National Cemetery. On June 1, Trump made a rare trip to Camp David with the entire family—including Tiffany—but without Melania or Barron. On June 4, she finally reappeared; the occasion was an annual White House event honoring Gold Star families. She had not been seen for twenty-four days, not since her appearance on May 10, just after her "Be Best" debut.

On June 21, during a surprise trip to a shelter for migrant children in Texas, she was photographed in a Zara jacket with a legend scrawled across the back: I REALLY DON'T CARE, DO U?

The president insisted that she was referring to the fake news media.

8

MICHAEL FLYNN

In early June, the Mueller team prepared to oppose what it believed was soon to come: the president's pardon of Michael Flynn, the bumptious and fleeting former national security advisor who had been indicted for lying to the FBI.

A frequent Trump riff was about whom he could pardon. His list included both contemporary and historical figures. Aides were urged to offer ideas about who could be added to the list. Jared sought to have his father, Charlie Kushner, pardoned; that effort went nowhere (Trump wasn't a fan of Charlie Kushner's). But Sheriff Joe Arpaio, an anti-immigration figure and Trump supporter, got a pardon. So did Scooter Libby, the Bush administration leaker whom President Bush, a frequent target of Trump derision, had failed to pardon, and so did Dinesh D'Souza, the right-wing author. Martha Stewart was a possibility. So was the corrupt former Illinois governor Rod Blagojevich, who was brazen and overweening in a Trumpian way. Trump pardons were less judicial corrections or acts of forbearance and kindness than statements of defiance.

But Trump needed constant reassurance about the extent of this power. He wanted to know just how absolute "absolute" really was. His lawyers went out of their way to assure him that his power was, indeed, truly absolute, thus reassuring him that he had ultimate control of his own fate: in a pinch, he could even pardon himself. At the same time, they urged him to keep his powder dry, at least for the moment. Everyone, they said, now understands that you have the power to pardon and are willing to use it, which sends the signal you want to send.

"It really is a get-out-of-jail-free card," Trump proudly marveled to one frequent caller. "I am told there is nothing anyone can do if I pardon someone. I'm totally protected. And I can protect anyone for anything. I can totally pardon myself. Really." Trump, said the caller, often revisited the topic.

For Trump, pardons had become something like the Nixon tapes. Here was a subject he had some deep feelings about: if Nixon had only burned the tapes, no problem. Likewise, if Trump simply pardoned everybody, no problem.

Hearing this kind of conjecture, Don McGahn worried about the fine line he walked. Was he merely explaining the pardon powers afforded the president or effectively counseling Trump on how to use these powers to obstruct justice? Pardons became yet another third-rail topic in the White House—everyone knew they did not want to have to recount a discussion about pardons before a grand jury or congressional panel.

* * *

Trump continued to convince himself that Mueller was an insult but not a threat. The White House senior staff, by contrast, was uniquely afraid of Mueller. There were various running office pool–type calculations of whether Mueller's best case would be for obstruction, collusion, perjury, election fraud, or financial crimes connected to Trump's Russian ambitions. Senior aides were most of all afraid of Mueller because they were afraid of Trump: nobody could have any reasonable confidence that he had not broken laws in multiple circumstances, nor did they have reason to believe that he had cleaned up after himself if he had. It was again that key element of his presidency: no one who worked for Trump had any illusions about him. "It's Donald Trump" was the umbrella explanation for their twilight-zone existence and the existential threat they faced every day.

As alarmingly, there was still no formal process in place that would enable the White House to deal with everything that an investigation of the president involved. Mueller's team began its work in May 2017; now a year had passed and, effectively, the president still had no real lawyers. There was no dedicated legal team, no deep litigation bench on the case, or cases, against him. Ty Cobb—who, after the ouster of John Dowd, shouldered all the blame, in the president's mind, for the ongoing investigation—was out in early May. Now Trump had only Jay Sekulow, a right-wing advocacy lawyer not attached to a law firm, and Rudy Giuliani, his designated television defender. And even Trump seemed to understand that whatever public relations advantage Giuliani's audacity might provide, he was likely to take it back almost immediately, drunk on a bid for further attention, or just drunk. Trump certainly wasn't relying on either of his lawyers. Indeed, he continued to solicit advice from everyone—and therefore to potentially implicate everyone.

Every day was a minefield. Trump constantly thought out loud. He perhaps had no solely private thoughts, and certainly no editing mechanism when he invariably expressed what was on his mind. Everyone was therefore potentially included in a wide conspiracy. Everybody was privy to the details of a cover-up.

Staffers even feared that plotting among themselves to avoid becoming part of a cover-up—"I didn't hear that" or "That's a meeting you definitely want to stay out of"—might be construed as a cover-up in its own right. Hence, there developed a back-channel network of shared lawyers. Bill Burck, for instance, represented Don McGahn, Steve Bannon, and Reince Priebus. As a consequence, all three men could communicate under the seal of their lawyer's privilege.

It was every man for himself. By the spring of 2018, the staff was experiencing the kind of panic you might not expect to see until all avenues and options had been exhausted, until the writing was clearly on the wall. Everyone had to acknowledge the real possibility that the Trump presidency would go down and take many people with it. Could the chances be as high as 50/50? Those were the odds John Kelly sometimes gave to friends; Kelly's wife whispered that they were even higher. The nearly apocalyptic mood led virtually all of the senior players in the West Wing to contemplate contingency plans: When could they reasonably exit? Don

McGahn, deeply depressed, found himself trapped because he felt honor-bound not to leave the job until someone else agreed to take it—and that was a hard sell.

Lawyer after lawyer was approached to join the White House counsel's office specifically to anticipate an impeachment. Emmet Flood, one of the most experienced attorneys in the rarefied field of white-collar political defense, had turned down the job earlier in the year after demanding the kind of autonomy that Trump was unwilling or incapable of giving. A succession of other turn-downs—combined with yet another threat of his own to resign—finally gave McGahn the leverage to insist that Trump meet Flood's demands. In May, Flood replaced Cobb, having been given assurances that, when fulfilling his responsibility to protect the interests of the presidency, he would have the autonomy he needed.

Unbeknownst to the president, McGahn, in late 2017, had begun to cooperate with the Mueller investigation. Bannon, aware of McGahn's move, could not get enough of this particular irony. Trump was obsessed with John Dean, the White House staffer who had exposed the Nixon presidency; Trump did not seem entirely aware, however, that Dean, like McGahn, was the White House counsel. And Trump now seemed quite unmindful of how much McGahn had come to hate him—"a black hatred," observed a McGahn friend.

Courtesy of McGahn, the Mueller team began to suspect that Trump, even though he had been advised to restrain himself, would move to pardon Flynn and thus try to deprive the investigation of a significant witness.

* * *

Bannon, in fact, believed that Mueller was in a far weaker position than the greater White House assumed. He thought Trump's instincts, thus far effectively diverted, were right: Mueller was more afraid of Trump than Trump ought to be of him. Donald Trump might be the target of the special counsel's office—a rich target—but he was also a lethal threat to it.

Trump had the upper hand, or at least he did for the moment. The president, still maintained his hold on Congress—and therefore his impunity. With the Republican majority in the House, Mueller was a paper tiger. He might be a bullet aimed at the president, but he lacked a triggering mechanism. He held the moral high ground but had no ability to defend it.

What's more, Bannon, after his testimony before the special counsel earlier in the year, had come to doubt that Mueller had the goods. Beyond finding that here, in the Trump camp, were some of the sloppiest, most unsophisticated, stupidest people on earth—who, to say the least, had little or no sensitivity "to, shall we say, accepting foreign assistance," as Bannon put it—what did the investigators have? Or, to put it another way, *who* did they have? Roger Stone, Carter Page, George Papadopoulos, Julian Assange?

Bannon was unimpressed: "No way you impeach the president over those dragoons." They were hopeless flotsam and jetsam.

Obstruction? "Give me a break."

With a Republican Congress in place, what Mueller needed was something that would undermine Trump with the something less than 35 percent of the electorate that had become fanatically his. As long as that support held, the Republican Congress, Bannon believed, would have to hold.

Shock and awe is what Mueller needed. Mueller had to give "the deplorables"—Bannon had adopted Hillary Clinton's disparaging term as his affirmative and affectionate label—a compelling reason to reevaluate Trump. That is, he had to produce a smoking gun far worse than anything anyone thought Trump might have done, and that was a high hurdle. It was not going to get the special counsel anywhere merely to confirm what people already knew Trump to be. Tell me something I don't know!

Bannon continued to advocate for firing Rosenstein and thereby waylaying Mueller. He worked his Greek chorus: Lewandowski, Bossie, Hannity, and Republican congressman and Freedom Caucus leader Mark Meadows. He also urged the Trump defense to follow the Clinton White House model, equating popularity with virtue. True, Bill Clinton's approval was always above 50 percent and Trump's nearer 40 percent, but Trump's support was hard-core, remarkably so. In Bannon's view, Trump was the most beloved president of his time—if, also, the most hated. Mueller, an ally of the people who hated Trump, was out to defy the will of the people who loved the president. That, Bannon believed, ought to be the fighting argument.

But the White House—in particular, Rudy Giuliani—seemed incapable of making a righteous case. Giuliani's was at best a backhanded defense. In effect, the argument he made was, Yes, the president might be guilty, but because he was the president he was *allowed* to be guilty. (This was a variation on Trump's own career refrain: yes, he might be a rotten son-of-a-bitch, but he was a successful rotten son-of-a-bitch.) Instead of discrediting the investigation, the White House, in its ambivalence, seemed to throw up its hands and once more acknowledge that Donald Trump was, for better or worse, Donald Trump. Say what you will, observed Bannon, there was actually a heavy dose of realism in the Trump White House, if not on the part of the president.

Even the most dedicated Trumpers certainly admitted that there was a lot of black-hole stuff about Russia. They believed Trump had an abiding good feeling for Putin, similar to what he felt for all men whose success he admired and whose money was greater than his own. They acknowledged that Trump was eager to be respected by Putin and might go out of his way to please him. They also understood that Trump, a sub-blue-chip borrower in the great age of Russian capital outflows, would, at the very least, have had to close his eyes to legal niceties to participate in this financing bonanza. And they certainly knew that Trump was not inclined to or capable of walking a meticulous line between private and public spheres.

What they yet found a hard time believing was that there was a plan, a scheme, a big picture. Donald Trump may have done any number of things that, given good sense and the letter of the law, he should not have done. But with his short attention span, inability to manage multiple variables, exclusive focus on his own immediate needs, and general disregard of all future outcomes, the notion of pinning a grand conspiracy on him seemed like a big stretch.

No, the Trumpers countered, this was just liberals and Mueller taking advantage of Trump being Trump, of a man who was always his own worst enemy. And you could defend Trump being Trump because he was the guy—even with his scuzzy associates, fantastic exaggerations, casual regard for the literal truth, and constant straddles of the line of the law—who had been elected, with all his flaws on view.

* * *

Hence, it wasn't Trump who was conspiring, it was . . . Obama.

In spring 2018, the exotic "deep state" theory, long embraced by the president, finally came together in some half-cogent form. The Democrats believed that Trump had conspired with the Russians to fix the election. Well, the Trumpers believed that the Obama administration had conspired with the intelligence community to make it *seem* as if Trump and his people had conspired with the Russians to fix the election. It was not Trump and the Russians who had successfully stolen the election; it was Obama and his cohorts who had tried and failed to steal it.

The conspiracy against Donald Trump, as it was related by the most hard-core Trumpers, began in 2014, when Obama's director of the Defense Intelligence Agency (DIA), retired General Michael Flynn, showed up at a spy meeting in Cambridge. (Trumpers would darkly note that Cambridge was where Christopher Steele, of the Steele dossier, was recruited to spy against Russia.) Most of the spies gathered for dinner in a university hall were cold warriors, wary of Flynn's willingness to tolerate if not embrace Russians because of his personal belief that Iran was the actual geopolitical devil. From this point on, in the Trumpers' view, there were intel eyes on Flynn. Indeed, it would be Flynn who helped bring Trump to a new appreciation of the Russian willingness to help oppose the radical Islamic scourge. That was the crux of the collusion case, such as it was, against Trump and company: it was the old-school, Russian-obsessed intelligence community against people like Flynn and Trump who appreciated our new enemies—the international terrorism cabal. In counterespionage fashion, the spy world, taking advantage of the Trumpworld's better disposition toward Russia, had in fact pushed the Trumpers in that gotcha direction.

Now, attempting to discredit Mueller, congressional Republicans pushed the Justice Department in late May to reveal exactly how it had come to target the Trump campaign. The name Stefan Halper surfaced, likely leaked by the White House.

In the Republican theory, Halper, an American in Cambridge, England, with close contacts to MI6, the British foreign intelligence arm, had, at the behest of the Obama administration acting through MI6, recruited two hapless Trump hangers-on, Carter Page and George Papadopoulos, into a plan to approach the Russians. This was the Trump side's new narrative: the Obama side had engaged in entrapment.

With hooded eyes and an overcoat in need of replacement, the seventy-four-year-old Halper was yet another spy vs. spy player in Cambridge, where, in Bannon's cryptic summation, "all worlds lead." (Bannon knew Cambridge well: he and Halper walked the same streets as members of the back-office staff of Cambridge Analytica, the shady tech company with which Bannon was associated that had more or less unscrupulously acquired vast amounts of election metadata.) Indeed, Stefan Halper *was* a spy, a heavy hitter in the U.S.-UK spy world, who had been married to the daughter of a legendary CIA figure, Ray Cline, who was on the case during the Cuban Missile Crisis. And Halper was also a professional spy recruiter—a flytrap in Cambridge. Now, Halper conveniently bubbled up from the *deep state* to recruit several Trump stumblebums.

In Bannon's view, the Obama White House and the intelligence community would of course have had close eyes on Trump during the campaign. Trump had been a suspicious character for years; how could responsible parties *not* take alarmed note of his sudden presence on the world stage? What's more, he was certainly not going to get elected—as not only all the polls indicated, but as a confident Obama privately assured Democratic donors throughout the fall of 2016—so, even as a major party nominee, he did not have to be treated as a serious candidate. But to the extent that he was a candidate, he certainly seemed like a Manchurian one, a small-time crook who had been suspiciously elevated. So of course you would be covertly tracking him.

There it was, almost in plain sight: the Obama administration was running a counterintelligence investigation against a presidential candidate, albeit one more fake than real.

But while it might be sensible to run a modest intelligence operation that kept track of a crook with dubious connections to Russia—who, by a ridiculous fluke, just happened to be a major party's candidate for president—the operation would become much harder to defend if the target actually became president. What had seemed prudent and responsible during the campaign would look, in hindsight, insidious and undemocratic.

"You would think that the deputy attorney general of these United States would be able to get his pen out and scratch a note that says, 'Of course there are no documents related to the surveillance of a presidential campaign or the transition of the duly elected president of the United States'—signed, Rod Rosenstein," said Bannon, outlining the case. "But"—Bannon suddenly clapped his hands—"he couldn't, for obvious reasons. Gotcha!"

It was, once again, the paradox of the Trump presidency: he was so unsuited, if not unfit, for the office, such an assault on the established order, that all the defenders of this established order were of course compelled to protect it from him. But then he won the election, which conferred on him the legitimacy of the established order—or at least he believed it conferred that legitimacy on him.

Trump was not, however, wily enough, or tempered or patient enough, to demonstrate and secure that legitimacy. Rather, he simply insisted on it. The same person who before the election was regarded as illegitimate by, arguably, the majority of voters now demanded, stamping his feet, that he be seen as legitimate. His argument was a simple inversion: the establishment—the deep state—regards me as illegitimate and violated democratic principles to deny me the White House. But I *won*; hence, they, not I, are illegitimate.

Devin Nunes, then the chairman of the House Intelligence Committee, became the Republican Don Quixote of the expose-the-deep-state initiative, demanding that the Justice Department break protocols and reveal the details of its early investigation of Trump. The hope, or Hail Mary pass, was to show that the Justice Department's actions, influenced by the Obama White House, were part of a fix-the-election conspiracy, or at least some muddy-the-waters dirty dealing—details of which were obsessively spelled out by Sean Hannity. This involved, in addition to Halper, two FBI agents, Peter Strzok and Lisa Page (lovers who had left a telltale trail of text messages about their contempt for Trump); former FBI director James Comey; former CIA director John Brennan; and former director of National Intelligence James Clapper. And contributing to this conspiracy were alleged abuses of the Foreign Intelligence Surveillance Court (FISA) and the Steele dossier, which the Republicans regarded as a Democratic piece of legerdemain and conspiracy mongering, and the corrupt basis for much of the case against the president.

To a degree, the Trumpers were correct. The powers that be had been so aghast at Trump personally, and at the peculiar and disturbing behavior of his campaign, and had responded to him so viscerally, that they had acted in ways they never would have acted toward a respectable candidate—or toward anyone they thought might actually win. But that did not change the fact that Trump was still Trump, and that virtually everything about him screamed that he ought to be investigated.

The inner circle of dedicated Trumpers—Bannon, Lewandowski, Bossie, Hannity—kept urging McGahn and the White House to join Devin Nunes and insist that Rod Rosenstein release all the files related to the Obama administration's moves to investigate the Trump-Russia connection. Rosenstein could delay and evade congressional requests almost indefinitely, but he would not be able to ignore his boss, the president. Issue the order, the Trumpers pressed, and then, if he fails to comply, fire him.

McGahn, already a secret Mueller witness, resisted. He worried about the global release of confidential intelligence documents, and the further effects of a White House confrontation with the Justice Department.

At about this time, the peak counterconspiracy moment, Lewandowski and Bossie were rushing to finish their second book about the Trump administration, one that focused on the deep state's efforts to undermine the president. Lewandowski and Bossie hired Sara Carter, a Fox News contributor and close Hannity colleague, as their ghost writer and sent her over to the Embassy to get further details on the conspiracy from Bannon. Certainly among the nimblest conspiracy provocateurs of the Trump age, Bannon spelled out the current narrative in powerful detail.

Still, Bannon felt obliged to warn Carter about the story that would shortly become the backbone of the Lewandowski and Bossie book *Trump's Enemies: How the Deep State Is Undermining the Presidency*. "You do realize," said Bannon, "that none of this is true."

* * *

The significance of Michael Flynn to the Mueller investigation was that he was, despite his mere twenty-five days in office, a player—this in a world where Trump permitted no one, other than himself, to be a genuine player. There might not have been anyone whom Trump had so bonded with during the campaign. Indeed, Flynn was, in the earliest days of the transition, one of the soon-to-be Trump White House's first official hires.

But now Flynn looked more and more like a smoking gun. At the direct behest of either Trump or Kushner—or, as likely, both—Flynn had reached out to the Russian ambassador during the transition and negotiated a separate peace around the Obama administration sanctions, or so the Mueller team seemed to indicate in its proposed obstruction indictment of Trump. An abiding historical regret for many Democrats was that Nixon had managed to get away with promising North Vietnamese negotiators working on a peace treaty in Paris that they would get a better deal if they waited for his administration to arrive in office. Here Trump and Flynn seemed to be up to similar dirty tricks.

What's more, Trump's apparent attempt to obstruct justice began with Flynn. Trying to deflect the FBI's investigation of Flynn had sent Trump down the path to firing Comey, which was the spark that lit the Mueller investigation.

* * *

If the pardon came, the special counsel was ready to go into federal court and ask for an injunction barring Trump from pardoning Flynn. The problem, however, was that the president's pardon power, just as Trump had been assured, was, practically speaking, ironclad.

"It appears likely," the special counsel's research on the topic concluded, "that the president can pardon his family members or close associates even for the purpose of impeding an investigation." When tested, courts have held that the president's pardon power "is plenary and absolute, with few exceptions." And it appeared that, in fact, the president could probably pardon himself. It might be "improper," in any reasonable understanding of basic standards of logic and propriety, but "a self-pardon is not expressly prohibited by the Constitution . . . If the president did not have the power to pardon himself, the *expressio unius textualist* reading says, the Framers would have added text specifically restricting the president's ability to self-pardon."

But having concluded that the pardon power was virtually unassailable, the Mueller legal team believed that Trump might yet present several unique exceptions to this power.

First, in the legal argument, Article II, Section 2, Clause 1 of the Constitution, which granted the pardon power, does offer two specific limitations. For one thing, the pardon power applies only to federal law, meaning that any state charges were excepted. For another, the power excludes anything to do with impeachment. The president can't stop an impeachment, his own or anyone else's, and he can't stop the Senate from convicting a federal official after impeachment and as a consequence depriving him or her of office. But that's it: otherwise, the pardon power was far-reaching.

Second, the special counsel's research fastened on a 1974 Supreme Court case, *Schick v. Reed*, while supporting the broad pardoning power, added a qualification: exercise of the power is legitimate if it "does not otherwise offend the Constitution." And in a 1915 case, *Burdick v. United States*, the Court invalidated a pardon because President Woodrow Wilson—who had pardoned a newspaper editor for any federal crimes he might have committed—had used this power expressly to negate the editor's Fifth Amendment rights and thus force him to testify. The Court therefore viewed the pardon as an infringement of the editor's constitutional rights. The research noted, however, that *Burdick* was the *only* instance where the Court had nullified a pardon.

Third, the president might issue a legal pardon, but by doing so, the team argued, he might himself commit a crime. The team's support here was an op-ed article in the *New York Times* from July 21, 2017. Its authors, Daniel Hemel and Eric Posner, wrote: "If a president sold pardons for cash . . . that would violate the federal bribery statute. And if a president can be prosecuted for exchanging pardons for bribes, then it follows that the broad and unreviewable nature of the pardon power does not shield the president from criminal liability for abusing it."

And, finally, the special counsel examined, in its legal plotting, what might be considered the mother of all disreputable pardons: Bill Clinton's pardon, in the hours before he left office in 2001, of the financier Marc Rich, who had fled to Switzerland to escape charges of financial fraud, racketeering, and tax evasion, and who, not coincidentally, had contrib-uted copiously to the Clinton campaign. In pardoning Rich, Clinton narrowly avoided prosecution himself for possible obstruction, bribery, money laundering, and other charges. The point here, grasping though it might appear, was that after Clinton's pardon of Rich, federal prose-cutors came very close to concluding that Clinton could be indicted for abusing his pardon power. In the end, the Justice Department chose not to go down that road. (The Rich pardon seemed also to be involved with diplomatic quid pro quos with Israel, where Rich was a likely Mossad asset.) But the fact that it was given serious consideration suggested that challenging a president for a self-serving pardon wasn't outside the realm of possibility.

* * *

Still, a pardon of Flynn—and for that matter anyone else whose own legal peril might induce him or her to testify against the president—would be a clear instance of the president using his authority to remove himself from the reach of the law. Such a pardon would, in the key phrase of *Schick v. Reed*, "offend the Constitution." Put simply, the president's absolute par-don power was up against that other constitutional guarantee: no one was above the law.

This was the argument—the offense against the Constitution—that few, if any, of the constitutional and Justice Department lawyers apprised of this approach thought had a chance in hell. But the draft of the special counsel's brief seeking to enjoin the anticipated presidential pardon of Michael Flynn tried to advance that argument with no apology or qual-ification:

"President Trump's attempted pardon is unique and unprecedented," read the draft. "Never before has a president so brazenly sought to obstruct an ongoing investigation by pardoning a defendant who is actively coop-erating with law enforcement. What makes the president's pardon even more unique, and farther beyond the bounds of constitutionally allow-able behavior, is that the president himself is a subject of the investigation that he attempts to impede by pardoning this key cooperating witness.

"The presidential pardon power, though broad, is not absolute. It is limited both by the text of the Pardon Clause, which prohibits exercise of pardon power in cases of impeachment, and by the Constitution as a whole, which prohibits any act that violates or otherwise offends the Constitution, including by unduly encroaching upon other, coordinate branches of government or by undermining the public interest in pur-pose or effect. President Trump's attempted pardon plainly violates both constitutional prohibitions."

This was at best a long-shot strategy, but you used what you had.

9

MIDTERMS

In May, with six months to go before the November midterm elections, twenty-five House races were highlighted for the president during three different meetings. A briefing had been prepared for each race. All would be held in critical swing districts, and all—at least in the view of some advisers—should get a visit from the president. Another view, strongly advocated by Jared Kushner, with quite some support from the Republican leadership, was that the president ought to keep as far away as possible from the midterm campaign.

In a sense, it didn't matter either way. Trump, in each of the three meetings, grew restive and inattentive within minutes. His behavior mirrored what happened in military presentations. Virtually innumerate, he was bored by both numbers and logistics—or, worse, they gave him something like brain freeze. He absorbed nothing.

There were too many members of the House. He couldn't remember their names. He launched into dramatic eye-rolling when told where they were from. "Flyovers," he said. "Men's shop salesmen."

It didn't help that his advisers were communicating two contradictory messages. The first was that the midterm House races could represent Armageddon for the Trump presidency. The second was that midterms were midterms, and that what happened in November would be more or less business as usual.

The business-as-usual model was that midterms invariably go against the party holding the White House. Hurting the GOP's prospects further was the fact that a precipitous number of Republicans—many simply giving up on Trump and Trump-age politics—were voluntarily leaving office. Add to this the painful results of several off-calendar elections in which Democratic turnout, traditionally unimpressive, had swamped Republicans. Now, with primaries wrapping up and the summer campaign season about to get under way, there were few pathways that would allow the Republicans to hold the House. Still, both Obama and Clinton had lost their majorities in their first midterm elections and yet both had served two terms.

In the Armageddon view, the current math suggested that Trump could be facing a two-year presidency. Now up by twenty-three seats, the Republicans would lose thirty, forty, fifty, or even sixty seats on November 6. At this polarized political moment, the country would likely be electing an impeachment Congress. And if the Senate fell to the Democrats, the country would likely be electing a conviction Congress.

True, the Republicans would probably hold the Senate. But Bannon, for one, had come to believe that the outcome of the House races was binary. If the Republicans held the House, Trump's presidency and the Trump agenda would remain viable; the president could hold back the determined forces against him. But if the GOP lost the House, Trump would not be able to endure a hostile Congress, one that would relish taking a deep dive into *all* of his affairs. Worse, his inevitable reaction—Bannon promised that it would be "psycho"—would undermine even his support among Republicans in the Senate.

And if the House fell, it would be a seething Republican Party. Five thousand Republican staffers could lose their jobs. Republican lobbying firms could easily go from billing $10 million a year to billing $1.5 million. Catastrophe—a Trump-caused catastrophe—in the D.C. apparat.

In the business-as-usual view, the math was actually pretty much the same. But in this scenario, a thirty- to sixty-seat loss would be, with a little critical interpretation, a gift to Trump—at least assuming the Republicans held the Senate. Just as he had run against Washington in 2016, now he would be able to do so again in 2020. Trump was at his best with an enemy: he needed the Democrats as his rabid and hysterical opposition. And enemies did not get any better than Nancy Pelosi as Speaker of the House.

Picking on Pelosi gave Trump energy. Ridiculing her gave him a special pleasure—and it was a plus that she was a woman. Impeachment? Bring it on. Since he had a fail-safe in the Senate, it would all be for show—*his* show.

Mano a mano played to Trump. It helped rouse him from his constant distraction. Fighting Congress would be a noble cause, Kushner felt; he also felt, all in all, that it was better now to keep Trump out of the confused midterm fray. This was part of the standard business as usual math: if you have an unpopular president—and Trump's numbers were about as low as any president's had ever been at this point before the midterms— you don't send him out to stump in iffy races.

And then there was Trump's own view: he found it very hard to feel in any way concerned about other people's political problems. The idea of party, of the president ultimately being a soldier in a larger effort, would never mean anything to him. Even the idea of giving a speech about someone else—*praising* someone else—was a large pill for him.

The minutiae of House districts presented yet another problem. All politics might be local, but local was noisome and small-time for Trump. Particularly irksome was the awkward dance of candidates who wanted his endorsement but simultaneously wanted to maintain their independence from him. He needed and demanded maximum deference and attention. But most of all he feared losers. All the enforced discussions about the midterm elections had focused on toss-up races, which meant that each of these candidates was a potential loser—and thus someone whose loser status might, malodorously, attach to him.

* * *

Mitch McConnell was not only telling people that the House was lost. He was turning it to his advantage, using the doomed House as the selling point to raise money for the Senate. He was sure the Senate Republican majority would be held—twenty-six Democratic seats were up, versus nine Republican seats. Further, he believed the Republicans might pick up two or even three seats. Trump would be safe in the Senate, assured McConnell. This is where to fall back and hold the line. McConnell, more and more cementing his reputation as the ultimate survivor, the one true political player of his generation, was already looking ahead to 2020, when the Senate might be considerably more difficult to defend.

Bannon believed that McConnell's willingness to let the House go—a strategic decision he made in concert with a cabal of major party donors—fell just short of conspiracy. If the Democrats were in an open and mortal war with Trump, the Republican leadership, or at least McConnell and Ryan, were in a secret mortal war with the president. Theirs was a fight for control of the party.

McConnell's contempt for Trump was boundless. He was not just the stupidest president McConnell had ever dealt with, he was the stupidest person McConnell had ever met in politics—and that was saying something. He and his wife, Elaine Chao, the secretary of transportation, regularly mocked and mimicked Trump, a set piece they would perform for friends.

Were the Republicans somehow able to hold the House in 2018, it would be, in Bannon's do-over version, a repeat victory for Trump. The anomalous, wild-card election of 2016 would now be incontrovertible. Failing to gain control of the House would have a nuclear effect on the Democrats, but a successful defense of the GOP's House majority would have a nearly equal effect on the Republicans. Even more than Trump's victory in 2016, it would spell death to the Republican establishment.

But if calamity hit the House, if the House flipped to the Democrats, Mitch McConnell would then hold virtually all the cards. Trump, who, in his own set piece, regularly belittled and mocked McConnell, would be, without a Republican House, entirely beholden to the Senate majority leader.

This, in McConnell's view, was the path to taking the party back from Trump. A Democratic House would mean that only McConnell would stand between Trump and his expulsion from office. Trump would be McConnell's prisoner.

It was Bannon's belief that McConnell had used this Machiavellian scenario to line up many of the party's major donors. McConnell *wanted* the Republicans to lose the House. He was working to that end.

* * *

Trump, to say the least, was not a natural political tactician. His organizational sense was limited. He was virtually incapable of acknowledging other people's purpose and talent. His political instincts were tone-deaf. And he dealt almost exclusively in visceral reactions.

In 2016, in make-or-break Florida, a political operative named Susie Wiles had helped Trump climb out of a steep deficit. But when, during the campaign, he met Wiles—whom he described as "looking like a refrigerator with a wig"—he demanded that she be fired. (She wasn't, and Trump won Florida.)

Now, in the spring of 2018, with the White House effectively denuded of anyone who might tell him what he did not want to hear—among the many types of people he eschewed were political head counters—Trump was happily able to put off any focus on the make-or-break midterm races.

Kushner, eager to keep his father-in-law's focus off the midterms, adopted the Trumpian "let's do big things" approach. The House might be lost, but the new opening to North Korea was going to be big. From Kushner's view, the more Trump focused on North Korea, the less he might make things worse in the midterm races.

At a moment when the White House should have been gearing up for the midterms, Trump's three closest political advisers were all outside the White House: David Bossie, Corey Lewandowski, and Sean Hannity. Each had a clear sense of what a dismal November could mean to Trump. But all three understood that their relationship with Trump depended on reinforcing what he already believed. "It's all about letting Trump be Trump," explained Hannity. "Let him go where he's going and encourage him to get there."

What's more, all three men saw the world as if from a bunker. They were fighters. They were martyrs. If the Republicans lost the House in November, they'd be in the place they knew best, defending Trump from the onslaught. They weren't operatives, they were believers, which is what Trump wanted them to be.

As for the sensible thought that the White House comms staff should get behind a political theme that would unite the White House and the party in a common fight toward November, forget it. Beyond the comms talent and leadership shortage—and the ongoing turf war among Sanders, Conway, and Mercedes Schlapp—the comms staff's job was not to be outward-looking; their mission was to look inward and please Trump by defending him in a way that met with his approval. This, of course, was impossible: they *never* pleased him. Consequently, the development of a coherent and considered piece of thinking about anything other than the boss's need to be reassured—however much of a no-win game that might be—was never going to happen.

Outside the White House walls, the party had by now settled on a strategy of its own, one that had nothing to do with the supposed virtues of Donald Trump. The Republican National Committee, the Republican House and Senate election operatives, and indeed most of the entire Republican establishment, supported by Ryan and McConnell, decided to run on the virtues of the tax reform bill that had been passed in late 2017. "It's tax reform, stupid," McConnell had taken to saying, wanting to make it as clear as possible that tax reform was a congressional accomplishment managed with scant contributions from the Trump White House.

* * *

As the midterm races heated up, it was hard to tell if Bannon's main mission was to frustrate McConnell or to save Trump. Equally, of course, he was trying to position himself. He was convinced that there was a movement beyond Trump—in which he could be kingmaker or, even, king—and that the key to it lay in taking on the Republican establishment. Hence, if his feelings about Trump were, to say the least, equivocal, he believed that on a sinking ship he had to be, in the eyes of the deplorables, the last man off the boat.

The Republican establishment, as well as many people in the White House, loathed Bannon as much as he loathed them. "Where does Steve's money come from?" was an oft-asked question in 2018. The Mercers—Bob, the hedge fund billionaire, and his daughter, Rebekah—had long supported Bannon and Breitbart News publicly. But this ended early in 2018, because of lacerating bad press and personal threats against the Mercers that, the family believed, came from their association with Trump, Bannon, and Breitbart.

After leaving the White House in August 2017, Bannon, like many other political entrepreneurs across the ideological spectrum, launched his own 501(c)(4) not-for-profit, which could raise money anonymously. In the months following his departure from the administration, Bannon had, with great discipline and attention, paid court to all of the top Trump donors.

This quiet campaign proved remarkably successful, provoking annoyance in the White House that some of the president's donors might be supporting Bannon, even supporting Bannon at the expense of Trump. It was an easy bond: many of Trump's big-money supporters admired most of Trump's policies, but almost all disliked Trump himself. Bannon became the Trump ambivalence whisperer. Trump was not the point, he argued. Where Trump could lead was the point—the destination mattered, not the man who would take you there. Bannon's pitch fell on sympathetic ears. There was a knowing rapport among people who found Trump ridiculous and yet necessary to support.

Still, Bannon needed an organizing premise, a sense of urgency. The urgency now was to save Trump from himself. So Bannon's C4, with no seeming shortage of funds, would support an election operation that would, if not rival the White House operation, ignore it—and meanwhile upstage the Republican effort to claim the election as its own.

By May, Bannon had assembled a staff and begun coordinating its efforts with a daily morning conference call. Working out of the Embassy, he quickly developed a consistent message, a surrogates operation that booked people on daily cable and talk radio shows, and a polling process to triage the sixty or so toss-up races.

It wasn't tax reform, stupid. It was Trump.

Bannon was convinced that Trump had to be on the ballot in each race. Politicians and operatives are often accused of always running the last race they had won, and for Bannon it was 2016 all over again. Only Trump could fire up the base with enough passion to turn the deplorables out for faceless congressional races. They needed to be voting for *him*.

* * *

The band was back together.

In came Sam Nunberg, David Bossie, Corey Lewandowski, Jason Miller, and several others—everybody whom Bannon had taken under his wing during the campaign.

The thing about Bannon's band was that it really *was* his band, with only a secondary, and often problematic, loyalty to Trump. As it was for Bannon, it was for them: Trump was the unaccountable, confounding, vastly annoying, but all-important centerpiece of their lives. Trump was their obsession. He ate at them.

A considerable part of the daily Trump narrative, and not the positive one, flowed from this group, beginning with Bannon, but filled in on a constant basis, sotto voce and otherwise, by the rest. Trump the clown, Trump the idiot, Trump the nutter. I-don't-give-a-shit Trump, What-me-worry Trump, Can't-put-on-my-pants Trump. The comic opera of Trump came from this crew.

Even as Bannon's bandmates worked to support Trump, they brought to this campaign mixed, if not tortured, feelings. In part this had to do with their proximity to Trump: they had all been embraced by Trump and burned by him. But it also had to do with the very nature of the people Trump pulled into his orbit. Each lived at quite some level of Trumpworld absurdity and emotional topsy-turvy; Trump was just part of their ongoing personal roller coaster.

Jason Miller, a long-suffering political operative and PR executive, had been brought into the Trump campaign by Ken Kurson, the editor of Kushner's newspaper, the *New York Observer*. Miller had become an able Trump whisperer—his stoic forbearance helpful here—and he seemed destined to be appointed the White House communications director. (During the campaign, Miller was the first caller of the morning. It was his task to sweet-talk the overnight and early morning bad press for Trump.) Then came news of Miller's relationship with another Trump campaign worker, a liaison that resulted in a pregnancy just as Miller's wife became pregnant, too. This nixed the comms director job, which was bad enough. But worse was to come, for Miller's campaign lover, A. J. Delgado—who moved in with her mother in Florida and went on to deliver and raise her and Miller's child—commenced a legal and media war meant to bankrupt and disgrace him. Along the way, Miller became a paid Trump defender on CNN, causing Trump to remark, "I get the people who no one else wants."

Corey Lewandowski, heretofore a lower-tier Republican political operative, got the campaign manager job because no one else wanted it. When Trump was casting around in 2015 for campaign staff, his calls were passed like hot potatoes even among operatives who undoubtedly needed the work. David Bossie, at the last minute declining to meet with Trump himself, passed the job off to Lewandowski. Lewandowski was known for a volatile temper, an attention-deficit problem, and his desperation for a job. Within a short time, he became wholly devoted to Trump. Corey, said Bannon, not necessarily as a compliment, would put his hand over an open flame and watch his fingers burn off before rolling on Trump.

For Trump, Lewandowski became "like my real son" (which, nevertheless, did not prevent Trump from mocking Lewandowski as an "ass kisser"). This caused seismic problems with Trump's actual sons, opening an ongoing rift between the Trump family and Lewandowski, with Lewandowski forced out in June 2016 by Don Jr. and Kushner. Ever since, Lewandowski had tried, often successfully, to work himself back into Trump's political family.

Bannon, who had worked in the past with David Bossie on a handful of right-wing agitprop films, brought Bossie into the campaign in September 2016. (Bossie had, in fact, first introduced Bannon to Trump in 2011, a meeting after which Bannon unequivocally dismissed Trump's seriousness as a current or future political candidate.) Bossie was the one person on the team with actual political organizing talents. Bossie focused on developing a robust door-to-door operation, a new concept for the Trump campaign. But Trump didn't fully trust him: Bossie looked "shifty—can't look me in the eye." Bossie, like Chris Christie, tended to get too close to Trump, physically crowding him. "They're bulls, they're bulls, they're all over me," complained Trump. Kushner regarded Bossie's past right-wing work—as an anti-Clinton investigator in the Whitewater years and as one of the prime organizers of the Citizens United lawsuit that unleashed unlimited corporate campaign contributions—as "vast right-wing conspiracy stuff." During the transition, Bossie was frozen out of a White House job.

Sam Nunberg, perhaps more than anyone, personified the peril and the absurdity of a relationship with Trump. Nunberg, a baby-faced thirty-six-year-old, was the son of prominent lawyers, and he had squeaked into a low-rent law degree of his own. With few prospects of a blue-chip legal career, he fell into volunteer political work and then into a position with Roger Stone, Trump's friend and adviser. Stone was a long-out-of-date Reagan-era political operative; variously disgraced and yet still an indefatigable self-promoter, he was ridiculous to virtually everyone except Trump—and even Trump treated him rather like a dog who kept creeping back into the house. Through Stone, Nunberg came to work full-time for Trump.

Starting in 2011, Nunberg was Trump's on-again, off-again political aide and adviser, loyal and dogged during the years when Trump was at best a political circus act. "There is no President Trump without Sam Nunberg," declared Bannon. "To the extent that Trump becomes even a half-legitimate political narrative, Nunberg invented it."

So, of course, Trump fired him. "He lives with his parents," Trump complained.

Lewandowski was Nunberg's replacement. During the campaign, Trump and Nunberg plunged into bitter litigation with each other, as though no one was watching.

Even after his firing, Nunberg never moved very far from the Trump orbit. This was partly because no other job, after Trump, was beckoning, but also because Nunberg—as a prime repository of institutional memory and the only person who really knew Trump—kept being pulled back into Trumpworld.

Nunberg was also a go-to, often astute, and always available source for almost every reporter covering Trump. Certainly Nunberg could be counted on to provide a confirmation of every negative story about Trump. When Trump criticized the media, he was in many instances criticizing Sam Nunberg.

Nunberg was frequently the connective tissue between Trump rumors and Trump news. Receiving a rumor, Nunberg in real time passed it off as breathless fact to one or more sources, ever increasing his own usefulness if not credibility. "I think of Maggie Haberman"—the *New York Times* reporter covering Trump—"the way I think of my grandmother," said Nunberg. "I always go running to her."

And yet, like others, he was wedded, no matter how bad the marriage, to Trump.

In late February, Nunberg was called to testify before the Mueller grand jury. Shortly before he was due to testify, he received word of some cutting remark Trump had made about him. Mightily hurt—once again mightily hurt—he took solace in a weekend of cocaine and prostitutes. On Monday morning, sleepless and high, he decided to refuse to show up for his grand jury appointment. He announced and reaffirmed his refusal—which he would reverse by the end of the day—on no fewer than eleven television and radio shows, one after the other, a real-time Trumpian melodrama and a train wreck of pain, recrimination, and substance abuse. It was also a media tour de force.

In 1998, Monica Lewinsky's lawyer William H. Ginsburg appeared on all five of the Sunday morning talk shows on the same day. This became known as the "full Ginsburg." The "full Nunberg" outdid Ginsburg's feat by no small amount, and after a bender weekend, too.

"Everybody said, 'You can't hire this guy, he got all coked up and went on eleven shows,'" said Bannon. "But how could I *not* hire him? He spent the weekend doing blow off a bunch of girls' asses and then got up and did eleven shows. It's all in the quality of the fuck you, and this was pretty high-quality fuck you."

* * *

You couldn't miss the sense of codependence here. Trump's key supporters worked for him because nobody else would have them.

For Bannon, bitter about many things, but now, at sixty-four, having the time of his life, electing Trump was the ultimate fuck you. Part of his mission was to elect Trump precisely to shock and outrage all of the people who so passionately didn't want him elected. "What is the point of democracy if not of an upset?" he would ask. The fact that Trump was Trump was a separate issue; yes, he was an imperfect weapon, but he was the weapon at hand.

For Bannon, Trump's campaign and his presidency were partly a dare. Stop me if you can—and if you can't, then you deserve Trump. His contempt for Democrats was, in its way, not directed at Democrats per se, but at what he regarded as the mediocrities they produced, a set of placeholders who did not have the necessary political gifts. He would enumerate their names in one breath: Hillary Clinton, Elizabeth Warren, Cory Booker, Kamala Harris, Kirsten Gillibrand. "That's who they've got? *That's* who they've got? Stop! You're killing me."

Even so, holding Congress was something that could only happen in spite of Trump. This was the real point: Trump couldn't manage or accomplish his own election. He couldn't execute, to say the least. Trump was merely a symbol, though, as it happened, an extraordinarily powerful one. Hence, the necessity of Steve Bannon.

In the presidential campaign, the goal had not been to win, but to reduce the margin from 17 to 20 points to a more respectable 6 points. For Bannon, that would have been adequate proof of concept; it would have demonstrated the power of the populist cause. Then Trump actually won, producing a whole other, not unproblematic, dynamic.

Now, in the midterms, a close loss might work better for Bannon. A twenty-five-seat loss—two over the majority—would mean that Trump would need every friend he had, including Bannon. Perhaps most of all Bannon.

"I think it is actually possible we'll pull this off and hold the House," said Nunberg. "It's possible—really. But, if not, it will be fun to watch Trump squirm. I'd pay for that."

10

KUSHNER

Just as Donald Trump was directing his "fire and fury" threat against North Korea in rambling remarks after a luncheon at his Bedminster, New Jersey, golf club in the summer of 2017, his son-in-law began a very different conversation.

The Chinese—aided by Henry Kissinger and deeply concerned about Trump's fixation on North Korea, while also aware of the leverage the North Korea situation might give them—reached out to Jared Kushner. The young man, absent any obvious experience, had quietly established himself with many world leaders and, similarly, with his father-in-law, as the brains, such as they were, behind the Trump foreign policy.

The president had often threatened to "dump" his secretary of state Rex Tillerson, whom he had quickly soured on, and replace him with Kushner. Kushner told friends he thought it was too soon; Kissinger had advised him to wait, counseling him to first put his name on a major initiative.

That summer, the Chinese put Kushner in touch with Gabriel Schulze, a U.S. investor. Schulze was part of a new class of international fortune hunters working at the intersection of international financial markets and troublesome regimes, including North Korea. Personal relationships, especially in parts of the world with autocratic rulers, were the most valuable currency. Since arriving in the White House, Kushner had worked hard at developing his own relationships with leaders who, with a word, could alter the shape of the world stage. These kinds of men could make things happen in a hurry, and both Kushner and Trump wanted to override the slow and cautious pace of the international world order.

Schulze was the emissary of a backdoor opening, encouraged by the Chinese, from North Korean leader Kim Jong-un. Trump had declared a virtual death match against the young despot. But the Chinese saw opportunity: during the meeting in April 2017 at Mar-a-Lago between Trump and President Xi—a meeting shepherded by Kissinger and Kushner—they had been amazed at Trump's openness, capriciousness, and lack of basic information.

The Chinese believed that Trump's stated views should not be taken all that seriously. Indeed, the Schulze initiative represented a sophisticated understanding of the new Trump diplomatic reality. In Trump's Washington it was possible to avoid the State Department, the foreign policy establishment, the intelligence community, and virtually every other normal diplomatic process or restraint. The chief work-around to institutional diplomacy was through Kushner, the self-appointed foreign policy expert. The White House joke, said with an amazed slap to the face, was that Kushner was a modern-day Metternich.

Through the fall of 2017 and into the winter, Kushner quietly urged his father-in-law to take a different view of the North Korea issue. He told Trump that if he made peace, he could win the Nobel Peace Prize, just like Obama.

Hence, on June 10, 2018, a bit less than a year after Schulze's approach to Kushner, the president arrived in Singapore to meet Kim Jong-un. The previous summer, all but unaware of the issues involved in the long stalemate with North Korea, Trump had threatened imminent war. Now, hardly better informed, he offered the North Korean leader one of the most fawning and peculiar embraces in diplomatic history.

* * *

Not long after his father-in-law's election, Kushner—encouraged by Rupert Murdoch, whom he had befriended when they were neighbors in a Trump-branded building on Park Avenue—reached out to Henry Kissinger for advice and counsel. Kushner had decided that he would take an official position in the Trump White House and that, given his family ties, he would be able to forge a role for himself as a direct conduit to the president. In this, he imagined that a new kind of clarity and efficiency could be brought to bear on the world's most pressing issues—the personal touch. It seemed of no significance that he knew very little about these issues beyond what he read in the *New York Times*.

Kushner saw Kissinger as a key to his great leap forward. The older man—he was then ninety-four—was flattered by the younger man's attentions. Kushner was not just deferential and solicitous, he enthusiastically embraced the Kissinger doctrine—the belief that mutual interest ought to form the basis for sagacious moves on the international chess board in the quest for ultimate advantage.

Kushner, without illusions about his father-in-law's lack of interest in foreign policy matters, saw himself, just as Kissinger had once seen himself, as the wiser and more focused adviser to a less sophisticated president. And while others might think Kissinger had become an elderly gas bag—and that he was, as ever, a shameless social climber—Kushner believed that Kissinger could provide him with special advantage in his new Washington world.

Kushner dropped his new friend's name shamelessly: "Henry says . . ." "I was just talking to Henry . . ." "I'd like to get Henry's take on that . . ." "Let's loop Henry in . . ."

"Jared's Uncle Henry" was Ivanka's perhaps not entirely approving designation.

For Kissinger—still globe-trotting, still at work at Kissinger Associates most days, still social climbing—the startling opportunity at his advanced age was to become the key adviser to one of the most significant foreign policy players, perhaps *the* most significant foreign policy player, in the U.S. government. And the essential point, as Kissinger explained to friends, was that Kushner, with zero experience in international relations, was a blank slate.

In the weeks after the election, Kissinger went out of his way to widely praise Jared's willingness to listen and the quickness with which he learned. Kushner, for his part, praised Kissinger's unfaltering acuity and renewed relevance in a complicated world. Kushner even floated the suggestion of Kissinger as secretary of state, relaying this idea back to Kissinger.

Trump told people that Kissinger was in full support of his hope for a new friendship with Russia, saying that Kissinger regarded Vladimir Putin with "fantastic respect—loves him."

Through much of the first year of the new administration, Jared continued to call on Kissinger. Even as Trump's foreign policy began to careen in uncharted directions—casual saber rattling, daily tariff threats, slavish embrace of despotic figures—Kissinger, enjoying his heightened prestige, remained tempered and supportive, reassuring his wide circle of concerned foreign policy experts and international businessmen that the drama and the tweets were irrelevant, that an impulsive Trump was contained by a thoughtful Kushner.

But in early 2017, Kissinger, lobbied by Kushner to write an encomium about the young man for *Time*'s annual list of the hundred most influential people, seemed forced to balance his own status-seeking inclinations against Kushner's lack of foreign policy bona fides.

> As part of the Trump family, Jared is familiar with the intangibles of the president. As a graduate of Harvard and NYU, he has a broad education; as a businessman, a knowledge of administration. All this should help him make a success of his daunting role flying close to the sun.

The subtle hedging of his bet on Kushner did not go unnoticed by the foreign policy professionals in the new Trump administration.

* * *

Through much of their first year in Washington, Jared and Ivanka seemed often to regret their move into official positions. The president too seemed to have frequent second thoughts. A beleaguered Kushner was perceived as having been blamed by his father-in-law for myriad bad decisions, including the Comey firing. He had been pummeled by Steve Bannon, viciously in public and murderously in private. In short order, Kushner had become one of the least sympathetic figures in modern politics. (Don

Jr. had become quite a sought-after surrogate for his father in right-wing circles, whereas an effort to enhance Jared's public face had ended very quickly.) The once-golden couple had, in the eyes of many, hopelessly lost their social cachet. Even their neighbors gave them the cold shoulder. "I don't know if anyone will ever understand what we've been through," Ivanka told friends.

But in the administration's second year, there began to be a new perception of what Rex Tillerson, the then secretary of state, called "the curious case of Jared Kushner." Tillerson had come to detest Kushner for his meddling, leaking, and personal agenda. Yet along with administration officials, as well as people in law enforcement, he had begun to notice that callow Jared Kushner, once an obvious victim of his own ineptness and hubris, seemed to be pursuing a much more calculated plan.

Kushner's personal wealth depended on a shaky business whose precarious financial foundation rested on less-than-creditworthy loans. These were the kinds of loans secured through personal relationships and, not unusually, the trading of favors and influence. Often, they were obtained from countries with lax regulatory rules.

Kushner's father, Charlie, famously malevolent and brutish, had gone to federal prison for tax fraud and witness tampering; he had tried to blackmail his own brother-in-law with a prostitute. But the sins of the father—whom Trump derided as a crook with no money—had largely been judged as having no bearing on Jared's nature as infinitely modulated and sober-minded.

Yet Jared's temperament did not change the fact that the family business was sorely overextended. Real estate development businesses frequently are, but the Kushner family's leap from garden-apartment builder in New Jersey to Manhattan tower owner and New York City landlord had been particularly headlong, much of it happening under Jared's titular leadership while his father was in prison. As the Trump administration began, the Kushners faced a looming refinancing of their premier property, 666 Fifth Avenue, and a strained market for their plan to build a tech center in the vast square footage they held in Brooklyn.

Jared's decision to enter the White House left the Kushner family business all the more public and exposed. What's more, it put his father-in-law in a terrible position. Powerful men are, inevitably, vulnerable through their families. Not only did Trump have myriad problems of his own, he now had the Kushners' problems.

Still, what initially seemed like naïveté and bad judgment began to seem like the moves of a high-risk player. Perhaps Kushner's seeming equanimity and restraint were just a proper poker face. Whatever you could say by the spring of 2018 about the Trump White House, Jared had, for the most part, successfully navigated it—the only person, other than his wife, to have done so. And in the back channels of a world that he was counting on to play an essential role in securing his wealth, he had had a singular impact.

* * *

Outside of Western democracies, much of the world's foreign policy was transactional in nature. Personal enrichment and an individual's hold on power were ruling concerns in all but the most stable states and regions. This had become more pronounced as private fortunes vied with governments or collaborated with them. The oligarch-billionaire world—from Russia to China, from South Asia to the Gulf states—ran its own diplomatic missions. People who had the money to bribe, who fundamentally believed that anyone could be bribed, and who had outsize influence on the legal structures that might otherwise restrict bribery, had become major foreign policy players in key parts of the world.

For decades, the United States had reliably frustrated transactional and freelance diplomatic efforts. The American government was too big, its institutions too entrenched, its bureaucracy too powerful, its foreign policy establishment too influential. The international world of fixers and operators, often referred to euphemistically as "investors" and "representatives," had to toil long and hard to be heard in Washington.

Enter Jared Kushner.

Almost immediately after his father-in-law's election, Kushner became the sought-after point man for any foreign government inclined to deal with a family rather than an array of institutions. Instead of depending on a vast and frequently unresponsive bureaucracy to arbitrate and process your concerns, you could go directly to Kushner, and Kushner could go to the president-elect. Once Trump was inaugurated, you had, through Kushner, an all but direct line to the president.

Side deals, personal introductions, quid pro quos, agents and subagents—all these quickly spawned a parallel diplomatic force, a legion of people representing themselves as having a direct relationship with the president. Michael Cohen, Trump's personal lawyer, opened for business and began collecting money from dubious characters and regimes. Chris Ruddy, who ran a conservative news site that marketed vitamin supplements and was a Palm Beach confidant of the president's, suddenly, in May 2018, had a $90 million investment offer from Qatar. David Pecker, the president's friend who ran the supermarket tabloid the *National Enquirer*, walked a high-placed Saudi intermediary into the White House and was suddenly talking to the Saudis about backing his quixotic, if not screwball, effort to acquire *Time* magazine.

But the most efficient point of contact was Trump's son-in-law. Russian, Chinese, and Middle Eastern diplomatic strategy centered on Kushner. European, Canadian, and British efforts did not, and they seemed to suffer for it.

In a side deal that was unprecedented in modern diplomatic history, intermediaries from Saudi Arabia's deputy Crown Prince, Mohammed bin Salman (MBS), approached Kushner during the transition period before the Trump administration entered the White House. The key issue for the House of Saud was financial—specifically, declining oil prices and an ever growing and more demanding royal family supported by oil output. The thirty-one-year-old deputy Crown Prince's solution was economic diversification. This would be funded by taking the Saudi-owned oil company Aramco public, at an anticipated $2 trillion valuation.

But first the plan would have to surmount a not inconsiderable obstacle: JASTA, the Justice Against Sponsors of Terrorism Act, which was expressly written to make it possible for 9/11 victims to sue Saudi Arabia. If Aramco were listed on a foreign exchange, it would be particularly vulnerable to anyone taking advantage of the opening provided by JASTA; in fact, Aramco's liability would be virtually unlimited. Hence, who would invest?

Not to worry: Kushner was on the case. If MBS would help Jared with a menu of items, including pressuring the Palestinians, Jared would help MBS. Indeed, MBS, to the consternation of the State Department—who backed his cousin the Crown Prince Muhammed bin Nayef (MBN)—would be one of the first state visitors to the White House. Three months later, without any White House objections, MBS ousted his cousin and became Crown Prince, the presumptive heir to the throne and the effective day-to-day Saudi leader.

It was the Trump administration's first coup.

To win favor with Kushner, the rich Gulf states—Qatar, the United Arab Emirates, and Saudi Arabia—competed with each other or partnered with each other. In this, Kushner found himself, or had positioned himself, as one of the essential players in one of the world's largest pools of unregulated free cash flow.

* * *

The Trump White House had, in an almost formal way, designated China as the number one enemy, replacing Russia and the former Soviet Union. Trump had a personal antipathy to the Chinese—not only were they the "yellow peril," they were unfair competitors. This complemented Bannon's unified field theory of the twenty-first century: China was both the rising power that would swamp the United States and the economic bubble that would burst, pulling the world into a fearful vortex.

Kushner's position was much less clear.

A key Kushner connection was Stephen Schwarzman, CEO of the Blackstone Group, one of the world's largest private equity funds, whose business view was significantly predicated on the continued growth of the Chinese consumer market. Kushner brought Schwarzman into the White House to head one of its business advisory groups; as a consequence, Schwarzman became Trump's most important blue-chip business contact.

Kushner and Schwarzman, along with other Wall Street figures in the administration, formed the opposition to Bannon and the architects of the Trump trade policy, Peter Navarro and Robert Lighthizer. The anti-China group proposed an all-out trade war with China. The Kushner group, with its deep and growing ties to China, sought to make a softer deal.

In early 2017, U.S. intelligence officials secretly briefed Kushner about Rupert Murdoch's former wife Wendi Deng. A decade earlier, Deng had facilitated both Kushner's relationship with Murdoch and Kushner's relationship with Ivanka, one of Deng's close friends. The Murdoch–Deng and Kushner–Trump relationships continued to blossom when they were neighbors in the Trump building on Park Avenue. Now, in the White House, Kushner was told that there was good reason to believe Deng was a spy for the Chinese. She was, Kushner was informed, regularly supplying information gleaned from her social and political contacts to Chinese officials and business figures.

This was, as it happened, just what her former husband was saying to almost anyone who would listen: Wendi was working for the Chinese, and she'd probably always been working for the Chinese. ("I knew it," declared Trump.) Kushner dismissed the intelligence assessment and said, confidently, that Murdoch was going a little senile.

Eight days after the election, Kushner, in an introduction aided by Deng, had had dinner with Wu Xiaohui, the chairman of Anbang Insurance Group, the Chinese financial conglomerate. Wu, who had partnered with Schwarzman on a variety of deals, was a close associate of the Chinese leadership—Wu's wife was the granddaughter of former Chinese leader Deng Xiaoping. One of the current financial era's most successful global tycoons, Wu had built Anbang from a company with an annual turnover of a few million dollars to one with $300 billion in assets in just ten years.

The Kushner family, through the early months of the administration, negotiated with Wu and pushed for a bailout deal for 666 Fifth Avenue. In March 2017, following negative publicity about the deal, both sides backed away. In June, the Chinese government removed Wu from the company and later sentenced him to prison on financial corruption charges.

* * *

In the White House, Kushner and Bannon represented the opposite polls of liberal globalism and right-wing nationalism. Bannon, for one, believed that Kushner showed the true and deeply self-interested face of liberal globalism. The Kushner family's desperate need for cash was turning

U.S. foreign policy into an investment banking scheme dedicated to the refinancing of the Kushner family debt. Government service regularly greased the wheels for future private careers and wealth, but Kushner, in Bannon's view, was taking this to astounding new levels of self-dealing.

The personal and ideological blood score between Bannon and Kushner had continued even after Bannon was pushed out of the White House. Indeed, many believed that Bannon was merely waiting for Kushner to be exposed and exiled, thus opening the door to his own return. But Bannon had come to believe that you could not separate Jared from the president, and that Jared was now one more point of mortal exposure for Trump. "They would gladly throw each other under the bus," said Bannon, "but they are so in each other's business that if one gets run over so does the other."

The Trump–Kushner family soap opera played out on multiple levels of exposure, even beyond the constant attention to business opportunities. There was former New Jersey governor Chris Christie, who had prosecuted Charlie Kushner. Jared and Ivanka, urged on by Charlie Kushner, had blocked Christie's expected appointment to a high position in the Trump administration. Christie, well versed in Kushner family business practices, was—or so both the pro- and anti-Jared forces believed—eagerly and pitilessly talking to former colleagues in the Justice Department about the pressure points that might be applied to the family and its princeling. Christie was also supplying to journalists details of his investigation of the Kushner family while he had been a federal prosecutor.

* * *

Jared saw himself as a problem solver. He was clear-eyed and methodical. Success was all about pushing through the challenges. *Be clear about what you want. Be clear about what you can get. Focus on where you can make a difference.* "Jared's self-help, business-book-leadership talk was one of the things that attracted Ivanka to him," said a friend of the couple.

By the spring of 2018, however, Jared Kushner had become another front in the president's legal problems. He was a subject of the special counsel's investigation; he was being looked at by federal prosecutors in both the Southern and Eastern Districts of New York (the Eastern District was claiming its primacy in "all things Kushner"); and the Manhattan district attorney was fishing for its piece of the action.

One curious aspect of the investigation of Kushner involved Ken Kurson, a Kushner crony and lieutenant who in 2013 had stepped in to edit Kushner's newspaper, the *New York Observer*, after a string of editors had clashed with Kushner over his desire to use the paper to support his family's financial interests. More recently, Kushner had helped Kurson secure the offer of an appointment to the board of the National Endowment for the Humanities. The FBI's background check on Kurson during the spring of 2018 had focused on a string of allegations following the breakup of his marriage in 2013–14, including spousal abuse, stalking, and the targeting of his wife's best friend, a doctor at Mt. Sinai Hospital. The doctor was holding emails and other electronic information that might be damaging to Kurson, information related not only to the marriage but potentially to the *New York Observer* and Kushner.

Kurson's troubles then become an issue in Kushner's own security clearance background check. The Eastern District and the FBI were pursuing reports that Kushner had taken extreme measures to help his friend. The Mt. Sinai doctor had an apartment in the same building in which Kushner lived—a Trump building. (The doctor's presence in the building had, in better days, been facilitated by Kurson's wife through Kushner.) Prosecutors and the FBI had been told that Kushner, using a pass key from the building, had entered the doctor's apartment seeking to take her computer.

The quest to get Kushner had become almost as intense as the quest to get Trump. In addition to reviewing the Anbang deal, prosecutors were taking a close look at a $285 million 2016 Deutsche Bank loan to Kushner and his father, and at a direct pitch for a bailout made to the Qatar minister of finance in 2017.

By now it had become a constant topic of discussion and calculation among many media people and Democrats, not to mention all but the most buttoned-up Trump hands: the possible indictment of the president's son-in-law. And if the indictment came down, would it land before or after the indictment of the president's son Don Jr.?

Kushner's lawyer Abbe Lowell, a renowned gossip, speculated to friends about what could become an exquisitely difficult dilemma: having to choose between one's father and one's father-in-law, who happened to be the president. Lowell quite seemed to relish that devil's choice. At the same time, Lowell was everywhere, it seemed, saying that Kushner was out of danger—and claiming credit for it. Lowell had become one of the key advisers on not just Kushner legal issues, but Jared and Ivanka's larger political strategy.

For Kushner, the long game was the 2020 campaign. He was convinced the Republicans would lose the House in November 2018; so be it. But no matter who became the Democratic nominee in 2020, it would likely be a very close electoral race. That prospect could prove to be an advantage during the campaign: tight numbers would keep the party in line. As long as the Republican Party held, they could block the Democratic venom. And with a majority in the Senate, impeachment was a toothless threat.

Kushner's model, he told friends, was Israeli prime minister and family friend "Bibi" Netanyahu. Whatever charges were leveled against him, Bibi, ever attentive to his base, was able to fend them off because he could always be counted on to win his next election. Early in 2018, Kushner had installed his ally Brad Parscale—who had run the data effort for the 2016 presidential campaign—as the head of the 2020 campaign. Looking forward, Kushner planned, at the appropriate moment, to take the reins of the campaign himself.

What stood between now and then was his father-in-law's volatility. It was only inside the Kushner family, particularly in conversations with his father and brother, that Jared discussed the extraordinary challenges of working with and trying to manage Trump. Kushner's analysis was the same as nearly everyone's who spent a significant amount of time around the president. He was childlike—a hyperactive child at that. There was no clear reason for why something caught his interest, nor was there any way to predict his reaction or modulate his response to it. He had no ability to distinguish the important from the less important. There seemed to be no such thing as objective reality.

Kushner's brother Josh, fervently anti-Trump, was always trying to explain his brother's involvement in the Trump administration to friends. *He feels the same way as everyone else*, Josh emphasized. *He sees it clearly.*

But Jared's future depended on managing Trump. He would have to accomplish the near impossible—which, in fact, he believed he could do. The downside was great, but so was the upside. He and his wife saw a future in which they would parlay their moment in the international sun into something of stupendous value to them.

It was a central attribute of the Trump White House. To fully comprehend the desire of the first couple to advance, you had to appreciate their belief that, in front of them, they had an open path to their *own* White House. This Trump White House was merely their stepping-stone.

* * *

Although Kushner had been a prime mover in Comey's dismissal—the move that precipitated almost all of the crises that followed—he now had become a strong advocate for not firing Mueller or Rosenstein. Under Abbe Lowell's tutelage—"Jared loves a tutor," said one friend—he had come to see the legal process as one of containment and management.

What you did not want to do is give clarity to the issues, and here Trump's constant diversions were of considerable help. But you also did not want to increase the level of conflict, which was Trump's natural response to any problem. In Kushner's mind, his father Charlie's battle to upend the investigation undertaken by federal prosecutors became the model of what *not* to do.

"Let's not break anything," became Kushner's constant advice to his bull-in-a-china-shop father-in-law.

Where Bannon believed, more and more, that the longevity of the Trump administration would depend on the outcome of the midterm elections, Kushner believed that his father-in-law's fortunes—and his own as well—depended on successfully preparing for and participating in the 2020 campaign. You just had to get there, to keep moving Trump forward.

The key to managing his father-in-law—as everyone in Trump's family, in the Trump Organization, on *The Apprentice*, and now in the White House understood—was distraction. The more, for instance, Kushner could persuade Trump to get involved in foreign policy, the less he would obsess about his own more immediate political and legal issues. This became, too, a proof-positive aspect of Kushner's belief that he could in fact engage his father-in-law, that he, above everyone else in the White House, could understand and tap into Trump's real desires and agenda. Or, with more cunning yet, that he could make *his* agenda Trump's agenda.

* * *

In early 2018, as Kushner refined his strategy for shifting Trump's focus from his present troubles, his thinking reflected advice he had received from Kissinger, who had served as Nixon's national security advisor and secretary of state. Nixon had been distracted from his legal problems by foreign policy excursions, and, Kissinger noted, this had distracted the media, too.

Over lunch at Bedminster shortly after the New Year, Kushner told his father-in-law that he should completely rethink his approach to North Korea. Kushner sketched out the favorable consequences: not only would he change the world opinion of his presidency, he could rub the noses of so many Trump haters in his accomplishment. Taking on one of the world's most volatile situations and reversing it was a PR no-brainer.

It would be like Nixon going to China, Kushner told the president, a major historical development. *One for the history books*—a favorite Trump phrase and standard.

Kushner assured his father-in-law that he could declare victory in his campaign against North Korea and proclaim peace. Kushner had been told—or at least this is what he told his father-in-law—that not only was Kim ready to deal, he personally admired Trump. Flattery was flowing through the backdoor channels.

Over the course of that lunch—hamburgers were served—Trump's yearlong campaign to confront, demonize, and provoke North Korea, a personal enterprise supported by no one in the White House, was entirely put aside.

* * *

Bannon believed that Kushner and Trump were being duped by the Chinese. Keeping his eye on Kim's train rides from Pyongyang to Beijing,

Bannon concluded that the Chinese client state would provide Trump with a great public relations opportunity, but this would also give China more leverage. After negotiating a flimsy handshake deal with Kim, Trump would be beholden to the Chinese, whom he would need to make the North Koreans deliver on their promises, such as they were.

News of the proposed summit with Kim broke in early March. Trump's foreign policy team—Tillerson, Mattis, McMaster, even the wholeheartedly loyal Pompeo—was relieved that the president was no longer issuing reckless threats, but confused and appalled that, in place of his taunts, he seemed ready to give away the store. With no revision of policy, no change in anything other than mood music, Trump had agreed to a radical alteration in the country's posture toward North Korea.

It was Mattis who was said to have identified the reverse Wag the Dog theory. In 1998, the Clinton administration sent air strikes against purported Osama bin Laden training camps, a largely pointless attack that, critics charged, was meant solely to draw attention away from the Monica Lewinsky scandal, and an event that eerily mirrored the plot of a recently released movie, *Wag the Dog*. The North Korea gambit might work equally well: it would offer up a phony peace that would distract the media and the opposition. But that was not all. Trump's foreign policy team also concluded that, although there would be no real alteration in the threat capabilities of North Korea, a hostile regime would nevertheless be converted to a seemingly much less hostile one. It would be an ass-backward but significant triumph of diplomacy.

A new theory, one that Kushner seemed to be acting on, began to emerge in the White House. The fear that Trump might go to war—that in a temper tantrum or a fit of megalomania, he would release the awesome power of the U.S. military—was misplaced. Modern warfare was data-driven; going to war required a decision tree involving ever more complex data points, meaning not just many hours but many months of meetings and PowerPoint presentations. But Trump had no patience for such meetings. Since he had begun to inveigh against North Korea, no one had been able to get him to spend more than a few minutes on the long-studied cause-and-effect matrix of what might happen in the event of military moves against North Korea.

The issue was not that he might act precipitously and recklessly because he didn't understand the consequences of doing so. The issue was that he could not comprehend the actual choices that needed to be made in order to act; indeed, he could not even stay in the room long enough to decide on a course of action. For Trump, the fog of war would waylay him before the first command could be given.

* * *

In the weeks before the grand trip to Singapore, worries about the difficulty of briefing the president became both a critical concern and a topic of high comedy. There was almost no particular—not geographic, not economic, not military, not historical—that he seemed to grasp. Could he even identify the Korean peninsula on a map?

But as the trip approached, Trump was full of increasing confidence and brio. He acted like a commander. He was inside the role. He seemed to feel not one iota of hesitation about how he would handle himself, even though, as the entire White House seemed to appreciate, he knew nothing whatsoever about the situation at hand.

For Mattis, incredulity battled with disgust. He began to tell people that he doubted he could make any contribution to the process, in terms of either how to restrain the president or how to move him.

Trump was promising "denuclearization," while the White House and foreign policy people trailed behind him and tried to clarify a nonexistent process for achieving this end, as well as the terms for this sometime-in-the-future denuclearization status. Then, in defiance of the most basic North and South Korean norms and assumptions—or, perhaps, just to fuck with the foreign policy people and, especially, Mattis, who increasingly irked him—Trump suddenly began talking about withdrawing U.S. troops from the Korean peninsula. That is, for perhaps nothing in return, he might give China and North Korea what they most wanted: the transformative change that would remove the United States from the region's power equation. Shortstopping this disaster quickly became the central goal of the foreign policy team. A successful summit would be one that did not permit China and North Korea to achieve total victory.

In the annals of American foreign policy, this might have been one of the most peculiar moments ever. The pugnacious president of the United States had abruptly begun to sound like a latter-day peacenik; soon he would be embracing his mortal enemy and, perhaps, talking about turning the other cheek. The media, having bitterly criticized Trump for his warlike posture, now, in confusion, appeared to decide that they must praise him for his new and sudden language of tolerance, patience, tranquility, and even affection.

* * *

The president arrived in Singapore on June 10. Mike Pompeo, John Bolton, John Kelly, Stephen Miller, Sarah Huckabee Sanders, and National Security Council aide Matt Pottinger accompanied him. Trump had invited Hannity to come; he would be something like the summit's official broadcaster. Almost as soon as it began, the trip was wholly celebratory—marred only by Trump's complaints about having to meet with the prime minister of Singapore, Lee Hsien Loong, the day after his arrival.

"As you know, we've got a very interesting meeting tomorrow," Trump said in his public remarks to Prime Minister Lee. "We've got a very interesting meeting in particular tomorrow, and I just think it's going to work out very nicely."

"The president is well-prepared for tomorrow's engagement with Chairman Kim," said Pompeo to reporters, even as he privately told friends that Trump had avoided anything beyond the most superficial preparation.

On June 12, the president and Chairman Kim convened shortly after 9:00 a.m.

"I feel really great," said the president at a photo op with Kim before their meeting. "We're going to have a great discussion and, I think, tremendous success. It will be tremendously successful. And it's my honor. And we will have a terrific relationship, I have no doubt."

"Well, it was not easy to get here," said Kim through his interpreter. "The past worked as fetters on our limbs, and the old prejudices and practices worked as obstacles on our way forward. But we overcame all of them, and we are here today."

They met for thirty-eight minutes.

This was not a summit in which the relationship between two nations would turn on the fine print of any ultimate agreement. Instead, this meeting marked the beginning of the new inverted relationship between two men, neither of whom spoke the other's language. Prior to the summit, they were hard-core enemies; afterward, they would become sincerely respectful friends. Any substantive policy discussion, even among aides, was largely dispensed with. Both men merely wanted to ratify their new relationship and their status as ultimate leaders.

"Brilliant," said Bannon, appreciating the Trump moment. "He achieves total command presence. Here's a thing he knows nothing about. He can't be briefed because he can't understand any of it. So they just give up trying. They tell him that nuclear is worse than all of them and hope he gets it. But he's got command presence. He looks the part."

It was, too, the moment when any pretense of an ordered, structured, cause-and-effect, expert-focused, process-led foreign policy went out the window. And it was also the moment that Trump appeared to have lost Jim Mattis, the last bridge to establishment thinking in the administration.

Mattis had begun to think that in Trump he had met his Captain Queeg.

11

HANNITY

By the second week of June, Immigration and Customs Enforcement agents were grabbing babies from their mothers. Images of ICE separations quickly became the daily face of Trumpism.

"When that little kid washed up on the beach in Greece"—three-year-old Alan Kurdi, a Syrian boy captured in a 2015 photo that gained international notice—"that was not the moment when snowflake revulsion called the world to moral attention," said Bannon, trying to explain the virtues of the new Trump policy of separating parents from their children as families came across the U.S. southern border. "That was the moment when the rest of the world said this immigration stuff is nuts and has got to stop. If you voted for Trump, every picture of a Mexican immigrant, a parent or a child, together or apart, reconfirms that vote."

Just as immigration had been the overriding issue in 2016, Bannon expected it to be the Trump payoff topic in the 2018 midterm elections. Immigration was not just Trumpism's sine qua non, it was the fundamental intellectual pillar that any dope could understand. "There are seven billion people in the world, and six billion want to come to the United States and Europe," said Bannon. "You do the math."

Immigration had also become, internal research indicated, Fox News's most consistently reliable prime-time theme. Teasers on Fox for upcoming immigration stories—scare stories—could be counted on to keep restive audiences in place. Channel flipping decreased dramatically during immigration pieces. Sean Hannity had built record ratings off of his holy war against immigration.

Privately, or not so privately, Bannon believed that Trump, if he made it through his first term, would have had quite enough of the presidency by 2020. "Dude, look at him," said Bannon, who didn't look all that good himself. In the event that Trump did not run in 2020, Bannon—ever revivified by the daily lurches, catastrophes, and lost opportunities of the Trump presidency—saw himself as the presidential candidate for the populist-nationalist movement and its radical immigration platform. He saw Sean Hannity as his running mate.

A contemptuous Hannity, with grandiose ambitions of his own, insisted that this scenario was ludicrous. *He* would top the ticket, with Bannon, "if he's lucky," taking the second spot.

* * *

Hannity was now one of the richest men in television news. In 2017, Roger Ailes, his former boss and the man who had plucked him from a $40,000-a-year television job, estimated Hannity's net worth at $300 million to $400 million. From his earliest days as a big earner at the network, Hannity had invested in rental properties across the country. "He may own every shitty piece of real estate in America," said Ailes, fondly. Bannon, never one to miss the obvious joke, wondered, "How many illegals live in Hannity's rentals?"

For twenty years, Hannity, like most people at Fox News, operated not just with loyalty and gratitude toward Ailes, but with the unambiguous understanding that Ailes was the brains of the operation, the unchallenged arbiter of the conservative political zeitgeist. At Ailes's funeral in Palm Beach in May 2017, Hannity, who had flown a group of Ailes's colleagues and friends down on his plane, found his plan to get back home for one of his children's sports matches delayed by the collective length of the many encomiums at the funeral. Stepping out to speak on the phone with his disappointed child, he said, "I'm sorry, I'm sorry. But, hey, wait a minute. Do you like our life? Well, we owe that all to Mr. Ailes. So I'm staying until his funeral is done."

With Ailes expelled from Fox in July 2016 because of sexual harassment charges, the network needed a new unifying mission and reason for being. For two decades, Ailes had created the messages, tone, and many of the personalities that the Republican Party embraced. Fox became the Republican brand, dramatizing and monetizing politics in a heretofore unimagined way. At $1.5 billion in annual profits, the Fox News Channel was the most valuable part of Rupert Murdoch's empire. But without Ailes creating the narrative and nursing the talent, a significant realignment occurred. Ailes had long warned about the dangers of the network becoming the mouthpiece of the White House: Fox's value and primacy came from leading rather than following. And, indeed, the Republican Party, and Republican White Houses, had once been beholden to Fox. But now Fox was beholden to Trump, the new zeitgeist mastermind.

After Ailes's ouster, the leadership at Fox was seized by the Murdoch family, which was ever consumed by its daily squabble about whether the father or one of his two sons had actual control. Rupert himself, after sixty-five years as the most aggressive and successful newspaperman on the planet, still had scant interest in television news; his sons, Lachlan and James, were political moderates and liberal society wannabes, and they were regularly embarrassed by Fox. The entire family, however, appreciated the cash windfall from the network—hence they were stuck, at least for the moment, with the Fox programming point of view. Compounding the leadership vacuum and the brand ambivalence in the months after Ailes's departure, Fox's two most prominent and highest-rated anchors, Megyn Kelly and Bill O'Reilly, left the network. Kelly was shunned by many of the network stars and bosses because she had spoken out against Ailes; O'Reilly was forced out in his own sexual harassment scandal.

Daily operation of the network defaulted to Ailes's loyal but undistinguished lieutenants, all of whom were accustomed to carrying out Ailes's directions and had little vision of their own. Fox's billion-dollar prime-time schedule was left to Hannity, the weaker player behind O'Reilly and Kelly; Tucker Carlson, a second-string replacement anchor; and, after a botched attempt at a panel show, Laura Ingraham, a conservative radio host who had never had a television success.

Hannity disdained Murdoch and his sons, not least because he was quite sure they found him contemptible. He figured they would fire him soon enough. But Hannity was sanguine: he believed his future was with Trump, and soon after Trump's inauguration he began telling people that he was staying at Fox only to "fight for Donald J. Trump." This was a programming approach—abject fealty to Donald Trump—that, buttressed by obsessive warnings about the evils of illegal immigration, suddenly turned Hannity into cable gold.

Carlson, a former magazine writer, had migrated to Fox via CNN and MSNBC, where he had struggled in the role of the young old-fogey conservative in a bow tie. As liberal channels shut down even their token conservative voices, he met a predictable end. At Fox, where Ailes saw Carlson as the kind of conservative that liberals like—that is, useful to the network, but not central to it—he warmed the bench for bigger stars who hard-core conservatives liked, each week shuttling up to New York from Washington to do the lower-rated weekend shows.

Off camera, Carlson was a funny, tempered, self-styled libertarian. He enjoyed Washington's chummy cliques, lunching every day at the Metropolitan Club; only two blocks from the White House, it was among the frumpiest and swampiest clubs in town. Over the years, Carlson had come to know Trump well, and when speaking privately he was a witty guide to Trumpworld outlandishness and lunacy. Inheriting, rather by default, Kelly's spot in the prime-time lineup, Carlson—with tax problems and financial troubles, and, now, approaching fifty—saw his last real chance to succeed in prime time. Carlson understood that the fight for Donald J. Trump, and the America First defense, provided both a narrative godsend and a clear avenue to big ratings. With a new tenacity and an everyman set of facial gestures—utter incredulity at the foolishness and hypocrisies of the left—he became, finally in his career, a conservative whom liberals loved to hate.

Ingraham, one of the keynote speakers at the 2016 Republican National Convention, might have been the most desperate of the three. Trump himself found her wanting: "She's never had a hit on television. I would ask, Why? Here's why: people don't like her. I like her okay. But I don't love her." He complained to both Murdoch and Hannity—"you gotta get me somebody better." In many ways, her standing at the network depended on an audience of one.

Fox as a coherent network—Ailes's enterprise was famously top-down, with its themes and messages of the day coordinated across every show—had retreated internally into mixed messages and turmoil. But the three evening anchors were in no way confused: they focused on the Trump message.

Fox was no longer the brand; Trump was the brand.

And the Trump-brand narrative was television genius. The establishment cadres—the elites, the media, the deep state, the great liberal conspiracy—were trying to bring Donald Trump down. At Fox, this was a big-ratings message: he had to be defended. And his most Trumpian instincts, especially those involving immigration, had to be supported, lest he waver from them.

Each of the Fox prime-time anchors privately acknowledged that were Trump to go down, they would likely go down, too. Each acknowledged that if Fox changed course, as they assumed it would, they would be out the door. They were tied to Donald Trump, not Fox.

Together the three—along with Fox's Judge Jeanine and Lou Dobbs—formed the sort of brain trust of presidential advisers and cheerleaders that heretofore had remained mostly out of view. This was new: the Fox team served as a public channel between the Trump base (the Fox audience) and the Trump White House. Likewise, many of the messages from the Bannon side of the Trump party were delivered through and supported by the Fox prime-time schedule—most consistently and succinctly, the message on immigration. And all this was constantly fed and reinforced by Hannity's incessant phone calls with Trump.

Two of Bannon's acolytes in the White House, Stephen Miller and Julie Hahn, the Trump anti-immigration brain trust, often lobbied Trump through Hannity. Indeed, Hahn's job was now divided between policy and comms, where she was the direct contact with Hannity—not only giving Hannity the White House position, but giving him the Bannon-Miller-Hahn position, which Hannity would recycle back to Trump.

* * *

Hannity and the president spoke as often as six or seven times a day. The calls sometimes lasted more than thirty minutes. John Kelly, astounded that there were days when the president spent as many as three hours talking to Hannity, had tried to limit these calls. But Hannity was a calming influence on Trump: he was both a distraction and a willing audience for Trump's endless complaints about almost everybody. Furthermore, Hannity supplied Trump with an ongoing report on TV ratings, one of the few things that could reliably hold Trump's interest. As always, Trump was keenly responsive to whatever words and actions might get him better ratings.

Hannity saw the daily talks as quite a professional opportunity; he also considered them a patriotic duty. He accepted Trump's volatility and his part in keeping the man from losing it.

"I calm him down," explained Hannity, with solemn modesty, to a group of Fox people about his conversations with the president.

Bannon had a different view. "Hannity's theories are crazier than even Trump's," he said, "so Trump becomes the voice of reason."

Hannity could press the president to do and say things that would, retold on the news, boost Hannity's ratings—and, as usually happened, almost everyone else's. A return in Trump's tweets to the Wall would often be Hannity's doing. This was old-fashioned politics, of course, a politician behaving in a way that would please his constituents. But this other angle—a television host directing the president to do whatever might most compel a television audience—took the game a big step further.

In part this was the Ailes formula, politicians doing what television, and specifically a highly targeted television audience, required. But Hannity was working Trump in a way that no president had ever quite been worked. "Trump is the star," Hannity would say. Hannity, the ultimate let-Trump-be-Trump-er, believed that it was his job, in television as well as in politics, to draw out Trump's performance—to encourage Trump to be his most Trumpian. Much of their conversations were about how this or that Trump utterance or tweet, or public dis or snarl, had played on television. Trump, rarely studious about anything, was a patient student of what played well.

He listened to Hannity partly because he believed that his own communications department was uniquely unable to offer him useful advice. They were "ignoramuses." Plus they looked terrible. Hannity was happy to support Trump's contempt for his own team. The comms department should have stood between Hannity and the president; instead, Hannity stood between the president and his comms team. Hannity was joined in this by Bannon, who saw himself functioning as shadow communications director (in addition to shadow everything else). Both men hugely enjoyed the abuse the comms team was forced to take from Trump. If Trump abused the press, he abused his own press team even more, issuing constant critiques on demeanor, dress, hair, and the passion of their defense of him. "Would you let your life depend on Kellyanne Conway, Mercedes Schlapp, or the Huckabee girl?" Bannon asked rhetorically. "That's some brain trust."

In June, Hannity seized the opportunity to push his person into the top comms job. Bill Shine, whom Hannity had been urging Trump to hire for almost a year, had been Ailes's right-hand man and Hannity's producer. At fifty-four, he had spent the better part of his career at Fox, much of it carrying out Ailes's orders. Shine, too, was forced out for his part in covering up Fox's ongoing sexual harassment scandals in 2017. Hannity's pitch to the president was that Shine, who officially joined the White House on July 5, not only could be as good a producer for Trump as he was for Hannity—"Lighting, lighting, I need better lighting," railed Trump—but could basically run Fox from the White House. He would be a pipeline right into the control booth. When Shine went to work in the West Wing, it was, and Hannity made this explicit, the realization of the network's effective new business model: Fox was the Trump network.

All that was needed now was . . . the Wall.

The Wall was the key branding element. Trump had at various points theorized about Wall alternatives: fancy fencing, or gun turrets and demilitarized guard posts, or maybe even an invisible wall, a force field that would deliver a shock, like the ones for dogs. But for Hannity, the Wall was literal, just as he believed it was for the rest of the Trump base. The Wall needed to be made of cement—"no virtual shit," Hannity would say. It needed to be the physical manifestation of Make American Great Again.

The mantra was simple: if there was no Wall, there was no Trump. Stopping immigration was the Trump story. Immigration was the passion. You could not be too tough on immigration. And the tougher you were, the better chance you'd have of winning in November.

* * *

Sean Hannity was correct: Rupert Murdoch and his sons could hardly stomach him. But in a sense Hannity was just part of the broader Trump effect on the Murdoch family. Trump had helped turn the final years of the eighty-seven-year-old Murdoch, a towering figure in conservative politics, into a sour time, with Murdoch having to kowtow to Trump, whom he considered to be a charlatan and a fool, and with his sons blaming him for his unwitting part in Trump's rise.

Murdoch regarded both Trump and Hannity as tabloid caricatures. They were the sorts of figures who populated his newspapers (he continued to think in newspaper rather than television terms); they were mass entertainment. But these were not the people in Murdoch's world who held power. Power was held by men who understood their own wider interests—and the wider interests of other men who held power—and who did not regularly risk their power. The elites Trump derided, at least the conservative ones, were exactly the people Murdoch respected.

Volatility was the enemy of power. Murdoch regarded Trump and Hannity as performers—clowns, both of them. Hannity was useful to him; Trump, before his election, was little more than fodder for Murdoch's *New York Post*.

Powerful men are often amused by the lesser attainments of lesser men who wish for power. For both Murdoch and Ailes, Trump and Hannity had been a shared bit of incredulity, a measure of how far you could go on lots of ambition and little brain power.

In 2016, Murdoch had refused to entertain the possibility of a Trump presidency and had directed Ailes to tilt the network's coverage to Clinton, the expected president. But after Trump's election, Murdoch, ever the practical man, forced himself into a relationship with the new president, who, in turn, could hardly believe he was finally being taken seriously by Murdoch.

"I can't get the asshole off the phone," said Murdoch to an associate after Trump entered the White House, holding out the phone as the president's voice rambled into the air.

Meanwhile, as a function of both his easy access to Trump and the rising ratings at Fox, Murdoch, now theoretically running the network himself, allowed his prime-time anchors to devote themselves to Trump. This move was bitterly opposed by his son James, who was revolted by both Trump and the prime-time lineup. James became increasingly confrontational with his father. James's wife, Kathryn, was particularly vocal about how much she detested Fox News, and, indeed, much of the Murdoch company's politics. Father and son had screaming fights over Hannity and Trump. The Murdoch family had become collaborators, declared the younger Murdoch. The world would remember. The future of their company was at stake.

But Murdoch was, agonizingly, tied to his network's Trump-dependent and ever-increasing profitability. Some around Murdoch thought that for the first time in his career, business needs and political expediency might be causing him to experience something like a crisis of conscience. He could not give Trump up, yet he could not abide him. He blamed Trump for the increasing estrangement with his son James. It was one more Shakespearean outcome: Trump, in the ultimate Fox result, was now tearing apart the Murdoch family.

Seeing no way to manage his own family's discord—Murdoch was by this time barely speaking to James, who had long been the designated heir—he began, six months into the Trump presidency, to plan for the sale of his company. His agreement with Disney, announced in December 2017, included most of the assets of the company, except for Fox News, which Disney did not want, and the Fox Network and local television stations, which would have caused issues with regulators. James would leave the company, and the remaining assets would be run by Murdoch's older son, Lachlan, until they, too, could be sold.

But there would be few corporate buyers for Fox and, the Murdochs believed, perhaps no buyers if Sean Hannity remained a vital part of the deal. Hannity's conspiracy mongering was not just absurd but intolerable: with his open political advocacy for Trump, he regularly flirted with FCC violations. And in the likely event that Trump fell, Hannity's value, and the network's value, would fall, too.

In May 2018, Fox was trying to move against on-air personality Kimberly Guilfoyle, romantically linked to Donald Trump Jr., and before that to Anthony Scaramucci, the short-lived Trump White House communications director. (Guilfoyle also spoke volubly about how often she believed Trump himself had hit on her.) Guilfoyle, who would shortly be ejected from the company, was being investigated for, among other behavior issues, circulating dick pics among co-workers. Lachlan Murdoch saw a possible opportunity here: he believed Sean Hannity might be implicated in compromising items that were on Guilfoyle's phone, which could potentially give the younger Murdoch the leverage he needed to persuade his father to oust Hannity.

But Hannity remained in place. Trump, Fox insiders believed, had interceded on Hannity's behalf with Murdoch. What's more, the Murdochs may have cringed at the mere mention of Hannity but he remained their ratings star.

* * *

Hannity and Bannon worried that Fox might ultimately insist on dialing down the focus on immigration, no matter its ratings fuel; they both heard reports of Murdoch saying enough was enough. Murdoch, an Australian, hewed to a belief in the ultimate economic benefits of a worldwide labor market. He was, as Bannon would often deride him to Trump, a standard-issue globalist. The conservative newspaper publisher, who had made his fortune promoting working-class xenophobia in multiple nations, was in fact a Davos man.

More critically, Hannity and Bannon doubted Trump's sticking power on immigration, or at least they could easily see him relenting on the details. The Wall would become an invisible wall, or a wall so far in the future that it would forever be only a theoretical wall. They didn't doubt Trump's feelings about the issue—he seemed to have a visceral dislike for and suspicion of immigrants, illegal or otherwise—nor did they believe he was looking for a middle ground that would accommodate all sides. But, as with all issues, the details bored him.

Hence, he became extremely susceptible to the last person who sold him on a different mix of details. In particular, Trump was the focus of a concerted effort by his daughter and son-in-law, and by the congressional leadership, to modify and soften the details of his immigration policy.

It became a consistent effort on Hannity's part, a kind of catechism of his daily calls with Trump. Over and over, Hannity would reiterate and reinforce the policy's zero-tolerance theme. This was rendered, of course, as effusive praise for Trump. Only he had the guts to stop the endless flow of immigrants across our borders. Only he had the courage to build the Wall.

Trump, galvanized, was suddenly demanding a new executive order that would fund the Wall and stop chain migration and birthright citizenship—"do it all," he said. Told the order wouldn't get through the Office of Legal Counsel, he reasoned, "If I sign it, people will know where I stand. I won't be blamed for the laws."

* * *

By mid-June, however, Hannity's cheerleading had begun to wear thin, and Trump started to turn on him. The vast disorganization of the zero-tolerance family-separation actions—of lost children, tent city–like facilities, and the prospect of a future of warehoused infants and minors—ought to have been blamed on an inept White House acting without a plan, but instead he blamed it on Hannity.

Once again, Ivanka had persuaded him that his reflexive harshness had to be walked back. He had, just as easily, been convinced—and would be so again—that draconian toughness on immigration had made him president and would keep him president. But now, especially when listening to his daughter, he believed Hannity had stuck him with a raw deal.

For all of Hannity's flattery, for all of his zealous commitment to the president, Trump, in almost equal proportion, had become disdainful of him. This was partly standard practice. Sooner or later, Trump felt contempt for anyone who showed him too much devotion. "Hating himself, he of course comes to hate anyone who seems to love him," analyzed Bannon. "If you seem to respect him, he thinks he's put something over on you—therefore you're a fool." Others believed that this was Trump's power principle at work. He demanded sycophancy from the people around him and then shamed them for their weakness.

And then there was money. Trump invariably despised anyone who came to profit off of him without sharing the financial benefit with him. For Trump, Hannity's high ratings were really his own; hence, he was being cheated.

In the Trump circle, Hannity was jocular, funny, and generous—the use of his plane was frequently on offer—and he injected a note of both energy and optimism into the nearly always beleaguered Trump camp. At the same time, virtually everybody, including most of the Trumpiest figures in Trumpworld, thought Hannity was a figure of rare daftness and incoherence. Even Trump would shout at his television, "No follow, Sean, no follow."

Bannon, too, though fond of Hannity and of his plane, was consistently amazed by the bizarre direction of Hannity's monologues, which echoed some of the most extreme online conspiracy forums. "Dude, dude, don't go bonkers on me," Bannon would mutter as he watched an evening broadcast.

The inside joke became—echoing Karl Rove as Bush's brain and later Steve Bannon as Trump's brain—that now it was Sean Hannity who had become Trump's resident genius. Trump had ended up with someone even stupider than he was. Yet this was fitting, because Trump deeply resented the implication that he ever needed to depend on someone else's acumen or intelligence—or, really, that there could possibly be anyone who was smarter than he was. But with Hannity as his sidekick, he could feel quite certain that no one would think he was relying on someone smarter. (This, in fact, was a frequent internal debate: Who was stupider, Trump or Hannity?)

Then, however, after signing an executive order on June 20 to reverse the family separation policy, Trump fell into a new funk, blaming everyone— though curiously not his daughter—for making him look weak.

But on June 26 the script flipped again when the Supreme Court reversed previous rulings and upheld the president's travel ban—the same travel ban that had been so contentious and seemed so outlandish in the first days of his administration. Now Trump fumed that if he hadn't signed the EO on family separation, he would have had a double win. "I would have had the magic touch," he told one aide. "My magic."

In fact, although it was known that the case involving the travel ban would be one of the last decided by the Court before its summer recess, no one in the White House was prepared for the decision. Even when handed a victory, there was a day's delay before a press release went out, and that was preceded by a flurry of squabbling emails in the comms department about who should write it.

Trump, weary of immigration, was suddenly excited, on June 27, to be handed the retirement of Justice Anthony Kennedy from the Supreme Court, thus opening a seat for a new conservative judge. Immigration became, overnight, a forgotten issue, and Hannity an annoyance. "Wetbacks, wetbacks, wetbacks. There's more to the world," said the president in a complaint to an evening caller. "Somebody should tell Sean."

12

TRUMP ABROAD

In its by now usual slapdash fashion, the White House, at Trump's sudden insistence, added two legs to the long-planned July 11–12 NATO meeting in Brussels: a stop in Britain to meet the Queen, and then a quick summit in Helsinki with President Putin.

On the morning of July 10, he spoke for a moment to the media before boarding the plane for Brussels. "So I have NATO, I have the UK—that's a situation with turmoil. And I have Putin. Frankly, Putin may be the easiest of all."

It was the UK leg that most worried Bannon. He had used every available channel to send out the message that the stop had disaster written all over it. There could be a million people in the streets to jeer Trump. Even before the trip began, Trump was urged to mostly keep out of London because of expected protests. And the audience with the Queen, whom Trump was dying to meet, was clearly more of a cold shoulder: the rest of the royal family would be "out of town." Jared and Ivanka, more sensitive to nuance than the president, understood a royal insult when they got one and bailed on the trip.

Trump, however, wanted to play golf, as well as meet the Queen. And he wanted to give Trump Aberdeen, his golf course in Scotland, a PR boost. Plus, the White House was constantly encouraging him to get out of town, preferably out of the country. "Far away and occupied," said an emphatic John Kelly.

But Bannon thought he might blow. Trump could "crack wide open. You don't want him walking into humiliation." Bannon, who had spent several years in the 1990s traveling back and forth to London as an investment banker, knew something about British upper-class disdain, which might well find its ultimate expression in a snub of Donald Trump. Then, too, there was left-wing British rage, which could hardly have a juicier target than Trump.

Bannon had his own reasons for not wanting Trump to have a meltdown in Europe. In recent months Bannon had vastly expanded the reach of his populist ambitions, promoting Trump as the new standard-bearer for right-wing Europe. If Brussels was the symbol, though a none-too-vibrant one, of a united globalist Europe, Trump was the symbol of a cohesive new right-wing Europe. That, anyway, was Bannon's message, or snake oil. What he had done for Trump he could do for the ever-lagging right-wing parties of Europe.

So Trump "losing his shit" on a European visit might not be the best thing for Bannon's business. And thus far, Bannon's business—exporting the Trump miracle, which provided proof positive that marginal right-wing parties could, with the help of Bannon's populist consciousness, actually take control of the levers of power—was fantastic.

Bannon, arguably—or arguably in his view—was the secret sauce behind Brexit. Early in 2016, Bannon, looking for ways to help his friend Nigel Farage and Farage's UKIP party, had launched a British Breitbart. UKIP and Brexit needed a platform, and "Farage will tell you," declared Bannon, "that Breitbart was the difference."

In the spring of 2018, Bannon became a string puller in Italy. The operative certainty in Italy was that its reliably factionalized electorate would ensure that some version of a compromised and ineffectual center coalition would always prevail. But Bannon had cozied up to Matteo Salvini, the leader of the right-wing nationalist League (its name recently changed from Northern League), and after a predictably divided result in the Italian election in March, Bannon parachuted in and helped negotiate a coalition deal between the League and the Five Star Movement (a left-wing populist party with some strong right-wing inclinations). Neither Salvini nor Five Star's Luigi Di Maio, in Bannon's formulation, would claim the prime minister spot, but together they could agree on a dupe to hold it. Here, for Bannon, was the perfect union of far right and far left.

Now, with the NATO trip looming, Bannon needed Trump to look the part of the American strongman, and not behave like a baby having a temper tantrum. That might spook Bannon's European clients.

* * *

The president and the First Lady arrived in a cool Brussels on the evening of July 10. The next morning Trump was full of complaints: he was sleepless; someone had misplaced a shirt; the food was wrong. He and his wife did not seem to be talking at all.

He had breakfast that morning with NATO secretary-general Jens Stoltenberg. Surrounded by his senior staff—Secretary of State Mike Pompeo, Defense Secretary James Mattis, White House chief of staff John Kelly, U.S. ambassador to NATO Kay Bailey Hutchison—Trump made his first odd remarks, accusing the Germans of conspiring with the Russians. "I think it's very sad when Germany makes a massive oil and gas deal with Russia . . . We're supposed to be guarding against Russia and Germany goes out and pays billions and billions of dollars a year to Russia . . . Where you're supposed to protect you against Russia but they're paying billions of dollars to Russia and I think that's very inappropriate . . . Germany is totally controlled by Russia."

NATO, Trump kept repeating to various people accompanying him, "bores the shit out of me." Indeed, NATO was a vast, complicated bureaucratic construct, a meticulous and uneven balance of interests. Trump's urge to disrupt it might be as much about his resistance to small-bore details—white papers, data backgrounders, endless coalition politics—as about policy and operational matters. He needed to tilt the conversation from small to large. The small, the calibrated, the item-by-item approach infuriated him. He even saw it as a power play against him, suspecting that people knew he could not absorb details.

"They're trying to get me to fall asleep in my soup," he complained. "They want that picture."

The other aspect of NATO summits he found irritating was that they were group meetings. He was almost invariably enthusiastic about one-on-one world leader meetings—no matter the subject, no matter the leader—and agitated about collective gatherings. He worried about being ganged up on; he suspected that plots had been laid to trick him.

His charm—or, really, sugary flattery—did not work on Angela Merkel, who was his closest leadership rival. (He didn't think so, but others did.) In previous encounters, he had tried laying it on thick with her, but this had gotten him nothing except her evident distaste. So he reverted to his basic approach: if maximum flattery doesn't work, if you can't get to a deal that way, then "shit on them." He practiced saying "Angela Merkel" correctly with a hard *g*, but in his version the *g* was mocking and mincing.

Trump did not like to share the stage with a group of so-called peers. But if he had to, he believed that such a situation required him to upstage everybody else. His standard method when distinguishing himself was negativity in utterance and body language. As he once said to a friend when explaining his strategy during the seventeen-candidate Republican presidential primary debates, "You want to make it seem that everyone else has a disgusting smell."

His stated goal at the summit was to persuade NATO member states to raise their financial contribution. This was a longtime conservative gripe: alliances and foreign aid did little except ensure that the United States got cheated. It was Lou Dobbs 101, said Bannon. "Elementary school eloquence. It's not complicated: he's been watching Lou Dobbs for thirty years. It's the only show he watches from beginning to end."

Others saw something weirder and darker. Trump wanted to undermine NATO. Trump wanted to undermine Europe as a whole. In his mind, if not also in some covert understanding, Trump had realigned the power axis from Europe to Russia, and was now, in Russia's interest if not at its behest, trying to weaken Europe.

Though Trump does not drink, there was a kind of drunkenness to his performance at the NATO summit: he canceled meetings with the leaders of Romania, Azerbaijan, Ukraine, and Georgia; he was late, without warning, for one of the key sessions; he delivered public as well as private rants, including a threat to unilaterally leave the sixty-nine-year-old alliance. With respect to policy, he could not get beyond his single point, the one element that overrode all others and stuck in his head: Europeans should pay more. His unhappiness with their resistance to this demand had seemed to harden into a deep enmity. He appeared to regard NATO as hostile territory: NATO, too clever by half, was the enemy.

In this, he had once more squared off against his own foreign policy advisers, most particularly his secretary of defense. Mattis, trying to act as the one U.S. voice of reassurance and reason at the summit, was telling his European counterparts that he was at the breaking point.

* * *

While Trump was disrupting—or acting out at—the NATO summit, Bannon teamed up with Hannity to go to London, hoping to catch a ride on Hannity's plane. Bannon knew that being close to Hannity was being close to Trump. Hannity's daily radio show, which during the trip would be broadcast from Europe, was almost as good as speaking directly to the president. In a way it was better, because someone else could talk and Trump had to listen. Bannon's voice, via Hannity's show, would be in Trump's head.

It was one of Bannon's active sleights of hand, the level of conversations he was having with the president. When asked, he did not say he was talking to Trump, but he didn't say he wasn't, either. Or, if he *did* say he wasn't, you might reasonably construe, given the parameters of confidentiality, that in fact he was. But even if he wasn't talking directly to Trump, Bannon was confident that Trump was listening to absolutely everything he had to say. In this way, Bannon could reasonably represent, or deftly imply, to his clients that, truly, he had Trump's ear.

What's more, Bannon, in campaign mode, now believed that the trends for the midterms in November were turning positive. Bannon carried fifty or sixty congressional races in his head, with an almost real-time sense of the movement in swing districts. If he could get Trump to focus and pay attention—"I can hardly believe I said that," Bannon chuckled—and get him into each key district one or more times in September and October, Republicans could hold the House.

In spite of his better instincts, Bannon had begun to think of himself in the White House again. There was something about the idea that seemed . . . destined. Except not.

Bannon understood that if the Republicans held the House in November, Trump could never have Bannon back as a *reward* for winning. That would mean Trump would have to acknowledge that Bannon had won the House for him. Nor could he have Bannon back if they lost the House, for that would be acknowledging his need for Bannon.

What's more, Trump continued to blame Bannon for getting him to support the man he called "the child molester"—Roy Moore in Alabama, the failed Senate candidate whom Bannon had backed. (More precisely, in Trump's locution, Bannon had persuaded him to support "the loser child molester.") Moore was said to have cruised Alabama shopping malls in a quest for teenage girls, an allegation that sunk his candidacy.

So yes, there was really no scenario in which Bannon and Trump could equitably align. Nevertheless, Bannon continued to imagine scenarios in which he would be recognized as the master political tactician, the visionary of the worldwide nationalist-populist cause, the person who brought a begging Trump back to him.

In London, ensconced in a $4,500-a-night suite at Brown's Hotel in Mayfair, Bannon played a cat-and-mouse game. Moving carefully through the scrum of reporters staking out his hotel, he calculated whom he should be seen with and whom he should avoid. In particular, knowing that Trump was always monitoring his moves, he did not want to be spotted with anyone who might aggravate the president.

* * *

Bannon's hotel suite was the locus that week of far right activity in Europe. His long-game plot was to storm the European Parliament elections in May 2019. The EU, resisted to a greater or lesser degree by all European right-wing parties, was controlled by the European Parliament. Hence, why not take over the EU and reform it—or break it—that way? Here was Bannon the political operative. Bannon knew that the European Parliament elections were always weakly subscribed: nobody came out to vote. The vote was therefore easy to sway. "The world's most leverageable elections," he declared, "with the lowest cost per vote."

Still, if Bannon was rating Italy as his great success and seeing the grim figure of Hungary's Viktor Orbán, whose ear he had, as a rising power, this was only a start. Italy and Hungary were not exactly the historic leaders of Europe; he needed France.

Bannon had turned several additional rooms at Brown's into a seminar venue for France's Front National. Louis Aliot—the "husband-partner" of Marine Le Pen, who had inherited the Front from her Nazi-leaning father—had come to London with a delegation. In investment banker style, Bannon was now going through the Front's financials line by line, as though getting ready to take the party public.

The problem was that the biggest investors in the Front were Russian gangsters likely fronting for Putin. For several years now, the Russians had been underwriting the Le Pens and their party. The optics, not to mention the unnerving political reality, were not good. If the Front were to help take over the European Parliament in 2019, that would mean Putin, or even worse Russians than Putin, would become a significant power in the internal politics of Europe.

In the shadowy world of purported efforts by the Russians to influence the West, here was a curiously naked fact: the Russians really were funding opposition parties. Many of the European right-wing parties had accepted Russian help. This support was only loosely hidden, and though there was nothing specifically illegal about it, the funding prompted an obvious question: If the Russians were supporting the Front National and almost every other right-wing party that came calling, why not support the Trump Party—which, in the figure of Steve Bannon, was itself supporting the Front National? It was a circle of Russia-inclined virtue.

Bannon's position toward Russian collusion was simple: whatever had happened, it did not involve him. He—and sometimes he would intimate that *only* he—was never in touch with the Russians during the campaign or through the transition. Still, he was perfectly in sync with Russian goals of using the European right wing to undermine European hegemony. Even for Bannon, however, overt Russian involvement was, to say the least, "not a good look."

His goal now was to pay the Russians back for their $13 million loan to the Front National (rebranded in mid-2018 as the National Rally) and replace the party's debt holdings with a more acceptable supporter. (In this, curiously, he was looking to right-wing Jews and supporters of Israel—looking to have them own what had heretofore been a neo-Nazi party.) To accomplish this, he needed to understand the Front's messy financials. The Front's delegation seemed at best to have only a sketchy knowledge of its own operations, and of who was being paid for what and how.

"I need to know all inflows and outflows," said Bannon the banker, met by largely unresponsive stares. "Really, we've got to go line by line on this."

Bannon struggled to contain his frustration with his clients. And no wonder: as Bannon talked, these would-be ministers of a future far-right-wing France glanced at each other with apparent worry and incomprehension. If this was the future of Europe, it had a certain small-time, Ruritania-like quality.

Nigel Farage—also at Brown's for a meeting with Bannon—seemed to tax Bannon's self-control as well. Bannon believed he had played a key role in expanding UKIP's influence and promoting Farage, but after the Brexit victory Farage had largely washed his hands of the party, sending the support for UKIP back to single digits. ("What do you mean, you fucking quit?" an incredulous Bannon had railed. "This is just the beginning!") The experience confirmed for Bannon the fundamental laziness of the European right—a result, he theorized, of the small material rewards provided by politics in Europe.

In Russia, joked Bannon, politics pays. Indeed, it pays even better than in the United States, which was why the Russians were taking over.

* * *

As Bannon predicted—and he was quick to remind everyone of his prediction—the Trump catastrophe in Britain unfolded.

Much noted by the media was a giant balloon that would shortly fly over London: Trump as an orange baby in diapers. The accusation that he behaved like a baby was a reliable Trump flash point, as well as a Trump refrain. "I'm not a baby! Do you think I'm a baby? *You're* a baby, not me!"

Trump was coming to the UK carrying a pro-Brexit message with little or no sense of the knife edge on which Brexit had put the UK. Nor did he care: for Trump, the Brexit controversy prompted dismissive impatience. Obviously it was right. Obviously England—he did not make the distinction between England and the rest of the UK—wouldn't want to be part of Europe. Here he defaulted to Churchill, World War II, and the "special relationship" between Britain and the United States. England, he announced, not necessarily as a joke, should become the fifty-first state.

On July 12, just before 2:00 p.m., Trump landed in London and was greeted by his old New York friend and crony Woody Johnson. Trump's ambassador to the Court of St. James's, Johnson was the Johnson & Johnson heir and owner of the New York Jets and much-mocked socialite and party boy in New York. ("Don't get me started," said Bannon. "In a long list of the unqualified, here you have the least qualified.") As Trump arrived with Johnson at Winfield House, the ambassador's residence on the edge of Regent's Park, the Beatles' "We Can Work It Out" was playing, competing with the jeers and chants of protesters.

Trump soon went directly into an interview with the Murdoch-owned tabloid the *Sun*. At Murdoch's request, the conversation had been set up by Jared and Ivanka. The *Sun* had promised an interview with a positive spin, one that would avoid Brexit and lean heavily on the special relationship. But Trump's mood, coming out of Brussels, was a Trumpian mix of combativeness, self-satisfaction, and sleeplessness.

Perhaps as much as any Trump interview ever—and there was lots of competition—this conversation with the *Sun* was heedless and unfiltered. He seemed genuinely pleased to put everything on the table. He was the devil-may-care boss who was perfectly comfortable with his unquestioned authority, the blowhard extraordinaire who was seldom on topic. He answered to no one.

Over the course of the interview, Trump blithely waded into the most volatile situation in British politics in recent memory. Each point he made was a quintessential, albeit shocking, Trump pearl:

If the UK does the Brexit deal favored by Theresa May's government, well then, naw—here he seemed to shrug—no trade deal. Yup, that would end a major trade relationship with the United States.

He would have negotiated much differently with the EU than May had done. He told her, but she didn't listen. He would have been prepared to walk away. "I did give her my views on what she should do and how she should negotiate. But she didn't follow those views. That's fine . . . but it's too bad what's going on."

The Brexit deal that the prime minister was now proposing "was a much different deal than the people voted on. It was not the deal that was in the referendum." (There was, in fact, no deal in the referendum, other than unspecified departure from the EU.) The deal, as now proposed, would "definitely affect trade with the United States—unfortunately in a negative way."

He then heaped praise on one of May's main Tory Party antagonists, Boris Johnson, who had just resigned from her cabinet as foreign minister over the May government's more cautious Brexit plan. Commenting on the speculation that Johnson would shortly commence a leadership fight against May, Trump said: "I think he would make a great prime minister. I think he's got what it takes."

On British defense spending: it ought to be doubled.

Immigration to Europe was "a shame—it changed the fabric of Europe." And "it was never going to be what it was—and I don't mean that in a positive way . . . I think you're losing your culture."

On the mayor of London, Sadiq Khan, the highest Muslim officeholder in the UK: "He's done a terrible job. Take a long look at what's going on in London. I think he's done a terrible job . . . All of this immigration . . . all of the crime that's being brought in." And "he's not been hospitable to a very important government." So, he said, "When they make you feel unwelcome, why would I stay there?"

And: "You don't hear the name England as much as you should. I miss the name England."

Trump was not just absent any diplomatic filter. He might as well have been talking to himself, ticking off the kinds of grievances that, on a long and soulful list, might put him to sleep at night.

* * *

Getting all this off his chest—and thereby tossing a bomb into the UK's relationship with the United States, as well as roiling Britain's own internal politics—apparently seemed to Trump to be entirely disconnected from the event he would shortly be attending: Prime Minister Theresa May was hosting a black-tie dinner in his honor.

The president and the First Lady, riding in "The Beast," the presidential limousine that had been flown in on the presidential cavalcade, soon arrived at Blenheim Palace, the ancestral home of the Churchill family and the birthplace of Winston. They were greeted on the red carpet by Mrs. May—in red gown and red heels—and her husband, while the Queen's Guard, a uniformed band in red jackets and furry hats, played a medley including "Amazing Grace" on bagpipes.

It had been a difficult struggle for May and Downing Street to fill the room with top-level British politicians and businessmen, most, as it happened, skeptical about the advantages of close proximity to Trump. The interview in the *Sun* appeared during the three-hour dinner, and through the evening a rolling awareness of it spread to many of the guests. Trump himself appeared unconcerned or unaware; in an affable mood, he was perfectly convivial with the prime minister.

Taken through the interview on the way back from dinner, he seemed disbelieving, even shocked. And dismissive, too: the interview had nothing to do with what he said. Really, he told aides, this was fabricated. "Fake news," he declared.

Murdoch, in New York, heard this comment and scoffed. "He's mentally out of it."

When the *Sun*, on Murdoch's instructions, posted a videotape of the interview, confirming the validity of its report, Trump barely skipped a beat.

Fake. Untrue. All wrong. Totally made up.

* * *

From any point of view, this was bad. From the point of view of statecraft, it was calamitous. So calamitous, in fact—so inexplicable and off the wall—that the interview was already being discounted. You had to grin and bear Trump and then assume that his words had only minimal relationship to ultimate policies and actions.

Bannon believed this, certainly. He had long discounted Trump by a significant factor—the man was a storm line of tantrums that inevitably passed. While the outcome of Trump's trip to Europe thus far would have called into question the competence and mental faculties of any other world leader, Bannon yet pushed to explain its usefulness.

Power, via expertise, had passed to a select group—the Davos gang. In Bannon's view, this group self-dealt at a historic level of wealth appropriation. It controlled the intellectual, economic, and diplomatic establishment. Trump, whether he knew it or not, represented intellectual, economic, and diplomatic disorder, the opposite of expertise and establishment power—and, hence, inspiration for the populist cause.

Even so, as Bannon appreciated as much as anyone, this was Donald Trump. Crazy was a potent enemy against the establishment, but how to predict what a crazy man will do?

* * *

On the morning of July 13, Trump left for Sandhurst, the royal military academy, to observe a joint exercise of UK and U.S. Special Forces with the prime minister. Then, together, they went on to Chequers, the country retreat of British prime ministers, for lunch and their official meeting and a news conference. Trump and May traveled by helicopter, with aides observing that, fortunately, it would be too noisy to allow for much conversation.

Many observers wondered how Trump would navigate the aftermath of one of the most extraordinarily undiplomatic interviews in diplomatic history. But he seemed entirely upbeat, if not unmindful of his previous remarks: "We're talking trade, we're talking military, we just moved some incredible antiterrorism things," Trump declared to reporters upon his arrival at Chequers. "The relationship is very, very strong . . . very, very good."

During a news conference with May after the lunch and meeting, Trump attacked the media, again largely denying what he had said in the *Sun* interview.

> I didn't criticize the prime minister. I have a lot of respect for the prime minister. And, unfortunately, there was a story that was done, which was generally fine, but it didn't put in what I said about the prime minister. And I said tremendous things.

> And, fortunately, we tend to record stories now, so we have it for
> your enjoyment, if you'd like it. But we record when we deal with
> reporters. It's called fake news. You know, we solve a lot of prob-
> lems with the good, old recording instrument.

Then he waved away any inference that he might have damaged the relationship between the United States and the UK. The prime minister looked on with excruciating forbearance. The scene in the movie *Love Actually*, where the prime minister—played by Hugh Grant—upbraids and humiliates a boorish U.S. president, instantly became a UK meme.

* * *

Then it was on to Windsor Castle and his meeting with the Queen.

Notably, the ninety-two-year-old Queen met with Trump alone. Her husband, Prince Philip, usually joined her in meetings with heads of state, but in this instance he was absent, as were all other royals.

The palace had deftly maneuvered around an official state visit by the U.S. president. Prince Charles, now in a careful campaign to burnish himself as the future king, did not want to be saddled with a lasting image of him with Donald Trump. His sons, the British princes, were even more appalled at the prospect of meeting with the president. No, leave it to the Queen. Even Donald Trump could not reduce her.

The president and the Queen performed a brief and awkward inspection of the grounds, reviewed the Honor Guard—largely minus any chit-chat, with the president, averse to listening to instructions, bungling where he was supposed to stand—and then went into the castle for a quick tea.

All unremarkable, as it should be. But during the tea, in a seeming warning to the U.S. president and a calculated affront to the Russian president Trump would shortly be on his way to meet, Robert Mueller indicted twelve Russians for hacking the Democrats in 2016.

13

TRUMP AND PUTIN

One focus of the Mueller investigation was on the concerted effort by the Trump campaign to purchase Hillary Clinton's 33,000 missing emails. Shopping in a dark-web bazaar, the Trump campaign had allegedly connected to Russian state hackers.

For Bannon here was a full and ironic circle. In 2015, Breitbart had funded the research for *Clinton Cash*, a book by Peter Schweizer (and later a documentary) that tried to trace the sources of the considerable funds that had flowed to Hillary and Bill Clinton's enterprises. It was the nearly nonstop Freedom of Information requests for Clinton's emails when she was secretary of state by Schweizer and several right-wing groups that helped shine the light on Clinton's email practices.

The ensuing scandal prompted an FBI investigation, which, especially when it was reopened weeks before the 2016 election, may have dealt the single greatest blow to Clinton's campaign. But even after Clinton had turned over most of her private-server emails, 33,000 emails she deemed "personal" remained unaccounted for. Bannon, along with many other Republicans, suspected that in this cache of emails was a clear road map of how Bill and Hillary were funding the Clinton Foundation, trading, they suspected, on her position in the Obama administration for cash contributions. In July 2016, Trump made a clarion call for Russian hackers to find those emails.

By that point Bannon and Breitbart had been in the hunt for the missing emails for more than a year. Taking a deep dive down the rabbit hole of international hacking, they met "finders" and eager sellers galore. The only problem was that many different collections and many different versions of the emails seemed to be available. Said Bannon: "It was like buying bricks from the Texas School Book Depository"—the building from which Lee Harvey Oswald shot JFK. "Don't tell the guy with the kiln that the building is still standing."

By the time Bannon came into the Trump campaign in August 2016, he knew that there was no holy grail of Clinton emails—or at least no reliable one. But various gofers and fetch dogs from the campaign, among them people in the candidate's family, still sought to curry favor with Trump by trying to obtain the emails, which Trump believed would damage Clinton.

These efforts confirmed for Bannon both the haplessness of the Trump campaign and, later, the weakness of the Mueller collusion case. The best Mueller would be able to do was make a case for screwball stuff, Trumpers vainly trying to find something that did not exist. The investigation would only prove the campaign's—and the candidate's—stupidity.

* * *

The indictment obtained by the special counsel's office against the twelve Russian intelligence agents, announced during the president's visit with the Queen, came three days before Trump was due to head from his golfing holiday in Scotland to his summit in Helsinki with Vladimir Putin, the Russian president.

The indictment made clear that on July 27, 2016, Russian hackers tried to break into Clinton's private email server—the same day that Trump had publicly called for the Russians to do exactly this. (Trump would later insist that this was a joke, with campaign staffers attesting that he was reading a prepared line and barely knew what he was saying.) These hackers then proceeded to infiltrate both the Clinton campaign—hacking into Clinton campaign chair John Podesta's pesonal email account—and the Democratic National Committee; subsequently, they leaked material they had stolen, deeply embarrassing the Clinton campaign and the Democrats.

The indictment outlined an operation of cyber spy versus cyber spy. Indeed, one implication here was that the U.S. intelligence community knew what the Russians were doing even as they were doing it but chose not to stop them—because, then, following conventional spy theory, the Russians would know that they had been found out.

The hackers, the indictment maintained, were in touch with a person with ties to senior members of the campaign. This was, by the clearest inference, Roger Stone. If there was anyone who best represented the irregular nature of the Trump campaign, it was Stone, a vivid if unstable combination of publicity seeker, performance artist, sexual adventurer, and conspiracist whom no one took seriously, probably not even Donald Trump.

"If all Mueller has is Stone, he doesn't have much," said Bannon, ever trying to parse what exactly Mueller had.

But the special counsel's indictment, it turned out, also appeared to be a cliff-hanger, for he was about to go quiet. It was now midsummer; always inclined to go by the book, Mueller was unlikely to do much else that could have an impact on the November elections. What's more, Mueller's small team had to prepare for the two trials of Paul Manafort that would take place sequentially in August and September, their first significant public performance and accounting.

The fact that the season finale came hours before Trump was to meet with Putin—well, Bannon observed, that's what coppers do. They turn up the heat on their subject and watch for the reaction.

* * *

It was just going to be Trump and Putin, with translators at their elbows. A straight-up discussion between two men. Two presidents sitting at a table in Helsinki, a favorite spot for Russian-American summits.

Trump was adamant about not having anybody else in the room. Mike Pompeo, one of the few people to whom the president was at least somewhat respectful, told him he couldn't do this, that at the very least his secretary of state ought to be in the room with him. But Trump blew him off: "I'm afraid of leaks, leakers." Which, by inference, seemed to mean Pompeo.

The entire foreign policy establishment—including Pompeo, NSC chief Bolton, and Kushner, with his vast foreign policy portfolio—was on the verge of a professional breakdown. The presidents of the United States and Russia meeting alone? It was unheard-of, but especially given the Russia investigation it was just this side of insane. Yet with a kind of bureaucratic heave, the foreign policy people readjusted. It was Trump— what could they do?

Trump had a plan, Mike Pompeo and John Bolton concluded: the plan was "happy talk."

Trump often boasted of his persuasive powers. "There's nobody who can butter up somebody like me," he bragged. In the Trump circle, this was understood as the anchor-tenant strategy. Jared and Ivanka were big proponents of this explanation of Trump's behavior. In the real estate business, you would do anything to get your big-brand anchor tenant for your retail space. Trump was famously single-minded in pursuit of his star tenant. If a hot retail prospect said he was sleeping with Trump's wife, Trump would say, Hey, let me get you some champagne. Until he got a signature and a deposit, there was no level of self-abasement that Trump wouldn't tolerate. Then, in the winter, he would withhold the heat.

Look at how well it had worked in Singapore with Kim Jong-un! Trump had buttered Kim up and, in return, Kim had buttered Trump up. And even if nothing else changed, the temper changed. Public hostility became public accommodation, even tenderness—albeit yet with nukes. That was a win, wasn't it? And it was all thanks to happy talk.

If Trump emerged from his meeting with Putin walking hand in hand with the Russian bear, that would be a win, too. He, Trump, would have used charm and personal diplomacy to win over the beast—all by himself. To Trump, this seemed like a no-brainer. It would be the perfect example of another of his favorite business maxims: "Pick the low-hanging fruit." If Trump and Putin flattered each other, they were much less likely to threaten each other or demand things of each other.

For now, Trump just needed a handshake. Later he could withhold the heat.

* * *

On Friday, July 13, three days before the Helsinki summit, the president and his team arrived late in the day at Trump Turnberry golf resort in Scotland, after passing on their way from the airport cow pastures and cheering citizens—but no protesters.

Mike Pompeo and John Bolton were carrying copious briefing books. This was meant to be a weekend of preparation interspersed with golf. John Kelly, Sarah Huckabee Sanders, Bill Shine, and several other aides had come along, too.

Saturday was sunny and in the mid-seventies, with nothing on the agenda except golf. But by now a few protesters had made their way to Turnberry. "No Trump, No KKK, No Racist USA," shouted a small group of them during the president's afternoon golf game.

Trump, energized by his NATO and UK meetings—"we roughed them up"—was in no mood to prepare for his Putin meeting. Even his typical, exceedingly casual level of preparation—prep masked as gossip—wasn't happening. Pompeo and Bolton reduced the boxed briefing binders to a one-pager. The president wouldn't focus on it.

He was fine. And why shouldn't he be? He had walked into his meeting with Kim unable to pick out North Korea on a map, but it didn't matter. He was in charge, a strong man making peace.

Don't box me in, he told his advisers. *I need to be open*, he kept repeating, as though this was a therapeutic process. Pompeo and Bolton urgently pressed him about the basic talking points for the summit, now just hours away—but nothing doing.

The next morning he played golf, and then it started to rain.

* * *

The presidential party arrived in Helsinki at 9:00 p.m. that Sunday, still an hour and a half before the sun would set, and then headed to the Hilton Hotel. While they were in the air, France had beaten Croatia for the

Russian-hosted World Cup at Luzhniki Stadium, Moscow, in a match attended by President Putin.

The morning of Monday, July 16, was occupied with ceremonial meetings and greetings with the Finnish president, but Trump found time to tweet about the Mueller indictments and the "rigged witch hunt" pursuing him.

Putin arrived in Helsinki later than expected—Putin was invariably late—keeping Trump waiting for almost an hour. After the hold, Trump and his party reached the Finnish Presidential Palace at about 2:00 p.m. Trump and Putin sat down together, posed for photos, and offered a few minutes of public remarks, with Trump congratulating the Russian president on a successful World Cup. Then the doors were closed, and their one-on-one private session commenced.

The meeting ran for a little more than two hours. For an additional hour or so, Russian and U.S. advisers and diplomats joined the two leaders. Finally Trump and Putin were led into the hall for a post-meeting press conference—where the world, and more specifically Trump's own people, saw a wholly unfamiliar figure.

Bannon's characterization of Trump quickly became the almost universal one in the Trump circle: "He looked like a beaten dog." Even Jared, likely unclear that the description originated with Bannon, repeated it.

For everyone in Trumpworld there was but one question: What could have possibly happened in there?

Trump and Putin went in as equals and came out as victim and victor. How had Trump's "happy talk" agenda been turned into such an obvious humiliation? Putin must have cornered the president with some dreadful unpleasantness—perhaps even some life-threatening unpleasantness! But exactly what was this order of pressure? What did Putin have? Almost everyone in the White House joined the debate.

"What could it be?" titillated staffers asked.

Bannon checked off the possibilities.

The pee tape? "I guarantee," said Bannon, "that if such a thing exists, and if it surfaced, he would simply, baldly, absolutely say that the spitting image of Donald J. Trump was not him. Fake. Fake. It wouldn't slow him down."

Don Jr. is said to try to buy the emails? "He doesn't care about Don Junior. Are you kidding?"

Proof that the oligarchs had bailed him out, that Russian billionaires had bought Trump properties at inflated prices? "Nobody gives a fuck. Trump knows that. Wouldn't faze him."

Possibly more devastating than a blackmail gambit, perhaps Putin had launched a concerted assault on Trump's intelligence.

"Forget the tax return, what if they have his college transcript?" This was a familiar White House riff. Many of Trump's friends believed that a root of his shame and intellectual insecurity was his steady semesters of Ds.

Or, what if Putin had turned the meeting from happy talk into geopolitical quizzing? How cruel, Bannon wondered, might Putin really be? Would he ask Trump to point out Crimea on a map? "Oh my God, not the relationship between Crimea and the Ukraine. Don't ask him that, please!"

Bannon believed that here were two narcissistic, cult-leader-type presidents on the world stage. Both had populist talents, yet both were ultimately out for their own benefit. Of the two, Putin was the far cleverer one.

For years, Donald Trump had stroked Vladimir Putin from afar, constantly calling out to him, the equivalent of overeager text messages. Putin remained aloof, making it clear that there was a ranking system. When, in 2013, Trump showed up in Moscow with his beauty pageant—when the pee tape was supposedly made—Putin let him think they would meet, that he would make an appearance at Trump's pageant. Instead, Putin snubbed him. Not rudely: he was smoother than that. Rather, the message was, Yes, someday we might meet, but not now. Bannon theorized that Trump may not have been interested in Russian help during the campaign; he may have merely wanted Russian attention, Russian interest— Putin's recognition.

Now, in Helsinki, after two hours in a room together, Trump had in theory finally gotten what he wished for. He was Putin's equal.

But then why did he look like a beaten dog?

* * *

The press conference surely ranked among the most devastating and damaging public performances by a president ever.

It wasn't even that Trump had fumbled a showdown with the Russian leader by delivering a performance something like Kennedy's famously botched first meeting with Khrushchev. Quite the opposite. Trump made no effort to stand tall. He was deferential, obsequious, servile. It really did seem like *Manchurian Candidate* stuff, with Trump under the thumb of his handler.

At the press conference, Putin audaciously offered to address the Mueller indictments of the twelve Russians. He would let them be questioned if, in turn, the United States would let Russia question American citizens it regarded as its enemies. This notion, Putin indicated, had been received positively by the U.S. president, who stood, deflated or uncomprehending, by his side.

Trying to rally, Trump blithely, with signature incoherence, exonerated Putin.

> My people came to me, they said they think it's Russia. I have President Putin; he just said it's not Russia. I will say this: I don't see any reason why it would be, but I really do want to see the server. But I have—I have confidence in both parties. I really believe that this will probably go on for a while, but I don't think it can go on without finding out what happened to the server. What happened to the servers of the Pakistani gentleman that worked on the DNC? Where are those servers? They're missing. Where are they? What happened to Hillary Clinton's emails? Thirty-three thousand emails—gone, just gone. I think, in Russia, they wouldn't be gone so easily. I think it's a disgrace that we can't get Hillary Clinton's thirty-three thousand emails.

Putin, for his part, casually dismissed Trump. The pee tape? Surveillance? Why? Trump was a nobody when he had visited Russia in 2013. A construction company executive. Not a guy who ran a branded high-end resort and casino business and was a major television star, but a run-of-the-mill, nothing-special business guy, Putin said with Trump wilting next to him. What reason would he have for taking an interest in Donald Trump?

Why didn't Shine stop it? How could the press conference have run so long? How had Trump been allowed to carry on, every comment worse than the previous one, digging himself deeper and deeper? And all the while, Putin stood next to him, watching, the coolest cat who ever swallowed a canary.

"We've had a reversal of fortune," said Bannon. "That was Little Big Horn."

But Bannon also recognized that Trump had been outplayed by a master. "God," he said, "Putin is a *badass*."

* * *

When Trump's public humiliation was finally over, he seemed unaware of what had happened. With Melania, Shine, and John Kelly following, he headed directly from the press conference into a small room in the presidential palace that had been converted into a television studio.

Trump had agreed to do a post-meeting interview with Fox's Tucker Carlson—Carlson, who had also come to Helsinki to cover the summit, had gotten the interview by calling Trump directly on his cell phone. But Sean Hannity, Carlson's colleague, also following Trump across Europe, had had a tantrum. Urged on by Bannon—"You're Sean Hannity! You get to interview Donald Trump!"—Hannity called Trump himself and begged. So Trump, always inclined to embrace anybody's servility, not to mention every opportunity for friendly publicity, was suddenly giving two interviews in back-to-back time slots to the same network in the same makeshift studio, everybody crowded in together.

There was hardly any room to stand: along with Trump, Melania, Shine, and Kelly, there were Carlson, Hannity, a camera crew, and two executive producers. Trump seemed yet undisturbed by the disastrous press conference. Kelly, snarling, could barely contain his fury and incomprehension, physically pushing people out of the way, including Carlson. Melania—rarely approached and certainly never hugged by anyone on

Trump's staff or in his entourage—visibly recoiled from Hannity's too-close embrace.

Hannity, like Trump, seemed to have missed the import of the press conference. Their interview proceeded in a flirty way—Trump playing hard to get and dismissive, Hannity excruciatingly unctuous.

Watching Hannity's performance, Carlson's executive producer said, "I'm gay and I've never hit on a man that hard."

Trump began the interview with Hannity by needling him for incorrectly identifying the number of NATO nations in his first question (with everyone surprised that Trump in fact seemed to know the correct number). "Tucker wouldn't screw that up," Trump said to a stricken Hannity. "He knows how many NATO countries there are. You ever watch his show? I watch it every night. I'll let you redo the question, go ahead."

Then, in his interview with Carlson—still unaware that he had incurred the condemnation as well as stupefaction of the free world for his slavishness to Putin—Trump went after NATO again. All in all, he said, he would be quite ambivalent about coming to the defense of NATO allies, thus effectively abandoning both the entire point of NATO and the foundation of the postwar order.

Carlson looked bewildered. "Membership in NATO obligates any other member to defend any member who is attacked," he pointed out.

Trump, noting that Montenegro is a NATO member, said he certainly would not want to fight for Montenegro.

* * *

On the plane ride home it only got worse.

At first, Trump looked eagerly for affirmation, but soon the disastrous coverage of his press conference began to sink in. His own perception of what had happened and the world's stood at nearly a 180-degree difference. Trump—almost never voluntarily alone, and absolutely never alone and awake without the television on—retreated into his bedroom cabin in silence.

As Air Force One flew west, he resisted all efforts to persuade him to brief his advisers about his meeting with Putin. He had had two hours of private conversation with the Russian president, yet no one in the U.S. government knew what he or Putin had said. The Russian government presumably knew everything.

The presidential party arrived back in the United States just after 9:00 p.m. that Monday. The president was followed off the plane by Bill Shine and John Bolton. Trump still refused to speak to anyone.

The next day, the president sat down with members of Congress to talk about tax reform, waving away efforts to engage him in discussions about the Helsinki summit.

Pompeo, Bolton, Mattis, the entire U.S. foreign policy leadership—everyone remained in the dark about what had been discussed. Nobody was read in. Did the president not listen to what was said, did he not understand, did he not remember? The Russians, meanwhile, started to leak details of what appeared to be a range of agreements that were reached during the summit. These included—incredibly, bizarrely—support for a plebiscite in Eastern Ukraine and a promise that U.S. officials would testify in a Russian judicial inquiry.

Many in the White House expressed a shocked appreciation of Putin's chutzpah: Had he really made such fantastical propositions, much less gotten the president to agree to them? In some surreal sense, this was a moment when effectively the entire U.S. government realized that its leader was not only tragically—or comically—out of his depth, but a pitiable mark. It was almost impossible to overstate the absolute bewilderment in the government or the rising panic in the Republican Party.

* * *

On Tuesday, July 17, Vice President Pence was delegated the responsibility to go into the Oval Office and tell the president that he had to walk back his Helsinki remarks. Pence stressed that it wasn't just Democrats; Republicans on the Hill were coming unglued. And there were about to be mass resignations in the White House.

Lewandowski and Hannity actually thought that the House might be hours away from voting articles of impeachment.

Derek Harvey, on the majority staff of the House Intelligence

Committee, frantically called the White House to say that six Republicans might vote to subpoena the interpreter who had worked for the American side during the Trump-Putin meeting.

Finally, after a further meeting with members of Congress that afternoon, Trump took questions from the press and performed his walkback. John Kelly, Ivanka Trump, Bill Shine, John Bolton, Mike Pence, and Steve Mnuchin were all standing close by.

"I'll begin by stating that I have full faith and support for America's great intelligence agencies," the president said stiffly. "I accept our intelligence community conclusion that Russia's meddling in the 2016 election took place." Oh, and also, he insisted, there was "no collusion."

Earlier, Trump had been huddling with Ivanka—even he couldn't find a way to talk himself out of this one. Ivanka called Anthony Scaramucci—"the Mooch"—the New York hedge fund executive who had, in July 2017, in a comic opera of drunkenness and ranting to the press, served for just eleven days as head of the White House communications team. Ivanka and Scaramucci proposed that Trump simply deny saying what he had said and blame it on misspeaking. Ivanka, pointing out that her father often misspoke and had "lazy speech patterns," ventured that this was at least a somewhat plausible explanation.

Trump had seized on this plan, and now he added: "It should have been obvious, I thought it would be obvious, but I would like to clarify just in case it wasn't. In a key sentence in my remarks I said the word 'would' instead of 'wouldn't.' The sentence should have been, 'I don't see any reason why it wouldn't be Russia,' so, just to repeat it, I said the word 'would' instead of 'wouldn't.'" It was, he continued, "sort of a double negative."

While Trump was in the middle of his walk-back remarks, carried live on national television, the lights went out. A puzzled Trump continued speaking, his face briefly darkened. Ivanka later accused John Kelly of purposely turning the lights off. It wasn't an accident or a sign from God, she insisted; it was John Kelly saying shut up.

Bannon was, once again, gobsmacked. "When Ivanka and the Mooch can talk the commander in chief of the United States into thinking that people will believe that you had a double negative problem, you've left the Cartesian universe."

* * *

A cabinet meeting was hastily arranged for the next day, Wednesday. To demonstrate that it was business as usual at the White House, the meeting was open to the press. Ivanka Trump gave the main presentation and offered an array of ideas for new job programs. "Wow," noted the president afterward. "If that were Ivanka 'Smith,' the press would say that was totally brilliant!"

Answering a question as the meeting finished, Trump said, No, he didn't believe the Russians were targeting U.S. elections any longer. A short time later, a clarification was issued: when the president said "No," he was saying, No, he wouldn't answer questions.

Jim Mattis, very publicly in town, openly incredulous and deeply alarmed—and, after Helsinki, more uncertain about whether he should remain in his position than at any time since he had joined the Trump administration—pointedly failed to show up for the cabinet meeting. Rumors everywhere, many seeming to come from people very close to the secretary of defense, had Mattis resigning in protest within hours.

And yet, as bad as it was, it got still worse when Trump suddenly announced that he was inviting Putin to come to the White House.

The furor raged on. Responding with hurt and explosive anger, he now looked for someone to blame. Mattis, with his apocalyptic hints of resignation, seemed an ideal target. Trump suddenly began screaming to aides about Mattis and his transgender tolerance. "He wants to give trannies operations. 'Learn to fire a gun and I'll give you an operation,'" Trump mimicked in his mincing voice.

The White House quickly tried to measure the likely reaction if Mattis—who, in the view of both parties, was the designated adult in the White House—was forced out. Firing the secretary of defense, they were told by members of the congressional leadership, might make the Saturday Night Massacre look like a peaceful evening.

"If he loses Mattis," said Bannon, more concerned than he had ever been about Trump's mental state, "he loses the presidency." Mattis was the link to the bipartisan establishment, such as it was. Without Mattis, the center truly might not hold.

Persuaded to turn his attention away from Mattis, the president next focused his guns on Kelly, who had hinted at his own resignation after Helsinki. But then Dan Coats, the director of National Intelligence, stepped into the line of fire.

Coats was out of town attending a conference on global security issues in Aspen. While being interviewed onstage, he was informed that Trump had just invited Putin to the White House. Coats, his eyes seeming to pop out of his head, couldn't stifle his amazement, nor did he try. "Say that again?" he asked. As the audience burst into laughter, he continued, "Okay . . . that's going to be special."

Within minutes, almost all the television news outlets were playing the tape of Coats's unfiltered reaction. Trump was furious: "He was shitting all over me!"

Making Coats's gaffe worse, news of the incident preempted the White House's planned distraction: with Ivanka at his side, the president was set to sign a new executive order creating the Council for the American Worker as part of his daughter's job-training program. The president, meanwhile, would sign a new executive order appointing Jared Kushner head of a new labor council. But there was no TV!

Trump vowed to fire Coats. Kelly immediately objected: if you fire Coats, Kelly said, ten other guys will resign. And if Congress doesn't impeach you over firing Coats, they will certainly censure you.

Trump began to crazily flip through the cable dial, looking for his defenders and finding no one. Where was Kellyanne? he demanded to know. Where was Sarah? Where was *anybody*?

Afraid that Hannity would call for Trump to fire Coats and that this would seal Coats's fate, the White House went into yet another panic. Before an interview with CBS in the Roosevelt Room, Kelly, Shine, Sarah Huckabee Sanders, and Mercedes Schlapp had a near throw-down fight about who would tell the president that he had to defend Coats. The job fell to Kelly.

On the air, the president seemed strangely eager to please. Sitting in a chair with his hands between his legs like a monster shrimp, he bent over the interviewer, Jeff Glor. Perhaps finally starting to appreciate his peril, he seemed, spirit broken, eager to give the right answers.

GLOR: You say you agree with U.S. intelligence that Russia meddled in the election in 2016.

TRUMP: Yeah and I've said that before, Jeff. I have said that numerous times before, and I would say that is true, yeah.

GLOR: But you haven't condemned Putin, specifically. Do you hold him personally responsible?

TRUMP: Well I would, because he's in charge of the country. Just like I consider myself to be responsible for things that happen in this country. So certainly as the leader of a country you would have to hold him responsible, yes.

GLOR: What did you say to him?

TRUMP: Very strong on the fact that we can't have meddling, we can't have any of that . . .

As the show wrapped, Kelly hit bottom. "This time he's not going to get away with it," he said, muttering to himself. "This shit is out of control. Nobody can carry this anymore."

And yet no one resigned—not that day, or the next, or the next. If Trump did not quite "get away with it," no one in his inner circle could come up with a good answer to the essential question: What are we going to *do* about this mess?

Bannon, in a public statement, declared: "You are either with Trump or against him." The comment resolved nothing and yet somehow summed up everything.

On Friday, July 20, the president headed off to Bedminster. On Saturday, he played golf. On Sunday, he tweeted that Russian interference in the 2016 elections "was all a big hoax."

* * *

Not long after the Putin summit, an ad hoc circle of Republicans started to talk. This group included representatives from the Senate majority

leader's office, the Speaker of the House's office, and some of the party's
most significant donors, notably Paul Singer and Charles Koch. Although
this was hardly yet an organized move against the president, it was the
beginning of an exploratory committee. The group's primary objectives
were to assess the president's strengths and weaknesses, and to look
toward 2020 and the possibility of a primary challenge.

14

100 DAYS

Sunday, July 29, marked one hundred days to go until the midterm elections.

Reince Priebus, Trump's chief of staff for the first six months of his administration, invited Bannon to have dinner with him at his country club in suburban Virginia. A year had passed since Priebus departed his White House job, the president dismissing him in a tweet as Priebus, disembarking from Air Force One, stood on the airport tarmac. Since then he had failed to land the kind of prestige position that customarily went to a former chief of staff. Now slated to step into one of the Trump campaign operations, Priebus was hesitating, foreseeing more backlash toward anyone connected to the president.

Bannon was encouraging him to take the job. "I don't know," said Priebus. "Mitch McConnell is a pretty smart guy, and he has us down by forty seats in the House. Paul Ryan is a pretty smart guy and thinks forty is optimistic."

In politics, one hundred days was ordinarily an eternity, but right now many Republicans felt like time had stopped and there was no way forward. Sometimes it seemed as if the whole campaign consisted only of Don Jr. and his girlfriend, former Fox star Kimberly Guilfoyle, out on the road supporting Trump, with Don Jr. finally getting the personal acknowledgment from the base that he had never gotten from his father.

It was a largely skeptical party, no matter how much it was theoretically bent to Trump's will.

"It's over," Jason Miller, the White House's designated CNN messenger and among Trump's most indefatigable surrogates, told Bannon.

Meanwhile, there was the continual and unprecedented departure of White House staffers; the day-by-day attrition from the senior ranks was relentless. The latest to go was legislative director Marc Short. To be the legislative director for a party that controls both houses of Congress is one of the plum jobs in politics. You're the point person for the push to deliver on your party's promises. You're the can-do guy. For all practical purposes, you can't fail, and your big-money future career is ensured. But Short couldn't wait to get out.

Ordinarily, a flood of résumés would stream into the White House in the wake of a departure like Short's. But the number of résumés that came in from people eager to take his job was . . . zero. The position was finally filled by Shahira Knight, a low-profile lobbyist and former aide to Gary Cohn.

Bill Shine, only weeks into the job, was beside himself with fury, telling everyone that this wasn't what he had signed up for. There was no organization. There was no plan. There were literally no bodies to do anything—he had to do everything himself. Plus, it was a full-time job just to deal with Trump, a vastly more difficult star than anyone at Fox. Trump was worse, said Shine, than Bill O'Reilly, who, by almost all accounts, was the most difficult man in television (in the *history* of television, according to long-time Fox boss Roger Ailes). But Trump, in Shine's telling, needed an even higher level of stroking, reassurance, and attention to his appearance.

Trump was at least as unhappy with Shine. "Hannity said Shine was talented," he groused. "He's a no-talent. Hannity said I was getting Ailes. Shine's no Ailes."

A year and a half into Trump's administration, it often seemed as if nobody worked at the White House anymore. One hundred days out from the most consequential midterm elections in a generation, no one was pushing out the White House message; even Kellyanne Conway seemed to have disappeared. ("Into witness protection," said Bannon.) Worse, there *was* no message. Jason Miller, the president's chief defender on CNN, was writing his own talking points for his appearances.

Bannon, however, was back in campaign mode. It was all war all the time: no matter how dismal your prospects, you could only believe in a positive outcome—that was the nature of a campaign. His war-room operation in the Embassy in full swing, he tried to revert to his August 2016 Trump Tower mindset, when he had arrived to take over a failing campaign. But at that critical moment he had a huge advantage: his enemy was asleep, fat and happy in the conviction that Hillary Clinton had the presidency locked. Now he was facing an enemy totally on the trigger, watching every opportunity to pour in more resources. Whatever happened, the other side would not be caught sleeping this time around; that arrogance did not exist. The Democrats, Bannon understood, had their existential boots on. If they blew this, they blew everything.

In the White House, there was lassitude, fatalism, and, above all, a disinclination to take responsibility for the woeful outcome that now seemed inevitable. The Democrats may have dramatically altered their mindset from 2016, but not the Trumpers: as in 2016, they assumed they would lose, even *should* lose.

It wasn't lost on anybody that Don Jr., in everybody's estimation a very weak link in the Trump family's march forward, was his father's chief booster. (This was a development that worried even the president. "He's a pretty stupid boy," said a realistic Trump.) Enjoying his new visibility, his son was now telling everyone that it didn't matter if they lost, and that impeachment would be a good thing. "Let them try it. Bring it on. I'm glad. This is going to be the best thing that could ever happen," said Don Jr., hitting his fists against his chest. "The Democrats are going to be very, very sorry."

"I just hope people don't really believe this shit," Bannon said to Priebus. "When the Dems get the gavel and start running through everything, if you think Trump is King Lear now, wait until every day is hearings, investigations, subpoenas. He will lose his shit."

* * *

Bannon, spending more and more time in New York, was being urged to dump Trump by some of the contributors and media figures he had befriended since leaving the White House. His reinvented career, from marginal political participant to kingmaker and international political celebrity, might well die if Trump died. Bannon understood that. "I'm just a movement guy staying with Trump because he's part of this movement," said Bannon, hardly affirming his passionate enthusiasm for Trump.

Curiously, at the same time that Bannon, along with the rest of the party, had grown more and more weary of Trump—for many, a pitiless exhaustion—there was now wide addiction to Trump's wild-card genius. He had imagination or instincts or a shamelessness so beyond the boundaries of traditional political conduct that no conventional politician—and politics remained the province of conventional politicians—had yet found a way to anticipate and counter Trump's disruptive behavior. "This is a herculean struggle, but at the end of the day we've got Trump, and no one in American politics has yet figured out how to deal with that," said Bannon.

This was just as true of the Republicans as the Democrats. In a sense, the Republicans—the RNC and the congressional leadership—were hardly mounting a midterm campaign. The elections in November weren't, after all, about the Republican Party. They were about Donald Trump. The party was just going through the motions, waiting for Trump to pull off a miracle. Somehow.

The Republicans were set to spend more than $500 million on House races (they would ultimately spend $690 million). But that was separate from Trump's own campaign—or, in his view, the real campaign—which would focus on what Trump liked doing best and what he had concluded was the singular reason for his victory in 2016: rallies.

In some perhaps unconscious but none-too-subtle sense, the purpose of Trump's presidency—its style and emphasis and daily bid for attention—was not so much about winning votes but about filling stadiums. Here, Trump was fed by Bannon's nearly constant exhortations that the election needed to be *only* about him. On T minus 102 days, Bannon had appeared on Hannity's Fox show, with both men speaking directly to the president: only you can save yourself.

Trump's fate, Bannon declared, rested with the deplorables, who had to be brought to the kind of fearful emotional pitch that would get them to the polls. Trump alone could accomplish this.

* * *

The feeling of resignation among the Republican ranks was overwhelming. The prospect of losing provided the only rationale for winning. "If we don't win, our situation will be so catastrophic we can't even think about it," said Bannon. "The internecine warfare between Mitch McConnell, the establishment, the donors, the bloodletting—no one will be left standing."

This rationale held equally for the Democrats, however. The party that lost the midterms would implode and be consumed by internal strife. Bannon, as though operating a political hedge fund, was hoping to benefit from either side's civil war.

If the Republicans lost their House majority, Trump would surely be the key reason for that loss. Just as surely, he would off-load the blame, in his most withering and abusive terms, on the Republican leadership. Trump flourished most of all as a contrast gainer to his enemies. Corry Bliss, the Republican operative running the party's efforts to hold the House, told people he wasn't so much afraid of losing the House, but of losing the House and having Donald Trump still in the White House. Given the certainty that Trump was not going to blame himself, nor give credit to the Democrats, then the fault was going to fall on the heads of the congressional Republicans and their donors.

Trump, as Bannon had to regularly remind his Republican friends, was not in fact a Republican. His party affiliation was purely a relationship of convenience, ready to be broken at any moment. "If you think Trump is dangerous now," said Bannon, "a wounded Trump knows no bounds."

For Bannon, losing the House could in fact be quite the perfect plan. A good part of his bitter fight with Trump—beyond the fact that everyone fought bitterly with Trump—had to do with Trump's willingness to let the Republican leadership substitute its agenda for his. Trump and Bannon's populist revolution had, too often, defaulted to standard Republican politics. So here, in defeat, Bannon might get his all-out war with the Republican Party. It was the RINOs—the Republicans in Name Only—who had not adequately defended Trump; hence, if the House was lost, it was the RINOs who would be responsible for his impeachment.

If the House flipped and Trump was threatened with impeachment, the deplorable wing of the party would be energized and ascendant (although even for Bannon the nature of that energy had its fearsome prospects). What would rouse this beast more than anything was its leader's destruction. Depending on Bannon's mood, he was ready to bring it on, and he could see how the martyrdom of Donald Trump might be a net positive for himself and the populist movement. Trump would be turned into a powerful symbol, victim and martyr, and in the end that might play better than Trump as the movement's infuriating and unpredictable standard-bearer.

But if the Democrats failed to win the House, this outcome, too, held all manner of advantages for Bannon. Here would be an epochal accounting. Universal revulsion toward Donald Trump across the liberal bandwidth had brought the Democrats together after the 2016 election. They had blamed Trump for stealing the election; they had not, more logically, blamed themselves for losing it. But if they could not take him on now—with money, righteousness, ground troops, and minus the drag of Hillary Clinton—then surely they would have to accept that the problem was the identity of the Democratic Party itself. In this scenario as well, it would be the establishment against the party's own great unwashed. The left wing, searching for new meaning and leadership, would, in Bannon's view, embrace its own militant version of populism.

And in this polarization and realignment would lie Bannon's opportunity—and amusement. Indeed, Bannon found himself drawn equally to the left and the right. His insight, yet to be shared by the left, was that he could be one of its natural leaders. Italy was his proof of concept: he had helped bring together the nationalist Northern League and the populist Five Star Movement. Both parties felt deep antipathy toward corporate influence, elite power brokers, a mordant status quo, and self-sustaining expertise—that was unifying. The rest was just details.

Since leaving the White House in August 2017 and then exiting Breitbart at the beginning of 2018, Bannon had paid increasing amounts of attention to liberal media, even as liberal media reviled him all the more. There was his widely discussed *60 Minutes* interview. There was his list of go-to liberal reporters and producers: Costa at the *Washington Post*, Gabe Sherman at *Vanity Fair*, Maggie Haberman at the *Times*, Ira Rosen at *60 Minutes*, seemingly almost anyone who called him from the *Daily Beast*.

Bannon had heard that Steve Jobs's wife, Laurene Powell—who was now using her billions to build a progressive media company—had said she was "a huge fan" of his. He had heard that a character in the forthcoming spy thriller *Mile 22*, starring Mark Wahlberg, was based on him. And Michael Moore's soon-to-be-released *Fahrenheit 11/9*—he appeared in that, too. He was also, while traveling the globe, being followed by a full-time documentary team.

Bannon was most especially looking forward to an Errol Morris documentary, which was due to be literally all about him—a 110-minute single-subject interview. One of Morris's most famous documentaries, *The Fog of War*, focused exclusively on Robert McNamara, secretary of defense under Kennedy and Johnson, an epochal and tragic figure of the Vietnam War. Morris's new film would, ipso facto, confirm that Bannon was just as epochal. The film—originally titled *American Carnage*, after Trump's dark inaugural speech, which Bannon had written—was now, for fear of offending liberal audiences before they had even seen the film, called *American Dharma*. It would play at the Venice, Toronto, and New York film festivals in the fall, thereby thrusting Bannon's views straight into the center of the liberal bleeding heart.

While Bannon was courting the mainstream and lefty media, he was also hard at work on a right-wing—*far*-right-wing—piece of propaganda. One of Bannon's peripatetic occupations was as an independent filmmaker; he had produced some eighteen films, most of them conservative documentaries, but also three Hollywood feature films. *Trump @War* was a bellicose, head-splitting, often surreal work, a fusillade of punches, screaming, fires, and bitter confrontations at the barricade. Bannon believed that the Left would have gladly made this film about the Right's merciless attacks on the Left's good people; instead, in his film, the Left mercilessly attacked the Right's good people.

The film was meant to have, after its release in September, a viral life driven by tens of millions of downloads. But it was also meant for an audience of one. And, indeed, when Trump was shown the Bannon film later in the summer, he was full of praise: "Very talented guy. You have to admit, very talented guy. Can really hold your attention."

In mid-July, in the days after Trump's Helsinki debacle, Bannon saw yet another opportunity to take center stage: he was due to appear as a surprise guest at a music-and-culture rally in New York's Central Park. Alexandra Preate, his dogged PR adviser, was more than dubious about the benefits of participating in this event, and she was intently trying to talk him out of appearing before a live Manhattan audience.

Yet Bannon would not be deterred. "I'm going to say you're a bunch of fucking suckers. You put your heart and soul into the gig economy, and you've got nothing. A bunch of serfs—no ownership, no benefits, no equity, your savings account at zero."

But then he added: "The problem with the speech is that this is New York, and all these people are either rich or sure they *will* be rich. They want to be the owners. Preate is praying I'll be rained out."

Which he was.

* * *

After Helsinki, Trump began a new riff about what in his administration needed to change. This was perhaps an indication that his progress was less random than it invariably seemed, that there was at least an atavistic desire to survive, if not a clear strategy.

Back into his conversation came the forbidden subject of Steve Bannon. Not that the reintroduction was positive: Bannon was a loser, a turncoat, a mess of a human being. But by trashing his former strategist and setting people up to agree with his criticism, he could then disagree with them. Yes, Bannon was an asshole and a leaker, but at least he wasn't an idiot like all the other White House assholes and leakers.

This reevaluation of Bannon was partly directed at Jared, at Jared's proxy Brad Parscale, and at Jared's intention to run the reelection campaign. That was now Jared's plan. He no longer intended to return to New York after the midterms, an outcome Trump seemed to be promoting among people who could promote it to Jared. Instead, he would stay in D.C. and take over the 2020 reelection campaign. Trump was resisting this because he didn't like to think ahead—bad luck to make too many plans. But another reason for Trump's new negative attitude toward his son-in-law was a sudden profusion of rumors about Jared's possible indictment. As it happened, many of these rumors were spread by Bannon. They were also spread by Trump himself, who discussed the chances of his son-in-law's indictment freely and to a large call list, causing the rumors to circle back. But that didn't matter: rumors were rumors.

So with Trump's blessing, White House intermediaries floated the question: Would Bannon consider coming back?

Bannon's intermediaries sent back his answer: "Fuck, no."

Yet Trump couldn't quite let the idea go. What if, he wondered, Bannon were to take over the campaign? The what-if was not so much about what this would mean for Bannon, but what it would mean for Trump. Would it mean that he didn't believe he could win without Bannon? Or would it appear that he was so confident he could be magnanimous and bring Bannon back?

Another question was floated: If the president asked, would Bannon come in to see him?

Bannon would . . . *if* the visit took place in the residence and not in the Oval. Specifically: "I will get there early in the morning and come to the residence, and after you watch TV we'll talk."

Bannon knew precisely what he would say to Trump if the meeting came through: "If you get your fucking relatives and Parscale out of there, I will run the fucking campaign. No promises after that."

Hearing Bannon's conditional assent to the notion of a visit, Trump seemed on the verge of inviting him. "I'm going to call him," he told a friend in New York. But then, to the same friend, he immediately said: "Jared's hearing bad stuff about him." Later, he debated the issue with Hannity. Should I call him? he asked.

In the end, the call never came. Bannon understood that Trump was incapable of publicly admitting he was in so much trouble that he needed help. "I know this guy," Bannon said. "Psychologically he can't handle dependence. In fact, I *wouldn't* be able to save him, because if it started to look like I was saving him, or if I got credit for saving him, he'd crack in front of everybody."

* * *

"Exogenous events"—these were the unknowable, almost mystical, forces and alignment of the stars that would, Bannon believed, determine the outcome of the midterm elections. As party loyalty eroded, as suspicion of all politicians increased, as the donor class on both sides ponied up the money to saturate all media markets, what happened in the final weeks of a campaign was likely to be determinative. Especially in the age of Trump, when the most recent event often eclipsed all that had come before it—with Trump's brinksmanship and showmanship amping up the drama—earlier advantages or deficits might not matter in the least. Even the stunning success of the Trump economy—the unemployment rate was the lowest it had been in years—would likely mean very little. More and more, elections represented a snapshot in time, not a cumulative experience. That, certainly, was the lesson of 2016: Trump probably won the White House because at the eleventh hour James Comey had revisited Hillary Clinton's email issues.

What *might* happen—that, Bannon believed, was the game to play. So what did Donald Trump or the gods have up their sleeves? Bannon imagined the wealth of exogenous events that might happen before November 6.

The hedge fund guys might return from the Hamptons in September and, with their big gains already made for the year, start to wonder where the off-ramp would be for the growing conflict with China. Threats were one thing, but a take-no-prisoners trade war was another. If the market movers turned negative and began taking profits, the market could swoon. A big correction could shatter Trump's confidence and cause him to behave even more erratically.

Or: if Trump did not get his funding for the Wall in the fiscal year beginning October 1, he might force the government to shut down. This time, weeks before the election, he might accept chaos, even revel in it. In February, after bitterly accepting his last humiliating compromise, he had vowed never again to let a budget pass without funding for the Wall. Now, at the end of July, he was still making the threat: no Wall, no budget. If he accepted anything less, the base would remember it.

Or: the confirmation of Brett Kavanaugh to the Supreme Court, which would play out in September, might deliver to the base the raw meat of cultural war. Kavanaugh, a conservative, would move the Court decisively to the right, and the Republicans hoped that the Democrats would launch a furious, foam-at-the-mouth, and ultimately futile campaign of opposition.

Or: Bob Woodward, the Nixon-slayer and backstage chronicler of every administration since Watergate—the purest voice of the Washington establishment—might deliver a knockout verdict on the Trump presidency. Indeed, the book, scheduled for mid-September publication, was precisely timed to disrupt the midterm elections and help put Trump's presidency in serious jeopardy.

Or: Trump might yet fire Sessions, or Rosenstein, or Mueller—or all three of them. He might try to blow up "the Russia thing," which in turn could work to his advantage or his mortal detriment.

"Just assume," said Bannon in late July, "that this thing is going to get insane."

15

MANAFORT

On July 31, in the Eastern District of Virginia, Robert Mueller brought Paul Manafort—the former international lobbyist and political adviser, and, more recently, chairman of Donald Trump's presidential campaign—to trial. He faced eighteen counts of tax evasion and other financial frauds.

Mueller would soon be trying Manafort on other charges—conspiracy, money laundering, witness tampering—in U.S. district court in Washington. The prosecutors had sought to consolidate all the charges in D.C., but the Manafort legal team, believing it had leverage where in fact it had none, refused to agree to the consolidation. The government therefore proceeded with a plan to conduct back-to-back trials, doubling its chances for convictions and, as it attempted to squeeze Manafort to testify against Trump, virtually guaranteeing his personal bankruptcy.

For Bannon, Manafort had long been an incomprehensible and comic presence, and the opening of the trial prompted something of a reverie from him. It was an absurdist tale, with Manafort a quintessential Trump sort of character, useful and amusing to Trump, and, as well, a potential mortal threat to him.

"Here," said Bannon, reminiscing one summer day at his dining table in the Embassy, "is how I met Paul Manafort . . .

"I was in New York, sitting in Bryant Park and reading the paper. This was the eleventh or twelfth of August [2016], and I saw Maggie Haberman's ohmygod story in the *Times* about the total, unremitting collapse of the Trump campaign. I called Rebekah Mercer. 'Did you know,' I say, 'that this thing was that fucked up?' She says, 'Let me make some calls.' Five minutes later she calls me back and says, 'It's even worse. It's a death spiral. McConnell and Ryan are already saying that by Tuesday or Wednesday they are going to cut Trump loose from the RNC and focus all the money on the House and Senate. They're telling donors this Trump thing is over.' Then Bob [Bob Mercer, Rebekah's father] gets on the phone and I say, 'You know, we're going to get blamed for this. It's going to be Breitbart, Bannon, and the Mercers who foisted this guy on the Republicans. That's why they don't have Rubio or Jeb Bush or even Ted Cruz.' So Bob says, 'Steve, you can't do worse than this. You could run this thing and tighten it up to losing by only five or six—not twenty!' I say, 'Hey, you know, I still think this thing is winnable—really.'

"So that's when they call Woody Johnson. Bob and Rebekah fly out to this fundraising thing he's got scheduled in the Hamptons for Saturday where they know Trump is going to be. They set things up to see Trump beforehand and they pitch him on me and Kellyanne taking over the campaign. Mnuchin was there but they threw him out. Rebekah has no bedside manner, so it was like, 'Who are you?' 'I'm Steve Mnuchin, I'm doing high-net-worth contributions,' Rebekah says. 'Well, you're doing a terrible job because no big donors are giving.' In fact, Woody has a tent for a thousand. Of course, everybody in the Hamptons reads the *New York Times* and knows you'd be a total loser to show up—and only fifty guys show up, thirty already tapped out. Trump walks out there and sees nothing but a handful of schmendricks and loses it. Doesn't shake any hands, just glares and leaves.

"It's set up for me to talk to Trump [from New York] later that evening. We're on the phone for like three hours. I'm father-confessor. He's saying, 'The campaign is fucked. Manafort is to blame. Manafort—fucking Manafort.' He's saying, 'Fucking Manafort. Fucking Manafort. Fucking Manafort.' And I'm saying, 'Listen to me, we've got this. Really. Really.' So we set up to have breakfast next morning. He says, 'I'm playing golf at eight so let's have breakfast at seven.' Fine. Done. Six forty-five I traipse into Trump

Tower. There's a black dude at that little guard stand. Place is totally empty. He says, 'We're not open to the public right now.' I say, 'I know, but I'm here to have breakfast with Mr. Trump.' He says, 'You came to the wrong place. This is Trump Tower. The residence is around the corner. But,' he says, 'not sure you'll find Mr. Trump there, just saying.' I say, 'Why not?' He says, 'Well, if you're supposed to have breakfast with him, you should know where he is.' Eyeing me like a kook. He's about to throw me out.

"So I go and call Trump and he says, 'Where are you?' I say, 'I'm sitting in the lobby of Trump Tower.' He says, 'What the fuck are you doing there? You're supposed to be here for breakfast!' 'Well,' I say, 'I thought that meant Trump Tower.' 'No,' he says, 'I'm here in Bedminster.' Well, I'd never heard of Bedminster in my life. So I say, 'What's that?' 'My golf course. A great golf course. The greatest. So be out here at noon.' Then he starts to explain in great detail how to get there because, honestly, he has no earthly idea what a phone can do. He is literally like my dad, who is ninety-six. For ten minutes—'You go over the bridge, exit, remember road splits, veer this way . . .' I'm saying, 'Just give me an address.' '. . . Get off Rattlesnake Road, come down by the church, but don't take that right . . . keep going . . . hard right . . .' On and on, he's from the land that time's forgotten. I swear he doesn't know how to use a phone.

"I get a driver to take me out, pull up, say, 'Mr. Bannon for Mr. Trump.' 'Oh yeah, you're going to the lunch. Go to the clubhouse.' I'm sitting there thinking, 'The lunch. *The* lunch.' I thought I was there to have lunch, not for *the* lunch. Then we pull up at this colonial thing, guy walks out and says, 'Mr. Bannon, you're early. Mr. Ailes and the mayor aren't here yet.' I go, 'Fuck me. I'm out here to *audition*.' I go into this gazebo thing and they're setting up and it's a table like for six. So I'm really pissed. They're putting hot dogs on the grill. It's like a Jersey shore cookout. Hot dogs—and not good hot dogs. I later realize that's what he eats. Nathan's franks, burgers. I am so ripshit. He's got me out there to audition. I'm not auditioning; I don't need this. I'm not going to be some fucking monkey. In front of Ailes, how embarrassing is this?

"Then Ailes shows up and says, 'What the fuck are you doing here? Don't fuckin' tell me he brought you out here for debate prep!' [The debate was scheduled for September 26.] Then I realize, 'Nobody has any idea why

I'm here.' So I say, 'Hey, he's tired of hearing your war stories. He wants to get some fucking work done.' I'm giving Ailes shit. Then Rudy piles in. Then fat-boy Christie shows up. It's like the Three Stooges. And Trump comes in, he's got the full Cleveland—white golf shoes, white pants, white belt. And red ball cap. It's gotta be ninety-five degrees, ninety-five humidity, and he's just played eighteen. He's sweating like something you've never seen. But he maxes down two hot dogs right off the bat. He's still the guy from Queens. Just played eighteen and needs his dogs. He goes, 'Look, I gotta go shower, guys. And hey, by the way, Steve's part of the team.' Thirty minutes later, he comes back, and we're all sitting there.

"And a few minutes later, in walks Paul Manafort. Holy Christ. He has on those sort of see-through white culottes, see your skivvies underneath, he's wearing those with the blazer with the kerchief and the crest. He's Thurston Howell III from *Gilligan's Island*. The only time before I had seen Manafort was on Sunday morning TV, live from Southampton. This whole populist thing was broadcasting live from *Southampton*. Anyway, we're sitting there, and Trump comes back and immediately goes after Manafort.

"I have never seen a guy mauled in front of people like Trump mauled Paul Manafort. 'You're terrible, you can't defend me, you're a lazy fuck.' It was brutal. I was the peacemaker. The other guys just sat there wide-eyed. 'Am I a fucking baby? Am I a fucking baby? You think you have to talk to me through TV? Am I a fucking baby? I see you on there saying what you think I should do? Hey, you know what, you *suck* on TV.' Then he rips into Manafort about the *Times* story. And I say, 'Hey, you know they make this shit up.' And he says, 'Really?' 'Sure,' I say. 'It's true,' he says, and then goes on a rant about the polling guys. 'They take your money and just make these numbers up. It's all made up.' He's screaming.

"Manafort creeps out early. There's no debate prep. Rudy, Ailes, and Christie are having a fine time. But no debate prep. A clusterfuck. Oh, and Trump hasn't told them I've come to run the campaign. I'm just part of the team. I hang back as the thing breaks up and tell him we've got to announce this, and that I'm not going to fire Manafort. He stays as chairman. We don't need more stories about how fucked we are.

"So I go immediately back into the city and go up to the fourteenth floor of Trump Tower. This time the guard lets me up. I walk into the place. It's Sunday afternoon now, about five or six. First of all, I've never been in a campaign headquarters in my life. I think I'll be walking into a scene out of *The Candidate*. Or *The West Wing*. I think I'm going to see incredibly smart young people. People walking around with data print-outs. Packed with people. Activity everywhere. Electric. But it's empty. When I say empty, I mean nobody. Closed. Shut.

"I walk around the fourteenth floor. Every office is empty and dark. I finally wander around this rabbit warren and get to the rapid response war room and there's one guy. Little Andy Surabian. One guy. I go, 'Where is everybody?' He says, 'What do you mean?' I say, 'Is this headquarters? Or maybe the actual headquarters is in Washington?' He says, 'No, no, it's here.' I say, 'You sure?' So I say, 'Then where is everybody?' and he says, 'The Trump campaign doesn't work weekends. They'll all be getting in around ten tomorrow.' I say, 'But there's like eighty-eight days to go!' I say, 'I don't know much, but I know that campaigns work seven days a week. There's no days off.' He looks at me, and says, 'This is not exactly a campaign. This is what it is.'

"So I realize the *New York Times* didn't even scratch the surface. There's nothing going on here. It's not a disorganized campaign. It's not a campaign. But I'm thinking, 'Well, this is a shit show.' But because of that, there's no downside for me. I'll cover myself on the downside and let people know what kind of joke this is. And I'm thinking I don't even know if there's a chance to close this up to within five or six points. I'm thinking, 'Trump *says* he's on board.' But you don't know what he hears because he just talks.

"Then my phone goes off and it's Manafort and he says, 'Where are you?' I say, 'I'm in the campaign headquarters,' and then I go, 'So nobody works weekends?' And he goes, 'What are you talking about?' I say, 'There's nobody here.' He says, 'Really?' I say, 'It's dark.' He says, 'I don't know. I go out to the Hamptons on Thursday nights. I thought everybody was there.' Then he says, 'Can you come up and see me?' I say, 'What do you mean, come up and see you? I'm in Trump Tower.' He says, 'Yeah, come up and see me. I'm on the forty-third floor.' Then he starts to describe this long, convoluted way to get up to the residence side from the business side, just like Trump telling me how to get to Bedminster. I say, 'Can't I just walk around to the other side of the building?' 'Yeah, yeah,' he says, 'you can do that.'

"I go up and walk in and he's got a beautiful apartment and there's a lady of a certain age in a white caftan spread on the sofa. When Manafort's daughter's phone got hacked in 2017, we learned that Paul likes to see multiple guys fuck his wife—his daughter asks her sister in one of the emails, 'Has Mom been tested for STDs?' Well, that's Mom lying on the sofa.

"Anyway, he goes, 'They say you're a good media guy, maybe you've got a good idea of what to do here—take a look at this.' Headline on this thing he hands me, which is going to break in the *Times*, is MANAFORT TAKES $14 MILLION FOR FOREIGN CAMPAIGN WORK. I say, 'Fourteen million dollars! What? Fourteen million dollars from where? How? For what?' He says, 'From Ukraine.' I say, 'What the fuck? The *Ukraine*?' He says, 'Hey, hey, hey. Hold on. I had a lot of expenses.' I say, 'Paul, how long have you known about this?' He says, 'I don't know, a couple of months.' 'A couple of *months*?' Then I say, 'When do they say it's coming out?' He says, 'I don't know, I don't know. Maybe it goes online tonight, they say.' 'Tonight!' Then I say, 'Does Trump know about this?' He says, 'Maybe a little. Maybe not the details.' I say, 'Dude, you got to go see him right now. I told you, you're the chairman, I'm the CEO, you got no authority, but I'm not going to embarrass you. You seem like an okay guy. But this is . . . He's going to go fucking nuts. You've known about this for two months? Why didn't you tell anybody?' 'Well, my attorney said I shouldn't.' I said, 'You need new attorneys, that's the dumbest thing I ever heard.' He says, 'Yeah, I'm getting new representation.' I said, 'Brother, there's no way you survive this.'

"He went up and saw him, and fucking Trump calls me and says, 'Fourteen million dollars! Fourteen million dollars! For his *expenses*!'

"And that was how I met Paul Manafort."

* * *

Bannon told this story not as a broadside against Trump and Manafort, but as an excuse for them. Here, he meant to say, were the kinds of people Mueller had caught in his net, people who did not know which end was up. Trump surrounded himself with the dysfunctional and the inept; in truth, Trump needed to surround himself with the dysfunctional and the inept, because *he* was dysfunctional and inept. Only in the land of the blind could he be king. And if you thought Paul Manafort was any sort of linchpin, you had bought into the same sort of fantasies that Paul Manafort seemed to buy into about himself.

But prosecutors don't care about the class and intellectual bona fides of the people they prosecute. Prosecutors do care—and here Manafort could hardly provide a better demonstration—when your fantasies of who you are, or who you think you should be, cross over into deed.

* * *

Manafort was hired to run the Trump campaign at the suggestion of Tom Barrack, Trump's longtime friend and sometime business partner. Barrack specialized in distressed real estate debt investments. With considerable business interests in single-leader states trying to influence Washington, he was not typically the sort of person you would want to serve as a senior adviser in a presidential campaign. After the election, when Trump asked him to become White House chief of staff, Barrack, recognizing his own conflicts and exposure, declined. But he did agree to manage the 2017 Trump inaugural, raising more money than an inaugural had ever raised in the past.

Barrack had suggested Manafort because the Trump campaign, by the spring of 2016, was in hopeless disarray, not least because it was operating without anyone who had presidential campaign experience. Barrack knew Manafort partly because Manafort had built a consulting company that operated in some of the countries where Barrack also did business. Though Manafort's political experience was a generation out of date, he was eager and available, and—an exceptional recommendation to Trump—willing to work for free. Another plus was the fact that he had an apartment in Trump Tower.

Manafort's connections and business arrangements all seemed so suspicious and dubious that it was difficult to see how they could be legitimate. As Mueller would allege, of the tens of millions of dollars that had passed through Manafort's hands in the past decade, nearly all were pilfered, or laundered, or fraudulently gotten. And that was not the worst of it: many of his associates operated in a lawless zone of international corruption, plunder, and despotism—not to mention mayhem and murder.

To boot, Manafort was lazy, as in no-show lazy. And yet here he had been given a 24/7 job, a high-pressure, low-support position that meant he would be working at the center of the storm and making critical decisions almost on a constant basis.

In the Trump team's view, nobody with any dark intent or design (or, for that matter, nobody with any other options) would have hired this man. But in the prosecutor's view, nobody would have hired this man other than in furtherance of a criminal conspiracy.

* * *

On top of all this, Manafort, in quite the movie plot, was being pursued by one of the world's most ruthless oligarchs, a Russian from whom he had pilfered millions.

Providing expertise to corrupt, unstable, one-man governments is a highly profitable niche for American consultants—blue chip as well as shadowy ones. If you help keep a corrupt man in power, the amounts you can make have few limits. Manafort's high-margin, easy-money opportunity was Ukraine. Every new introduction to top government officials and their industry counterparts—or to the apparatchiks, agents, bankers, and out-and-out criminals who shuttled between them—became a revenue opportunity.

Such was the time in which Paul Manafort met Oleg Deripaska, a.k.a. "Mr. D." Deripaska sat atop the hierarchy of Russian oligarchs because of his wealth, his ruthlessness—or at least the legend of his ruthlessness—and his closeness to Putin. Even other oligarchs raised their eyes at the mention of Mr. D. His own associates tended not so much to deny the rumors about him, but to excuse his actions and behavior as situational.

In the mid-2000s, Mr. D. hired Manafort, one of the significant figures on the Russia-backed side of Ukrainian politics, who then became one more player in Deripaska's own effort to leverage political power in Ukraine. This relationship lasted for six or seven years, until Manafort, in *Ocean's Eleven* fashion, seemed to have conned Deripaska into an investment ruse that enabled Manafort to abscond with at least $19 million, incurring in Mr. D.'s mind something of a blood debt. Deripaska and his people had been relentlessly pursuing Manafort and Mr. D.'s $19 million through the courts, in the Cayman Islands and in New York State, and through a forensic accounting of the long paper trail of Manafort's treacheries—an accounting that Mr. D.'s people may or may not have shared with U.S. officials. (Mr. D., denied a visa by the United States because of his suspected criminal activities, had been trying to curry favor with U.S. law enforcement.)

Manafort, meanwhile, was trying to somehow make good on his debt. In March 2016, an all-but-broke Manafort agreed to become a senior operative in Donald Trump's presidential campaign pro bono. In Trump's view, this was a fair price for helping to run a race that he was wholly convinced he would not win no matter who ran it. But in Manafort's view, joining Trump's campaign provided him with a golden opportunity to get Mr. D. off his back. And indeed, almost immediately after Manafort took the job, he offered Mr. D. access to the Trump campaign and intelligence from inside it in satisfaction of his debt.

It was either a bizarre but random coincidence that there was a direct line that ran from Donald Trump to Paul Manafort to Oleg Deripaska to Vladimir Putin—or not a coincidence at all. Either Manafort and Deripaska were the middlemen connecting Trump and Putin, or Manafort and Deripaska, in some cosmic joke of proximity, just happened to find themselves in their own crazy shit inside some other, larger crazy shit.

* * *

In the liberal imagination, unsurprisingly, the dots connected so clearly that a conspiracy was certain.

Jared Kushner, for one, pushed back on this idea. Ever since he took over active management of his father-in-law's presidential campaign, he had been telling people, Don't take things too literally with Trump. A lot of the time, nothing is at it seems. Conspiracy? Are you kidding?

Manafort, Kushner said, was a douche but not a plotter. And although Oleg Deripaska might seem to be a James Bond villain, with real estate on every sumptuous block of every glittering city, with lavish yachts always outfitted with willing beauties, and throwing the best party every year at Davos, he was really just a careful businessman. Punctilious in his habits, inverted in his person, averse to risk, he was quite the last person to step outside the most carefully proscribed lanes of power politics in Russia and the needs of RUSAL, variously the world's largest or second-largest aluminum company.

One evening in 2017, while having dinner with acquaintances in New York during UN week—the one time of the year, trailed by FBI agents, that he was allowed to come to New York—Deripaska was asked point-blank about whether Trump had a backdoor relationship with Putin. "No, this is not the way it is done in Mother Russia," he declared, suggesting that the nuances of power in the Putin circle were well beyond the understanding of U.S. politicians, prosecutors, and journalists.

"Was the Trump campaign provided any aid by the Russian government or people or entities connected to it?" he was asked.

"No. But I would not know about that."

"And Manafort?"

"He is not a good man."

"Did he try to use his position in the campaign to work out his issues with you?"

"He has not worked out his issues with me."

"But he tried?"

"He did not succeed."

In the spring of 2018, after Manafort's indictment, the Trump administration added new, harsh sanctions on Deripaska and his company. This was regarded by some as a warning from the White House to Deripaska to keep his distance from the Manafort trial, or perhaps an effort by the Justice Department to bargain for Deripaska's assistance in its pursuit of Manafort, or perhaps merely a random way to look tough on Russia. Whatever the motive, it was a move that, likely, no one had thought through, since it immediately created a worldwide spike in aluminum prices.

Deripaska told a friend he had become "a burden to the state" and was fearful for his life. This was taken to mean either that he was indeed a key connector between Trump and Putin and needed to be removed, or that he wanted to show that he really was not a Putin crony at all—quite the opposite. Or perhaps it was mere Russian melodrama and a precursor to a negotiation that he hoped would lift the sanctions from him. (Indeed, they were ultimately lifted.)

In any case, the essential question remained. Were these random associations among some of the world's most corrupt and dangerous men? Or was this conspiracy of an extraordinarily brazen kind?

* * *

As the Manafort trial proceeded, Trump—in the White House and then on summer holiday at Bedminster, often a place of increased fury on Trump's part—seemed to struggle with a sense that his adversaries were closing in on him. On August 1, he lashed out at his attorney general, demanding once again that Jeff Sessions put a stop to the Mueller investigation. On August 12, Trump's old *Apprentice* and White House sidekick Omarosa Manigault Newman accused him of having used the N-word on the set of *The Apprentice*, provoking a national discussion about whether the president was a racist. For his part, Trump took the bait and branded Manigault Newman a "dog" and "a crazed, crying lowlife." On August 13, under pressure from Trump, the FBI fired Peter Strzok, the agent whose texts, during the Russia investigation, showed him to be personally horrified at the prospect of a Trump victory. (Trump had repeatedly accused Strzok of being a deep state conspirator.) On August 15, Trump revoked the security clearance of Obama's CIA director John Brennan, who had become one of Trump's most acerbic and appalled critics. And on August 16, hundreds of newspapers joined together to condemn Trump's continuing attacks on the press as the "enemy of the people."

Then a bad month for Trump got worse. On August 21, Manafort was convicted of eight counts of various fraudulent financial activities in federal court in Virginia. (The jury was unable to reach a verdict on ten other counts.) No grand crimes were addressed in the trial; instead, it

was the sheer ordinariness and cravenness of Manafort's greed and financial scams that caught him up. These were not political crimes. This was
cheating on your taxes in order to buy an ostrich-leather bomber jacket.
Trump people might scoff at the lowliness of Manafort's criminal endeav-
ors, but prosecutors, their eyes aglint, knew that the more basic the crime,
the more inevitable the punishment.

But for Trump, there was a silver lining here: Manafort had not cut a
deal with Mueller's prosecutors.

Many Trumpers found it easy to dismiss Manafort's contributions to
the campaign, and they seemed genuinely to believe he had nothing to
tell. By now, Manafort had been branded as just one more in a long line
of Trump campaign and Trump presidency jokes. When you fell out of
the Trump circle, you became irrelevant to it—history was immediately
revised such that you were never really part of the circle. (Among some in
the White House, this was equated with Stalin's predilection for removing
faces of certain inner-circle cronies from photographs.) Indeed, in some
reasonable sense, everybody involved with Trump was inclined to believe
that everybody else involved with Trump was a joke.

Mueller's prosecutors had a different point of view about Manafort:
they believed he was waiting for a pardon from the president. Considering the prison sentence Manafort likely faced in the wake of his Virginia
conviction—as well as the prospect of more jail time if his second trial
also did not go well—a pardon seemed the only likely explanation for his
silence. But prosecutors also believed that a pardon, if it came, would not
be granted until after the midterms. If the Republicans were somehow
able to hold their majority in the House, the political price of a pardon
would almost certainly be more tolerable for Trump.

As the special counsel's team prepared for Manafort's second trial,
Andrew Weissmann tightened the screws on Trump's former campaign
manager even further. With only mild worries about the double jeopardy implications, Weissmann reached out to Cyrus Vance Jr., the district
attorney in Manhattan, and suggested that in the event of a presidential
pardon he might want to indict Manafort on the ten counts upon which
the federal jury in Virginia had deadlocked. If Manafort was tried in state
court, the president could not pardon a conviction.

On the eve of Manafort's second trial, he caved and agreed to take a deal—he would cooperate for a combined sentence in both cases of no more than ten years. But Manafort continued to play the game in Manafort fashion. He could rely on Mueller's goodwill for a reduced sentence, or he could rely on Trump's goodwill for a pardon, but he could hardly do both. Yet Manafort now proceeded to do precisely this. Courting disaster— which would shortly come when prosecutors again accused him of lying and then vacated their deal—he tried to minimally satisfy the prosecutor in case no pardon was forthcoming from the president, even as he tried to avoid antagonizing Trump in case a pardon might yet come.

16

PECKER, COHEN, WEISSELBERG

Editor man," said Donald Trump over dinner in the White House during the summer of 2017. "Editor man," he repeated, pleased with his patronizing nickname.

"Yes, Mr. President," replied Dylan Howard, an Australian from outside of Melbourne, who had risen in his career in tabloid news to the top editorial job at American Media, Inc. (AMI)—the parent company of the *National Enquirer*, the supermarket celebrity and scandal sheet—and now to a meal with the president of the United States. Indeed, in one more inversion of civic standards, Trump had brought David Pecker, the CEO of AMI and the king of kiss-and-tell journalism, along with Howard and other staff members, into the White House for dinner.

"How much more do you sell when I'm on the cover instead of just a celebrity?" Trump pressed Howard, meaning instead of people like Jennifer Aniston, Brad and Angelina, or the big-ratings reality television stars.

"Fifteen to twenty percent more," said Howard to a satisfied Trump, who, a few minutes later, reconfirmed: "So, I sell fifty percent more than any of the movie stars?"

"Well, like I said, fifteen to twenty percent more."

"Let's call it forty," said the president.

Whatever the number, it was increasingly less relevant to the publishing company. As the newsstand business dwindled in the United States—*Enquirer* sales were down 90 percent since the 1970s, and in the past decade almost 60 percent of newspaper and magazine sales outlets had closed or begun to sell other products—AMI had shifted important aspects of its business from checkout-counter sales to a "client-based" approach. Now the company, trying hard to impress with its new business-speak, partnered with celebrities in broader communications and branding strategies.

The sophisticated version of a celebrity-media partnership was currently something like what the women's magazine publisher Hearst had done for Oprah Winfrey with its co-ventured *Oprah* magazine—a "brand extension." In a markedly less polished approach, AMI, in an effort to attract investment from the Saudi kingdom, published a one-off magazine about the kingdom's laudatory virtues and amazing travel and business opportunities.

Pecker, once a magazine industry accountant, had transformed the *Enquirer* from a down-market tabloid to a lower-mid-market celebrity and gossip magazine, added multiple other titles to his stable, and, he and his allies argued, steered the company through several bankruptcies. (Others argued that he had also steered it *into* those bankruptcies.) But Pecker and Howard weren't cool branding and marketing types; they were Damon Runyon sorts, unreconstructed and proud tough guys, unsentimental about how they made their money.

Pecker realized, with Howard in tow, that instead of making a fortune by exposing stars, they could, in the new age of celebrity partnerships, make money by helping to protect them. As sex tapes, a wide variety of salacious hacked materials, and the booming confessional and revenge marketplace became factors in the careers of many celebrities, AMI adapted. The *Enquirer* team still gathered dirt, but for the appropriate incentive, and given a mutually beneficial relationship, they didn't publish it—a.k.a. "catch and kill."

The *Enquirer*, for instance, had worked closely with the film producer Harvey Weinstein, who set up a production deal for American Media in return for its agreement not to publish stories about the cascading sexual harassment and abuse allegations that would eventually doom him.

AMI also joined with Arnold Schwarzenegger, the ex-bodybuilder, former governor of California, and repeat sexual harasser, who, in exchange for the magazine's silence, used his influence to help the company buy a group of fitness magazines. But the company's perfect celebrity partner was perhaps Donald Trump.

Trump and Pecker defined a sort of mean regression. Trump, through much of his career, was always trying to make friends with major media moguls, most of whom, like Rupert Murdoch, snubbed him. Pecker, similarly, was always trying to make friends with A-list celebrities, who shunned him. Trump and Pecker eventually settled on each other in a certain mutuality of disrepute.

The two men had a similar view of media. They were tools of wealth, influence, and power—and only a chump would see it otherwise. In the early 1990s, when Pecker was running the U.S. magazine company owned by the French publisher Hachette—with titles like *Elle*, *Car & Driver*, and *Woman's Day*—he backed John F. Kennedy Jr.'s idea for a pop culture magazine about politics called *George*. In Pecker's view, this was a brilliant commercial confection: a celebrity magazine with a celebrity editor. But the relationship foundered because Kennedy, Pecker came to believe, was a classic chump, and an entitled one, who saw *George* as a magazine that actually was about politics.

Pecker, like Trump, imagined himself as not just a businessman but a media figure, too. Whenever he was profiled or written about, he would almost always call the top executive at the publication to lobby for better press for himself—just as Trump did.

They had plans together. Pecker had a Walter Mitty–style dream of owning *Time* magazine; Trump said he would help him with the purchase. Not long before his election to the presidency, Trump, expecting defeat, was plotting a Trump Channel; he told Pecker he wanted him in on that deal. Roger Ailes, the creator of Fox News, with whom Trump was actively discussing his media future in the fall of 2016, called Pecker "Trump's water-boy idiot." Added Ailes: "An idiot needs an even bigger idiot to get his water."

* * *

For Trump, meanwhile, there were the women—a constant and, to some degree, sporting problem throughout his three marriages. Managing the women whom Trump had disappointed or mauled or humiliated was a recognized process.

It was a point of pride for Trump that he led a Sinatra-style, rat-pack, "grab-them-by-the-pussy" sex life—and an equal point of pride that when a woman threatened him, he could fix the problem. "My people know how to take care of things" was a particular Trump boast.

The ultimate threat from any of these women was to go public. They could sue—but Trump's lawyers knew how to handle that with quick settlements. Or they could publish—and for that Michael Cohen and Marc Kasowitz, Trump's "personal" lawyers, could turn to Pecker.

Prior to the rapid rise of the internet free-for-all, Pecker, who had acquired the lion's share of supermarket tabloids (including *Globe*, *In Touch*, *OK!*, *Star*, and *Us Weekly*), effectively controlled the market for celebrity sex allegations. Not only were his publications among the few that would publish this kind of story, but Pecker was the one customer who would reliably and handsomely pay for dirt. But during the last decade, in the anything-can-be-published internet age, the market began to change radically. There were no longer effective gatekeepers; dirt flowed freely. What quickly evolved was a regular trade in celebrity humiliation.

In this new world, the Los Angeles lawyer Keith M. Davidson was a specialist. Davidson was a real-life Ray Donovan, a celebrity fixer who became one of the leading representatives of sex tapes for sale, including two of the most famous, Paris Hilton's and Hulk Hogan's. In another career-enhancing trade of confessions and secrets for Davidson, an array of Davidson clients—each, it seemed, trying to shake down the other— helped clear the path to proving that the television actor Charlie Sheen was HIV positive. Howard and Davidson had first met in 2010 over a story involving Lindsay Lohan, but it was the *Enquirer*'s pursuit of the Sheen story that helped to truly bond them. Indeed, Davidson, not just providing dirt and negotiating for people who had the dirt, but negotiating for people who wanted to avoid being tagged with dirt, became a steady source for Howard, a one-stop tabloid middleman.

At this seamy junction there was, in addition to Howard and Davidson, Trump's lawyer Michael Cohen, a source, confidant, and business associate of both men and of AMI chief Pecker. In a limited market, the major players tend to know each other, which lessens friction and facilitates deal making. Everybody understands each other, everybody understands what's reasonable, everybody knows whom to call. In the run-up to the 2016 election, Davidson conveniently came to represent both Karen McDougal, the 1998 *Playboy* Playmate of the Year, and Stormy Daniels, the porn actress—both claiming they had a sexual relationship with Trump.

In late spring 2015, Davidson called Howard about McDougal, saying she had a credible claim of having had an affair with Trump. Howard informed Pecker, and, in short order, Howard was put on a plane to L.A., where he met Davidson and McDougal. So far, this was all standard practice in the tabloid business: Howard would do a debrief and evaluate the direct evidence, including emails, texts, photos, and videos. But, unusually, Pecker also called Cohen about the claim—and Howard was told to keep Cohen in the loop.

But the problem here was McDougal, who, though more than willing to share details about the affair, was not willing to share evidence of it. Her phone, theoretically with texts from Trump, was in storage. The friends in whom she had confided were unavailable. Her receipts were lost. In other words, there just wasn't enough solid material for a story.

But suddenly McDougal was being paid for the story anyway. In the world of catch and kill, the *Enquirer* had caught something that, in publishing terms, did not exist—hence, it didn't have to be killed. Oddly, they were paying someone who seemed to have no intention of going public to . . . not go public.

The basic arrangement was clear: Pecker and Trump had agreed that, in the event of possible scandal, Pecker would use the resources of the *Enquirer* to protect his friend Trump. But, at least to Howard, quite an expert in scandal, there did not seem to be the necessary elements for a credible takedown.

Was this, Howard wondered to friends, a Cohen and Pecker setup? Were Cohen and Pecker, each in a perpetually subservient and unrequited relationship with Trump, in cahoots to increase their standing or leverage with Trump?

Yes, McDougal had had an affair with Trump. But it was unclear who was now playing whom—or who, in this particular cadre of lowlifes, held the leverage. It wasn't just women who were after Trump but, quite possibly, his own people. His people might well be helping to threaten his presidential aspirations in order to be in a position to clean up the problem—and then getting the credit for having done so.

Trump, in short, was being protected by people who had self-interested reasons to find problems that he needed to be protected from. Not too surprisingly, his most loyal henchmen were potentially double-dealing as well.

In the deal with McDougal, which was organized by Davidson and sanctioned by Cohen, Pecker, and Trump, the *Enquirer* agreed to buy McDougal's story for $150,000—the ask-no-questions price established by Kasowitz for a harassment complaint against Trump—but not run it. Furthermore, McDougal would be paid to write columns for the *Enquirer* and AMI would put her on the cover of one of the company's fitness magazines. As it happened, AMI ultimately failed to fulfill its part of this deal. Likewise, in more small-time-crook fashion, the company's arrangement with Trump also came apart: AMI never recouped its $150,000 from Trump or Cohen.

Later, in 2018, when Dylan Howard, with a grant of partial immunity, testified before prosecutors, he was shown an email from Pecker that said, "Dylan doesn't know about this"—"this" being the backdoor agreement among Cohen, Pecker, and Trump. Howard, according to a person in the room, broke down in tears, realizing then that he had likely been a hapless instrument of Pecker and Cohen trying to please or manipulate Donald Trump—or both.

* * *

Among Trump's personal lawyers, Kasowitz, a partner in a reputable New York law firm, yet tried to maintain his standing as an independent lawyer. Cohen, on the other hand, was delighted to be Trump's fixer. He often quoted Tom Hagen, the Corleone family consigliere and lawyer in *The Godfather*: "I have a special practice. I handle one client."

It delighted Cohen that he knew how everything worked—most especially, as he put it, "who deposited into and withdrew from the favor bank." You had to understand, he said, not just the deal, but the side deal. Everybody, except the chumps, operates this way; hence, so should you. In fact, do it more. At the same time, few in the Trump Organization, including Trump himself, felt confident that Cohen knew what he was doing. Trump frequently riffed about Cohen's clumsiness and limited brain power. Cohen, for his part, taped conversations with Trump out of fear that Trump would renege on their deals.

Certainly the Karen McDougal and, later, Stormy Daniels problems, both of which fell to Cohen to deal with, became, each in its own way, terrific screwups.

The Stormy Daniels screwup was even worse for Trump, and ultimately for Cohen, than McDougal. When Davidson approached Cohen about reaching an arrangement with Daniels, Cohen tried to work a deal similar to McDougal's through the *Enquirer*. But Pecker was getting spooked by the money trail and the possibility that the payoffs might qualify as illegal campaign contributions, and in any case AMI could hardly hire a porn star to write columns. Instead, Davidson negotiated a payment of $130,000 for Daniels's silence. Cohen, Trump, and Trump Organization CFO Allen Weisselberg agreed on a ruse wherein Cohen would pay the money and be reimbursed later through what would be described as payments for legal services.

Later, when this scheme was revealed, it struck some campaign officials and Trump Organization executives as a characteristic Cohen-Trump deal—the two men liked to act as fixers. It made much less sense for Trump to try to buy the silence of someone who would likely not stay silent than it did to merely take his licks for yet another accusation of infidelity.

Early in 2018, Daniels, hiring Michael Avenatti to represent her, sued both Davidson and Trump. Avenatti, a lawyer with a checkered past of bankruptcies, tax liens, and allegations of commingled accounts, was a new sort of ambulance chaser, one whose sophisticated understanding of the media allowed him to build a formidable public platform. In his relentless pursuit of Trump on television, impressing no one so much as Trump himself, he pointed the finger directly at Cohen, Davidson, Pecker, and Howard.

What Avenatti identified was not only a nexus of financial hanky-panky and double-dealing, but a potential lockbox of secrets and dirty linen held by a gang that was likely, without much of a push, to turn on each other. Indeed, Avenatti had followed the payments to both Daniels and McDougal and traced a line straight back to the Trump Organization. At the end of that line was the man arranging the payments, Allen Weisselberg—yet another true-to-type Trump-tale character.

Trump friends had been waiting for the seventy-two-year-old Weisselberg to be identified. An Orthodox Jew who had spent his entire career working for the Trumps, first for Fred Trump, then for Donald, he had served as the chief financial officer of the doomed Trump casino operation, as the CFO for the Trump Organization, and as a trustee of the trust that controlled Trump's holdings during his presidency. Weisselberg administered the family's personal expenses; he also prepared the Trump Organization checks and took them to Trump to sign.

In frequent television appearances beginning in early 2018, Avenatti pounded relentlessly on Trump, and on Cohen's payment to Daniels. The story took yet another turn after the FBI's raid on Cohen's office in April, following which attorneys and a court-ordered referee sorted through Cohen's records, sequestering any materials that might qualify for attorney-client confidentiality and admitting the rest into evidence, with most of Cohen's work being judged as, at best, extra-legal. Delving into Cohen's taxi medallion business, prosecutors identified a massive tax fraud even beyond his participation in the violations of campaign finance laws. Cohen was threatened with two hundred years in prison. His wife, who had signed their joint tax return, was threatened with a lengthy sentence as well. So was her father, Cohen's partner in the taxi business.

On August 21—the same day, in a news-cycle double whammy, that Paul Manafort was convicted in Virginia—Cohen, with prosecutors agreeing not to pursue his family, pleaded guilty to five counts of tax evasion, along with one count of making false statements to a bank and two counts of campaign-finance violations. In his plea, he directly implicated Trump in the campaign-finance violations.

On August 24, the *Wall Street Journal* reported that David Pecker had cut a deal to testify. The same day, the *Journal* reported that Weisselberg had also accepted an immunity deal and had testified several weeks before.

* * *

"The Jews always flip," said Trump.

In the days after Cohen's guilty plea, he took to referring to "the law firm of Pecker, Cohen, and Weisselberg." He developed a riff on the horrors that an Orthodox Jew would probably encounter in jail, one that sketched a vivid picture of a tattooed Nazi cell mate.

Considering Trump's generally low regard for his close associates, it was not difficult to imagine that they would be willing to testify against him. Trump might have called them "my people" or "my guys," but Cohen was "the only stupid Jew," and Weisselberg was the financial adviser whose name, after more than forty years, Trump took delight in mangling ("Weisselman," "Weisselstein," "Weisselwitz"). Pecker was often mocked by Trump as "Little Pecker," and his mustache was the target of derisive and obscene remarks. (Curiously, Pecker bore a resemblance to Trump's father, who also wore a mustache.) But even as it became apparent that Pecker's and Trump's interests were in direct conflict, AMI executives believed that Pecker and Trump were still talking and that Pecker was still, helplessly it seemed, trying to curry favor with Trump—while Trump was still trying to keep, as it were, Pecker in his pocket.

Even as Cohen and Manafort were admitting to or being convicted of crimes, a major new front had opened in the legal battle against the president—or, in Trump's view of it, the Justice Department's war against him. The Southern District of New York—where Geoffrey Berman, the Trump-appointed federal prosecutor, had recused himself in the Cohen investigation—reached an understanding with the special counsel and assumed jurisdiction over the Trump money trail. People around Trump were now saying that Mueller was the sideshow and the Southern District the main event.

In yet a further indication of the president's jeopardy, the *New York Times* on August 18 published a detailed article about White House counsel Don McGahn's extensive cooperation with the Mueller investigation, a level of cooperation unknown to Trump. Few questioned that the leak leading to the article had come from either McGahn—who, having tried to inoculate himself with prosecutors, was now eager to do the same with the media—or his proxies. For many months, McGahn had been talking about when and how to leave the White House, while promising, in good-soldier form, to stay until a replacement was found.

On August 29, without informing McGahn, and at a moment when the president's legal difficulties were becoming ever more intense, Trump tweeted that McGahn would be leaving his job in the fall. "I have worked with Don for a long time," Trump wrote, "and truly appreciate his service!"

Privately, Trump described his White House counsel differently. "McGahn," he said, "is a dirty rat."

* * *

How bad was it?

August had been one of the most difficult months of a presidency in which almost every month felt progressively grimmer. And if Cohen and Manafort could go down *on the same day*, what fresh hell might be just around the corner?

The addition of Pecker and the *National Enquirer* into this tale confirmed the larger concern of some aides and many Republicans on the Hill: not just that the Trump circle lacked experience and talent, but that it was the greatest concentration of ignominious lowlifes, scammers, and con artists ever seen in national politics, which was saying a lot.

As the summer ended, Trump spent the final days of his vacation in Bedminster. His mood, as ever, was changeable, but his resilience—perhaps his most underestimated quality—seemed undiminished. Directly ahead was a busy schedule of big rallies; he would be on the road almost full-time until the midterms. The raucous, free-form rallies, by now a highly ritualized call and response, left him uniquely content and sated; he always let the rallies run, almost without time limit, until he was fully gratified.

Despite all evidence and counsel to the contrary, he was convinced that the Republicans would win both the House and the Senate. It was a blind and happy confidence.

Mueller, meanwhile, observing Justice Department convention, seemed certain to do nothing that might have an impact on the coming election. Yet his team continued to grind silently away.

Partly in deference to Mueller's cease-fire, the White House had muzzled Giuliani. This was mostly McGahn's doing: in concert with his lawyer Bill Burck, McGahn was working on the nomination of Brett Kavanaugh to the Supreme Court, and they had decided that Giuliani only highlighted—or invited—the potential constitutional confrontation between Trump and Mueller that might be decided by Kavanaugh's vote on the Court.

Mueller and his team—having come this far, having somehow stayed in business despite Trump's many threats to shut down their investigation—now believed that they would safely make it past November, and that a Democratic victory would provide a firewall for them. What's more, the special counsel's budget request had been approved—they had survived that bureaucratic hurdle. (Trump may not have ever understood that the budget process was a weapon that he could have used against the special counsel—it appeared that no one had told him.) Indeed, for all of Trump's threats, he had made no real moves to interfere with the special counsel's work and mission.

As Mueller worked, many government lawyers outside the special counsel's office found the notion of getting a piece of the spreading case against the president nearly irresistible. If you were a government prosecutor and were not involved with the investigations of Donald Trump, you might be missing a major moment in your career.

The Mueller team, now more than fifteen months into its investigation, continued to pass evidence it had collected to other prosecutors, not just to ensure the long-term viability of its effort, but also because there were so many avenues of attack. Trump was vulnerable because he was an amateur who had run for high office in a complicated world governed by byzantine election rules. Trump was vulnerable because he couldn't control the many inept and undisciplined people around him.

Trump was vulnerable because he couldn't keep his mouth—or his Twitter feed—shut. And Trump was vulnerable because for forty years he had run what increasingly seemed to resemble a semi-criminal enterprise. ("I think we can drop the 'semi' part," chuckled Bannon.)

It wasn't just the president, either. There was his family, to whom he had closely bound his administration. John Kelly continued to tell people that Jared and Don Jr. would soon be indicted.

The Manhattan district attorney, Cy Vance—needing to make amends for pursuing neither an investigation of Harvey Weinstein on sex abuse charges nor one of Ivanka Trump and Donald Trump Jr. for their part in potentially fraudulent sales efforts at a New York Trump hotel—was now looking for political points in pursuit of the Trump and Kushner families. His team was circulating a long list of promising avenues:

1. Receiving stolen property from computer hackers
2. Financial crimes, including money laundering and falsifying business records
3. Bribery/gratuity and other corruption offenses
4. Official misconduct/obstruction
5. Violations of New York City lobbying laws
6. Tax fraud

The dogs were in full pursuit.

* * *

Many of the people most involved with Trump—from McGahn to Kelly, from the comms staff to Steve Bannon—lived the dual Trump realities most intensely: they accepted the likelihood that the president would be taken down by the forces pursuing him, but they also marveled at, and sometimes savored, the remarkable fact that he had not yet been taken down. Which led, however inexplicably, to the astonishing possibility that he might *never* be taken down.

Here was a curious equanimity, born, in part, from the fact that many in the president's inner circle didn't much care what happened to him—they wouldn't grieve, or be surprised, if he went down—but, too, of the fact that you couldn't begin to predict what might happen. Many in the White House saw themselves as bystanders to the drama rather than principals in it. No logic satisfactorily applied, so why worry? John Kelly, for one, took a fatalistic view. If God wanted Trump's head, He would take it—it was certainly there for the taking. And if He didn't take it, there must be a reason. So suck it up.

"He has incredible luck," said Sam Nunberg. "The most incredible luck. I can't tell you. It's not even believable how lucky he is. It will probably run out. But maybe not."

The defense of Trump, in some sense the only defense, continued to be that he had been elected president. It was clear who and what he was, and *still* he had been elected. The voters had spoken. The case against Trump was illegitimate—"fake"—not because he hadn't done much of what he was being accused of, but because no one was accusing him of doing something that most people did not already know he had done. (Were the nefarious actions of Michael Cohen and David Pecker really shocking to anyone?) In tangled teleological terms, everyone else masked their dishonesty, but Trump's was there for all to see.

In effect, the definition of the smoking gun, that high hurdle of evidence that was needed to bring down a president, had abruptly gotten much higher. To convict this president, to oust him, you were going to have to prove not just that Trump was Trump. Quibbling over the relative importance of this or that Trumper's unproductive conversations with the Russians seemed, arguably, too small time to matter. It seemed unfair, somehow, that entirely characteristic transgressions could take Trump down.

But clear to everyone nearest the president was that the law was literal, and that you could almost certainly build a strong case that he had, repeatedly, offended the letter of it. Hence, the real defense, the real legal strategy, was a belief in Trump's magical properties. In Bannon's appraisal, Trump was unique. "Nobody else," he said, "could get away with this shit."

Still, the ad hoc group of Republican leaders and major donors—which now had a name, Defending Democracy Together—was nothing less than a rump party organization considering a challenge to its own president. As the fall began, the group began to commission polls on the appetite for a challenge to Trump; thus far, his scandals were still seen as insider stuff, which was helping to maintain the president's strong support among the base. But that was precisely the problem for Trump: the country as a whole wasn't yet paying attention to the unfolding story of the president's corruption.

17

MCCAIN, WOODWARD, ANONYMOUS

Trump took John McCain's brain tumor, diagnosed in the summer of 2017, as something like personal validation. "You see?" he would say, raising his eyebrows. "You see what can happen?" Then he would mime an exploding head.

As McCain's illness progressed, Trump began to express annoyance that McCain "hung on." Or that he was not a "good enough sport" to resign his seat and let the Republican governor of Arizona appoint a more Trump-friendly senator. He often transferred his disdain for McCain to McCain's daughter Meghan, a regular panelist on ABC's *The View* and a stern anti-Trumper. He was obsessed with her weight gain. "Donut," he called her. "When she hears my name she always looks like she's going to cry. Like her father. Very, very tough family. Boo hoo, boo hoo."

McCain, in turn, took the opportunity of his mortal illness to draw a line in the sand between his American and Republican values and Trump's. In an epic political dis, McCain did not invite Trump to the funeral he was planning for himself. Two days after McCain's death, on August 25, the McCain family released his good-bye letter, a powerful statement of establishment principles and a direct rebuke to Trump.

Trump's relationship with his chief of staff the former marine general John Kelly—now an open cold war in which each stayed out of the other's way and each pronounced the other crazy—took a further bitter turn. Kelly, with a soldier's affinity for McCain, the former fighter pilot and prisoner of war, took Trump's comments to be both antimilitary and unpatriotic.

"John McCain," he said as the president made his exploding head gesture one day, "is an American hero." Then he turned his back and walked out of the Oval Office.

McCain's was a full dress funeral, second only to what might be given a president. Held on September 1 in Washington's National Cathedral, it was attended by Barack Obama, Bill Clinton, and George W. Bush, each personally invited by McCain, each magnifying Trump's exclusion. "The America of John McCain has no need to be made great again, because America was always great," said Meghan McCain in her eulogy, generating an unlikely applause line at a funeral.

The funeral attracted the establishment great and good on both sides of the aisle, and almost everyone there—save perhaps the representatives of the Trump family—bore a pointed witness against Trump. The many Republicans at the service wanted to be counted: the globalist Republicans, the military-minded cold war Republicans, and the national-security, maintain-the-world-order Republicans. Even if they did not know how to fight back against Trump, or were not yet ready to, they could raise a finger here at John McCain's funeral.

Trump, for his part, tried to out-tweet the funeral and then went to play golf.

* * *

By Labor Day weekend, establishment Washington and the mainstream media—largely one and the same, many Trump supporters argued—were eagerly awaiting the publication of Bob Woodward's new book *Fear*, about Trump's first year in office. Its publisher had embargoed the book before its September 11 publication, but the leaked teasers had built enormous anticipation and, equally, great consternation in the White House. As much as the book would deliver Woodward's own weighty statement about Trump, many in the GOP establishment believed Woodward could be counted on to reflect their views—and even to provide cover for their views.

Woodward and his partner Carl Bernstein had created the modern model of a political journalist with their Watergate reporting. Their subsequent books on Watergate and the movie about their pursuit of Richard Nixon had made them world famous. Woodward, ever attached to the *Washington Post*, had gone on to write more bestsellers and make more money than any other Washington reporter in history. At seventy-five, Woodward was one of the city's monuments, or at least one of its institutional fixtures.

Since Watergate, much of his career had been spent in careful parsing of the political bureaucracy, a.k.a. the swamp. At times, he seemed almost to become its voice. In a way, that was the ultimate lesson of Watergate. In periods of acute political stress, the bureaucracy looked out for itself and protected itself, so all a smart reporter needed to do was listen to it. The more acute the stress, the more active the leakers, the bigger the story. Now, more than ever, with an outsider and rank amateur in the White House, the swamp—so pilloried by Trump—was fighting back.

The particular part of the swamp bureaucracy that over the years had provided Woodward with so many scoops was the deepest and most entrenched part of it, the vast national security system. Upon publication of Woodward's new book, it was immediately evident that one of his key sources was H. R. McMaster, the three-star general who had joined the Trump administration in February 2017 as national security advisor, replacing Michael Flynn. Losing Flynn, the first casualty of the Russia investigation, had been an early dispiriting moment for Trump, and he had acceded to his staff's choice for Flynn's replacement without giving it much thought. In the initial interview, McMaster, detail- and plan-oriented, a PowerPoint general, had bored the president. Wanting just to be done with it and avoid a follow-up interview, Trump agreed to hire him.

Their relationship never got much better. McMaster became a target for Trump's mockery and derision. The general hit all of the Trump sweet spots: his looks, his earnestness, his pomposity, and his short stature.

"What are you writing there, Mr. Note-Taker?" Trump heckled McMaster, who was invariably scribbling in a little black notebook during meetings. "Are you the secretary?"

Late in the process of researching his book, Woodward had contacted Bannon. For Bannon, there was hardly anyone who represented the Washington establishment more perfectly than Woodward—here, for him, was the enemy. But after just a few minutes of conversation, he began to understand what Woodward had. It was access to McMaster's little black notebook, a detailed, sometimes nearly minute-by-minute chronicle of every meeting that McMaster had attended in his ten months in the White House. Bannon decided he needed to go into damage control.

Woodward's book, Bannon understood, was set up to be the revenge of Team America. This was the self-styled band of grown-ups, or professionals, or (as they would sometimes acknowledge) resisters, working in the Trump White House, who had come to see themselves as patriots protecting the country from the president they worked for. At different moments, the group included, along with McMaster, Jim Mattis, Rex Tillerson, Nikki Haley, Gary Cohn, Dina Powell, NSC's Matt Pottinger, NSC spokesperson Michael Anton, and, at certain points, John Kelly. The group excluded most people who were actively part of the Trump presidential campaign or others, like Mick Mulvaney, the Office of Management and Budget director, who had close Tea Party ties. Cohn was a Democrat, Mattis at least nearly one, and Pottinger's father was a well-known liberal lawyer in New York. The rest, all Republicans, were far closer to the GOP of John McCain and George Bush than to the party that was now Donald Trump's. In particular, each represented the antithesis of Trump's anti-free-trade, America First, nationalist view. These were the Democrats and globalists who—in the chaos of an unprepared staff having to create, overnight, a presidential team of advisers—had slipped into this nationalist White House.

If they had tried to hide or blur their beliefs during their time in the White House, now, more than ever, they wanted to be known for them. They also, without exception, bore Trump a high level of personal as well as professional animosity. He had tainted them. Now out of the administration, their message to Woodward was that they had defended the nation against Trump and tried to shift the direction of Trump's policies, or at least tried to create diversionary tactics as he veered off in some extreme or loopy direction.

Trump may not have been crueler to the globalists around him than he was to the nationalists, but that was not saying much. His derision of McMaster was a daily pastime; Rex Tillerson was "Rex, the family dog"; he accused Gary Cohn of being gay; he spread rumors about Dina Powell's personal life. While die-hard Trumpers had no choice but to rationalize his cruelties, sometimes even prizing them when they were directed at someone else, the less-than-faithful adopted a steady, low-level, I-don't-have-to-take-this, I-only-do-it-for-my-country umbrage. (At the same time, as Trump derided them, they derided Trump. Gary Cohn, for instance, would take Trump's calls while playing golf at the private Sebonack Golf Club in Southampton, holding out the phone so others could hear Trump's diatribes and meanwhile making crazy-man gestures.)

For Bannon the establishment's passive response to Trump—its willingness to yet tolerate a man they so openly detested—was somehow further proof of the establishment's weakness, and its cravenness. The behavior of the globalists and so-called professionals provided yet more evidence that they could not be trusted. They could not even stand up to someone they obviously hated and who hated them.

Even as members of this group cycled out of the White House, there seemed to be no will, or ability, or courage to openly oppose Trump. Gary Cohn could not get a new job, largely because of his association with Trump, but though he continued to privately dine out on Trump's outlandishness, he seemed to continue to be too concerned about his reputation to publicly express his alarm and disgust. Dina Powell, furious about the rumors Trump was spreading about her, but hoping to land the UN ambassador's job someday, said nothing. Nikki Haley, eyeing the exit, continued to cultivate her relationship with Jared and Ivanka while privately considering a primary run against Trump (and, indeed, hoping that Trump might be gone and that a primary challenge would not in the end be necessary to get her to the White House).

But Woodward and his book now provided cover for delivering a powerful message: Team America represented the collective resistance to Trump's extreme, manic, and uninformed behavior.

Communication of this message required a coordinated effort. Each person's willingness to talk to Woodward was cross-checked against the willingness of several others to talk to him. This was part of Woodward's standard method of establishing a critical mass of inside sources: he created a kind of in-group, and this also suggested that if you failed to participate, you would not only lose your opportunity to be part of the in-group but lose your place in history—indeed, you would become one of its dupes. But Woodward's sources now offered something greater than gossip or a self-serving telling of events. Here were members of the White House trying to distance themselves from the very White House they had helped create. They wanted to cast it off, and in fact many of the Trump administration's key participants were declaring it a failed administration, although through no fault of their own.

Appearing fifty-seven days before the midterm elections, Woodward's book became a political event, one that many clearly hoped would do what, forty-four years before, Woodward's first book had done: help bring down the president.

Inside the White House, Trump not only got this message, he suddenly couldn't stop talking about Richard Nixon and how much he had been wronged. Nixon, Trump announced, was the greatest president. The fact that the establishment players had gotten together and thrown Nixon out was *proof* that he was the greatest. His mistake was the tapes—he should have burned them. "Trump," said Trump, as he had often said before, "would burn them."

* * *

As the autumn campaign cycle began, with Trump planning to be on the road four or five days a week, the mood among the senior staff in the White House—never buoyant, seldom even hopeful—reached something of a new low.

It wasn't just that they were being attacked by former colleagues but that they had been left behind. Being a Trump staffer had become an existential predicament: even if you wanted to get out, and almost all of them did, there was nowhere to go. The internal view of Woodward's book—that those who had served as his sources, no matter how much virtue they now claimed, would be forever discredited by the fact that they had worked in the Trump White House—was hardly confidence-building. What it came back to, and this was relevant in a personal way to everyone who worked in the White House and who might want to work somewhere else, was Trump's fragile legitimacy. They all tried, some sheepishly, some pluckily, to insist on it: *He was elected, wasn't he?* But as it turned out, having been elected president did not, in fact, make you a legitimate president—at least not in the eyes of the establishment, which still seemed to be the final arbiter in such judgments.

"Woodward is part of the overthrow effort," said Bannon one early September morning while sitting at the Embassy's dining table. But he was not without some admiration for how well his former colleagues had played Woodward, and how well Woodward played them.

As much as anyone, Bannon understood why people who worked for Trump might naturally, or inevitably, turn against him. He understood all the empirical reasons why people might think Trump was unfit. He recognized, too, that part of the art of being president—which Trump might well be remembered most of all for sorely lacking—was keeping yourself from getting thrown out of office.

But Bannon also believed that if you could get around Trump's repellent character, intellectual deficiencies, and glaring mental health issues, you ought to be able to see that Trump was being savaged—with the powers that be trying to run him out of office—for doing much of what he had been elected to do. Trumpism, in fact, was working.

The European Union was about to cave to most of the U.S. demands. Mexico was buying the Trump shift on NAFTA, and Canada would surely follow. And China? It was in full panic. Trump's threats of $500 billion in tariffs were doing what Reagan's military buildup had done to the Soviet Union. This could be, if Trump held the line, the end of Chinese inevitability.

Here, Bannon believed, was the real nature of the effort to bring the president down: the establishment did not want Trump gone because he was a failed president, but because he was a successful one. Trump was a cold war president and China was his enemy—about this he could not have been clearer. If Trump was ill-informed and untrustworthy about everything else, he did have one bedrock belief, one idea he truly understood: China bad. This was the basis of powerful new policies that would put the United States toe to toe with China. If successful, these policies might topple China and, as a consequence, derail an economic future—the very future that Gary Cohn, Goldman Sachs, and much of Team America had staked *their* futures on—that was penalizing and even crippling the American working class.

Bannon, chopping the air with his hands, was exercised now. Cohn and McMaster and Tillerson and the National Security Council bureaucracy were selling out the country. What they were defending—along with everyone else who had spoken, none too sotto voce, to Woodward—was the status quo. Add to that crowd Paul Ryan and Mitch McConnell and their hedge-fund allies as they weighed the president's weaknesses and considered whether and when and with whom to move against him.

Forget that Trump was an idiot and had clearly invited everything that was coming his way. There was a coup in progress.

* * *

On September 5, the Wednesday after Labor Day, apparently timed to complement the imminent publication of the Woodward book—and, propitiously, in the days just after John McCain's funeral—the *New York Times* published an anonymous essay by "a senior official" in the Trump administration.

> President Trump is facing a test to his presidency unlike any faced by a modern American leader.
>
> It's not just that the special counsel looms large. Or that the country is bitterly divided over Mr. Trump's leadership. Or even that his party might well lose the House to an opposition hellbent on his downfall.
>
> The dilemma—which he does not fully grasp—is that many of the senior officials in his own administration are working diligently from within to frustrate parts of his agenda and his worst inclinations.
>
> I would know. I am one of them.

The essay portrayed Trump as the man nearly everyone knew him to be: erratic, unfocused, impetuous, likely not of sound mind. But the article seemed also to single out a higher concern: "Although he was elected as a Republican, the president shows little affinity for ideals long espoused by conservatives: free minds, free markets and free people. At best, he has invoked these ideals in scripted settings. At worst, he has attacked them outright."

The essay went on to argue, as Woodward's book would echo, that significant parts of the executive branch were actively trying to undermine Trump's will and policies. This was offered as a silver lining, or what the writer called "cold comfort," but it might also have been offered as proof of the administration's incompetence: Trump's presidency was, the article suggested, subverting itself. Pointedly, the essay ended with a reference to John McCain and his farewell letter.

For twenty-four hours, it quite seemed that something was happening in American government that had seldom happened before. One part of the government was in open civil rebellion against the other, with the aid of the nation's most influential media outlet.

The provenance of a newspaper article has seldom been so carefully dissected. "A senior official" meant what, exactly? An assistant to the president, a cabinet secretary or undersecretary, the head of a major agency? But the *Times*, in a cryptic response to a question about the essay's author, suggested that it might not even know who the writer was. ("The writer," said the editor responding to a query, "was introduced to us by an intermediary whom we know and trust.") Trump railed against "the Sulzbergers" and how they were out to get him, a trope sometimes employed by the right to remind people of the Jewish background of the family that controlled the *Times*.

Within the White House, speculation about the author became a feverish parlor game, with most guesses centering on the National Security Council and a joint effort by two or three present and former NSC officials. But it might also be anyone of high standing in the administration who had a close relationship with a lawyer who could serve as the go-between with the *Times* and, for reasons of attorney-client privilege, could protect the writer's identity if a formal investigation were to ensue. Furthermore, this lawyer would need to be someone whom the *Times* could trust. This last point was critically important if the *Times*, as seemed possible, did not know the exact identity of the author.

One top guess was Matthew Pottinger, who was on the China desk at the National Security Council, and who, although he might not be considered a "senior official," could have collaborated with H. R. McMaster and Michael Anton, McMaster's spokesperson, who had written widely read pseudonymous essays during the 2016 campaign. (His essays were pro-Trump, but Anton had since sided with McMaster in his war with the president.) Pottinger's father was the New York lawyer Stan Pottinger, well known in liberal circles and to the *Times*, not least for being a long-time consort of the feminist icon Gloria Steinem.

But, in fact, it was remarkable how many people in the administration might plausibly have written the article or contributed to it. Few could be excluded. "Treason"—a word seldom used in American politics, and never in the White House, but which had variously been applied to both the president and the president's son in reference to their dealings with the Russians—was now, particularly by the president and his family, used against the author or authors of the essay, with the president vowing swift retribution.

There was a dire sense in the White House that the letter could have earthshaking consequences. "This is Monica at the Ritz Hotel," said one person close to the vice president, referring to the moment when Monica Lewinsky was whisked off the street by the FBI and held at the Ritz in Washington until she admitted to her affair with President Clinton, which in turn led directly to his impeachment.

It could hardly be overlooked that establishment Republicans seemed less than shocked by what might be reasonably construed as an overt rebellion within the White House. Mitch McConnell, as he took pains not to criticize "Anonymous" or even express concern about the essay's appearance, seemed almost to chuckle. In fact, the same day the op-ed was published, McConnell used the controversy about the article to make another, but perhaps quite related, point. Addressing Trump's renewed attacks on his attorney general, McConnell said, "I'm a big supporter of

Jeff Sessions. I think he's done a good job and I hope he stays right where he is."

The other point White House insiders would make in the coming days was equally telling. The disarray and discord that arguably led to the essay's publication now contributed to a complete inability to discover who had written it.

18

KAVANAUGH

Following the announcement of Brett Kavanaugh's nomination on July 9, Trump had mostly seemed pleased with his choice—"he's very safe," Trump kept repeating, "big respect, slam dunk." But toward the end of the summer he began to express reservations in some of his after-dinner calls. Here was one more instance of a president who often seemed to feel that his own White House was working against him. Somebody was feeding him doubts. One friend speculated that it might be his sister Maryanne Trump Barry, a now-inactive federal judge, even though she and her brother were not particularly close. But the message, wherever it came from, became a sudden irritant for Trump: there were no Protestants on the Supreme Court. "Did you know this?" he demanded of one friend.

Of the eight justices currently serving, all were either Jews or Catholics. Kavanaugh was also a Catholic, as was the runner-up choice, Amy Coney Barrett. There was some confusion about Neil Gorsuch, and Trump was offered conflicting views. But Gorsuch was certainly raised a Catholic and had even gone to the same Catholic school that Brett Kavanaugh had attended.

Can't we find lawyers who *aren't* Catholics or Jews? Trump wondered. Weren't there any WASP lawyers anymore? (Yes, he was told—Bob Mueller.)

It seemed confounding to Trump that he hadn't been aware of this new and remarkable fact about the Supreme Court. Inexplicably, the tide of history had turned, yet no one had noticed—or informed him.

"You had all Protestants and then in a few years none. Doesn't that seem strange?" he ruminated. "None at all." The nominally Presbyterian Trump went on: "But I can't say, 'I want to put a Protestant on the Court for better representation.' No, you can't say that. But I should be able to. You should be able to have the main religion in this country represented on the Supreme Court."

Was this McGahn's doing? Trump wondered, now deeply suspicious of the White House counsel. He was the White House point person on Supreme Court nominations; he was also a Catholic. Was McGahn packing the Court? Kavanaugh, like Gorsuch, had been preapproved by the Federalist Society, and Leonard Leo, the society's key man, was (reportedly) a member of Opus Dei, the secretive, far-right Catholic organization. Trump said he had been told that Leo was in bed with the Vatican.

As though putting two and two together—a slow dawning—Trump started to focus on abortion. Here he was on thin ice: whenever the issue came up, after only a few sentences of discussion, he would often begin to waver. His now-standard right-to-life view would revert to his previous, pro-choice view. In late August, weeks after nominating Kavanaugh, Trump wanted to know: Was this guy part of a Catholic plot to abolish abortion?

Suddenly alive to the reality of a no-Protestant Court, he continued needing reassurance that Brett Kavanaugh was not just out to make abortion illegal. Kavanaugh, he was told, was a "textualist," meaning he was primarily concerned with curbing the ever growing and, in the textualist view, unconstitutional authority of the administrative state. Abortion was far from his number one issue.

Still, as the White House staff prepared for what they assumed would be a harshly contested confirmation, Trump felt like he wasn't getting the full story. This irritation fed into a larger theme that had surfaced during the Gorsuch nomination: Why wasn't he being allowed to choose people he knew? He knew a lot of lawyers; why couldn't he just pick one?

* * *

Almost every observer of Trump's presidency agreed that the appointment and confirmation of Neil Gorsuch had been one of the smoother White House maneuvers. They also agreed that the reason it had been so smooth was that the White House—and Trump himself—had had very little to do with it.

During the campaign, the Federalist Society had produced a list of judges that it deemed acceptable for any open seat on the Supreme Court. All the choices were well vetted, reputable, and graduates of top law schools; all were judges who subscribed to textualist views and had not supported pro-abortion decisions. This became a no-fault Trump talking point during the campaign: if given the opportunity, he would nominate someone from the list. (This approach sharply contrasted to the campaign's haphazard effort to come up with a slate of likely foreign policy advisers. That list was generated inside the campaign and included a largely random group of relative unknowns, notably Carter Page and George Papadopoulos, both of whom would later help ensnare the campaign and the future White House in the Russia mess.)

But no matter how solid the Federalist Society's list or how well the selection of Gorsuch had worked out, Trump yet rebelled. This was a plum job; why couldn't he give it to a friend? He may not *be* a lawyer, but he knew more than most lawyers. After all, he had hired and fired lawyers for almost fifty years. And in New York, this was standard operating procedure: you wanted judges who owed you.

Trump had pushed to nominate Giuliani (also, as it happened, a Catholic) as his first Supreme Court pick, but he was quietly talked down from this idea—Giuliani was pro-abortion. Now Kavanaugh, like Gorsuch, was presented as a done deal. There were runners-up, such as Barrett, but Kavanaugh was the McGahn-Federalist choice, the establishment choice. They had a clear plan: Kavanaugh would be rolled out over the summer and then hearings would begin right after Labor Day. The timing could not be better. Only weeks before the midterms, the Democrats would almost certainly take the bait and make a noisy, futile effort to obstruct the president's choice. The president would ably defend his solid and upright nominee, a judge who was acceptable to the legal establishment.

He would also deliver on his necessary promise to the base: a hard core conservative and right-to-life Supreme Court justice.

That Kavanaugh would be confirmed at the height of the midterm election season was the invaluable bonus. Here was the golden message to conservative voters: no matter how much Trump might grate on you, you could depend on him to deliver a rehabilitated Court. With Justice Kennedy gone, Kavanaugh would push the Court firmly to the right—and there might well be two more appointments to come.

But now a sanguine Trump became a more truculent Trump. He wanted more choices. He wanted to add his people to the list. If push came to shove, he would need people he could depend on. Lest anyone miss the point, he pressed the issue: he wanted "a get-out-of-jail-free card."

This then became the Trump focus. Given his myriad levels of personal exposure, the pursuit of the special counsel, and the prospects of a Democratic House barreling toward impeachment, he needed to know that Kavanaugh would protect him. Could McGahn and the others be sure Kavanaugh would have his back? Ever unsubtle in his desires, he pressed harder: Could they get a commitment from him?

Not a problem. Kavanaugh had already argued, Trump was told, that the office conferred a special status, that a sitting president was in effect exempt from personal legal culpability. (In fact, Kavanaugh, who had worked for Clinton prosecutor Ken Starr, had also argued quite the opposite during the Clinton investigation, and though he now seemed to advocate for a strong executive, the particulars still seemed fairly hazy.) Yes, Trump's advisers repeatedly assured him, all the Trump-related questions that might come before the Court—about his business interests, about executive privilege, about his possible indictment—seemed quite safe with Kavanaugh.

* * *

The Kavanaugh nomination was a bright red flag for Andrew Weissmann and the Mueller team. Were the special counsel to proceed with an indictment of the president, the issue of presidential immunity would undoubtedly come before the Supreme Court and yield a decision that could be as consequential as *Bush v. Gore* or the case involving the Nixon tapes. Indeed, the decision might either secure Trump's hold on the White House or unseat him. And if the Court came to that crossroads, what would be the Kavanaugh effect?

Almost from the beginning, Mueller's team had assumed that the president's fate, and quite possibly the fate of the special counsel's investigation, would be decided by the Supreme Court. But now the constitutional issues that lay at the heart of the likely case would be considered by someone who appeared to have already made up his mind about presidential fallibility—and to have judged the president quite infallible. Assuming the Senate confirmed Kavanaugh, a near certainty given the Republication majority, the Court's newest justice might provide just the sort of presidential exception that would render their investigation all but pointless.

But as the Trump team sought to make Kavanaugh the president's fail-safe mechanism, Weissmann looked for ways to override the likely new justice and the protection he would probably offer the president. On the eve of the Kavanaugh hearings, the special counsel's team gamed out what might happen if the Department of Justice demanded that Kavanaugh recuse himself.

This approach had virtue on its side, though not necessarily the law. If you were a judge and found yourself weighing the fate of someone about whom you might reasonably be biased—say if he had granted you a favor, like making you a judge—you ought to recuse yourself. This is what fair-minded judges did. If they did not, judges could be compelled to disqualify themselves through an appeal to higher courts. But although all judges in federal courts were subject to the same standards relating to conflicts of interest, it was less clear that this standard applied to justices on the Supreme Court—or, anyway, that there was someone who could enforce this standard on them.

The special counsel's own review of the law here did not provide much room for optimism: "The Rules of the Supreme Court make no provision for the filing of recusal motions. Predictably, such motions are seldom filed, and we have found no instance of one being granted," declared a research memo prepared for Mueller's team. "And we are aware of no examples of the U.S. government filing a motion for the recusal of a justice."

On the most basic matters of the law, the document was doleful: "The ethics code that generally governs the recusal decisions of federal judges—the Code of Conduct for United States Judges, promulgated by the Judicial Conference—by its terms does not bind the justices of the Supreme Court."

Still—and here was the continuing argument of the special counsel—there was, in the law, no ultimate exception, no imperial option: "The federal recusal statute . . . by its terms applies to '[a]ny justice, judge, or magistrate judge of the United States.' . . . Moreover, the decisions of the Supreme Court are clear that recusal is a fundamental matter of fairness and the appearance of justice, which implicates Due Process."

Alas there was "no mechanism for appealing from a decision of a justice of the Supreme Court not to recuse him- or herself, nor any means of addressing the question to any judicial audience apart from the justice alone."

Weissmann's proposed Kavanaugh work-around appeared to be a bust. If Brett Kavanaugh became a Supreme Court justice, the Department of Justice could demand that he recuse himself from what might be the case of the century. But Kavanaugh could simply refuse—and that would be the end of it.

* * *

As the special counsel's office weighed its options in the wake of the Kavanaugh nomination, so did the minority Senate Democrats. Their conclusion was that the Kavanaugh nomination could be derailed only by an attack on Kavanaugh's personal rectitude. An email from one Senate staffer listed some of the Hail Mary issues that might block Kavanaugh: "Sexual or financial improprieties, drugs, violence and anger management issues, plagiarism, gambling debts."

Throughout the summer, there was a low-level murmur about Kavanaugh's Yale fraternity, Delta Kappa Epsilon. A generation before, similar murmurs had trailed the presidential candidacy of George W. Bush; he, too, had been a DKE member, and rumors about extreme alcohol abuse and sexually aggressive behavior followed him.

But it was Kavanaugh's high school life that came to haunt him. Dianne Feinstein, the senator from California and ranking minority member of the Senate Judiciary Committee, confided to multiple friends that she had received a confidential letter containing allegations about Kavanaugh's behavior one night during a prep school party. Kavanaugh's accuser was a woman named Christine Blasey, who sometimes used her married name, Ford. A professor of psychology at Palo Alto University, she seemed credible and had a solid background. But she was fearful of coming forward; furthermore, Feinstein wondered if the single incident that Blasey Ford described would register with anyone. Feinstein wondered if the incident even *should* register. For weeks, Feinstein kept the letter under wraps.

The Kavanaugh confirmation hearings began on September 4. Initially, the hearings caused no great alarm for the nominee's supporters. But Kavanaugh's opponents were desperate, and after a series of leaks from Democrats on the Hill, Blasey Ford, whether she wanted to or not, became the designated weapon against the nominee. Forced out in the open, she described her one experience with Kavanaugh in an article published by the *Washington Post* on September 16.

The story she told took place in Maryland in the summer of 1982, when a small group of teenagers gathered one evening in one of their homes. Blasey Ford was then fifteen; Brett Kavanaugh, then seventeen, was a distant acquaintance, someone she had occasionally encountered in Montgomery County private school circles. That evening, according to Blasey Ford, as she went upstairs to look for a bathroom, a drunken Kavanaugh, with a drunken friend in tow, forced her into a bedroom, pushed her down on a bed, and jumped on her, pawing at her clothes and holding a hand over her mouth long enough for Blasey Ford to begin to panic.

* * *

Trump, it seemed, could not get enough of this story. "He pushed her down on the bed and that's it?" How long had he held her down? Trump wanted to know. "Did he just fall on her and go in for a kiss? Or was it humping?"

When Trump was told that Kavanaugh's friend Mark Judge, who Blasey Ford claimed was in the room, had written a book about his drunken exploits in high school, Trump whacked himself alongside the head. "What kind of idiots did you get me here?"

Then he went back to insisting that things would be going much better if he had chosen the nominee. "This is embarrassing," he said. "Catholic school boys." Which provoked a recollection of his exploits when *he* was seventeen: he hadn't just stolen kisses, that was for sure.

As Blasey Ford's story instantly came to dominate the news, Trump conceived quite a sudden level of dripping contempt for Kavanaugh. "He seems weak. Not strong. He was probably molested by a priest."

As Kavanaugh was put more and more on the defensive, the nomination abruptly seemed imperiled. The White House and the Kavanaugh team nixed a possible CBS interview, believing that the nominee couldn't hold up under hostile questioning. But by this point Kavanaugh needed to defend himself somehow, so the White House agreed to the promise of a soft interview at Fox, with the questions provided beforehand.

During this treacly sit-down on September 24, a defeated and self-pitying Kavanaugh said he was a virgin in high school and for a long time thereafter. Trump could barely believe it. "Stop! Who would say that? My virgin justice. This man has no pride! Man? Did I say *man*? I don't think so."

Trump seemed eager to cut his losses and move on. Only several bracing warnings by senior members of his staff highlighting the depressing effect that abandoning Kavanaugh would likely have on the Republican base in the midterms, now just weeks away, prevented the president from sending out a tweet dumping his nominee.

Adding to the turmoil, Ivanka was telling her father how poorly Kavanaugh was performing with women. He was doing serious damage to the Republicans' chances in the coming midterms. Democrats could hardly believe it, but the Kavanaugh battle seemed to be turning, quite inexorably, in their favor.

Trump's ire rose yet further when he learned that George W. Bush—among the politicians that Trump scorned most—had come to Kavanaugh's defense, and that many Republicans believed it was Bush who was keeping the nomination alive.

"The drunks stick together," said Trump. "If he's a Bush guy, he's not a Trump guy. It's bull that we can depend on him. Virgin-man will sell me out."

* * *

During the week of September 24, Blasey Ford's public testimony seemed to hang in the balance. Would she show up or not? The suspense created a level of uncertainty and tension that seemed especially to annoy Trump—Blasey Ford was commanding all of the attention.

Lewandowski and Bossie, egged on by Bannon, were telling Trump that if he lost Kavanaugh or, worse, dumped Kavanaugh, he would lose not only the House in November but the Senate, too.

Trump seemed to find new resolve by focusing on Michael Avenatti, Stormy Daniels's lawyer, and Ronan Farrow, a journalist whose stories often focused on sexual abuse, both of whom produced last-minute Kavanaugh accusers as Blasey Ford wavered in her willingness to testify. Avenatti's accuser told a tale of teenage gang rapes in suburban Washington, D.C. Farrow's accuser claimed she recognized Kavanaugh at a drunken party at Yale, and said he might have exposed himself to her.

"Pathetic," Trump declared, and then digressed into considerations of whether Farrow was the son of Frank Sinatra, as his mother, Mia Farrow, had suggested he might be, or of Woody Allen, adding, in a further digression, that he knew both Frank and Woody.

As the accusations against Kavanaugh mounted, Trump seemed to identify more with his nominee, or to recognize that the fury toward Kavanaugh was directed at him, too.

"They are after *me*," he said, as though proudly.

Once again in the fight, Trump had to be restrained from not leading the counterattack himself. His enforced efforts at something like judicious temperament were gut-busting to many in the White House and the subject of something like a silent White House pool: "When will he blow?"

When Blasey Ford again agreed to testify—her testimony now set for Thursday, September 27—Trump expressed further concern about whether Kavanaugh was capable of handling himself in a tense public situation. He began to pass instructions and advice: "Admit to nothing. Zero!" He wanted aggression.

In the days and hours before the testimony, Trump would call friends and repeat his now favorite theme: when *he* was accused, he toughed it out. He seemed to be polling everybody about how tough they thought Kavanaugh really was.

"I don't think he's that tough," Trump would then conclude.

Through it all, there seemed to be an implicit recognition on the president's part that what Blasey Ford had said was probably true. "If it wasn't true," he offered, "she would have claimed rape or something, not just a kiss."

* * *

On the morning of the twenty-seventh, Trump watched Blasey Ford's testimony in the residence before coming down to the West Wing. He was on the phone with friends almost the entire time. "She's good," he kept saying. He thought Kavanaugh was in "big trouble."

That afternoon, watching Kavanaugh's performance, he was deeply displeased. He seemed personally offended that Kavanaugh had cried during this testimony. "I wanted to slap him," he said afterward to a caller. "Virgin crybaby."

But he also claimed credit for the fact that Kavanaugh admitted to nothing. "You can't even admit to a handshake," he told the same caller. He digressed to "my friend Leslie Moonves," the chairman of CBS, who had recently been under fire after a series of #MeToo accusations. "Les admitted to a kiss. He's done. Forget about it. When I heard about the kiss, I thought, Done, finished. The only person who has survived this stuff is me. I knew you couldn't admit to anything. Try to explain, dead. Apologize, dead. If you admit to even knowing a broad, dead."

That evening, catching up to the coverage and seeing the strong Kavanaugh reviews on Fox, Trump's views seemed to shift. "Every man in this country thinks this could happen to him," he told a friend. "Thirty years ago you try to kiss a girl, thirty years later she's back—boom. And what kind of person remembers a kiss after forty years? After forty years she's still upset? Give me a break. Give. Me. A. Break."

The next day, Jeff Flake, the lame-duck senator from Arizona, confronted in an elevator by tearful and hectoring Blasey Ford supporters and Kavanaugh opponents, threatened to withhold his confirmation vote unless the FBI conducted a further investigation.

"Flakey Flake," Trump pronounced. But despite the setback he was feeling a certain confidence that Kavanaugh's nomination would go through. "It's a total bullshit investigation. Total bullshit."

Four days before the scheduled confirmation vote—as the FBI conducted its further round of vetting—Trump attended a rally in Mississippi. By now he was full of swagger.

"'I had one beer.' Right? 'I had one beer.' Well . . . you think it was . . . ? Nope! One beer. Oh, good. How did you get home? 'I don't remember.' How'd you get there? 'I don't remember.' Where is the place? 'I don't remember.' How many years ago was it? 'I don't know.' I don't know. I don't know. I don't know. What neighborhood was it in? 'I don't know.' Where's the house? 'I don't know.' Upstairs? Downstairs? Where was it? 'I don't know.' But I had one beer. That's the only thing I remember. And a man's life is in tatters. A man's life is shattered."

Trump's rudeness caught the tide: nothing was going to derail Kavanaugh's nomination now.

* * *

On October 6, Brett Kavanaugh was confirmed by the full Senate, 50 to 48.

After the vote, Bannon was practically hooting with pleasure. "Don't ever underestimate the Democrats' ability to overplay their hand and fuck things up. Kavanaugh *is* the presidency." Not only were the Democrats helpless in front of the nomination, they had revved it up into a make-or-break cause. Then, tasting victory, they had lost the fight in the final hour.

In Bannon's view, Trump had pulled to his side the people who did not believe the Democrats and Blasey Ford, as well as those who did not think a decades-old two-minute tussle had anything to do with the price of beans. But Bannon also understood that Trump may have irretrievably lost every woman in the country with a college education.

Still, Sean Hannity had 5.8 million viewers on the night of the Blasey Ford–Kavanaugh hearing. "That's a lot of fucking hobbits," said Bannon.

For Bannon, it was a line-in-the-sand moment. The surging Democrats saw the coming election as a mortal game. Now the hobbits did, too.

Pelosi's people, sure of sixty additional seats in the House four weeks ago, were now privately cutting their estimates to thirty seats.

Bannon could hardly believe that the midterms were swinging back his way. "Finally, fucking finally, Kavanaugh has nationalized this election."

He only wished that this was November 6 and not October 6. And he fervently hoped there would be no more exogenous events.

19

KHASHOGGI

Jamal Khashoggi—a Saudi citizen and U.S. resident, a journalist and high-stakes player in Persian Gulf politics, and an irritant to the thirty-two-year-old Crown Prince and Saudi ruler Mohammed bin Salman—entered the Saudi consulate in Istanbul on the afternoon of October 2, 2018, shortly after 1:00. He was met by an assassination squad. After Khashoggi's murder and dismemberment, Khashoggi appeared to have been dissolved in a vat of acid or his body parts flown out of Turkey in a diplomatic pouch.

Unbeknownst to the none-too-smooth Saudi assassination team, Turkish security services were recording most of Khashoggi's last moments. In the hours and days afterward, while the Saudis insisted that Khashoggi had walked out of the embassy unharmed, Turkish president Recep Tayyip Erdoğan—aligned with Saudi Arabia's enemies Qatar and Iran—authorized a drip-by-drip leak of the dark details of Khashoggi's disappearance and murder.

President Trump brushed off the first sketchy report of Khashoggi's disappearance and possible death. When more details started to emerge, he said he didn't trust the Turks. Finally he prodded Jared to "call your friend"—the Crown Prince—an international ally of Jared Kushner in his effort to be a dominant foreign policy voice in his father-in-law's administration.

"Mohammed," Jared reported back, "is looking into it. He doesn't know anything more about it than we do."

On October 4, the *Washington Post* ran a blank space where Khashoggi's column "should appear." The *Post* laid the suspicion of Khashoggi's murder on the Saudi ruler's doorstep. The next day the Turks confirmed that Khashoggi had entered but never left the Saudi embassy.

As so often happened in Trumpworld, an important, and rare, victory—the Kavanaugh confirmation vote—was now almost instantly subsumed by this new ugly reality, Trump and his family's close personal relationship with someone caught up in a murder investigation.

Saudi Arabia, with its complex and difficult royal family, alliances with terrorist organizations, cruelties of law and culture, vast amount of oil, and key position in the Middle East, had always required the greatest diplomatic finesse and legerdemain on the part of U.S. presidents. Absent those skills, the Trump administration, four weeks before a challenging election, found itself owning, and publicly defending what was being reported as a blatant act of torture and political revenge, with more gory details emerging every day.

In a dramatic example of Bannon's feared exogenous events, here was an open window—which no one could seem to close—into Trump and his family's strange dealings in the dubious corners of the world.

* * *

Mohammed bin Salman—MBS—spent hours every day planted in front of a screen playing video games. Like Trump, he was often described as a petulant child. Uncontrollable, he was determined to flatten any opposition to his rule within the vast royal family, and to use a level of brutality in service to this goal even greater than the kingdom's usual brand of savagery. MBS, the U.S. foreign policy and intelligence community understood, was, even for the Saudis, a piece of work.

What was harder to understand was Jared Kushner's exceptional embrace of the man. Not only had they become genuinely chummy, but Kushner spent time, effort, and significant political currency promoting the Crown Prince. The Saudis' already vast PR operation in the United States included Kushner as one of its important sponsors.

On October 5 and 6, with the president barnstorming the country in his now almost daily series of MAGA events in friendly stadiums, Kushner was left to get his friend MBS, as well as himself, out of the Khashoggi mess. In frequent contact with the Crown Prince, Kushner effectively became a crisis manager for him. To that end, he also become the White House's most prolific leaker of Saudi conspiracy theories and disinformation.

From White House sources came the Turkish plot: blaming MBS for Khashoggi's "disappearance" was part of Erdoğan's plan to reestablish the Ottoman caliphate and take control of Mecca from the Saudis. From White House sources came the UAE plot: the plane carrying the assassination squad departed from Riyadh but landed in Dubai on its way to Istanbul. MBS was once the protégé of Mohammed bin Zayed—MBZ—the ruler of the UAE, but recently their relationship had been souring, in part because of MBZ's disapproval of MBS. MBZ, it was falsely said, might well have had a number of assassins join the team in Dubai so he could lay the blame for the killing on MBS.

Kushner, in an off-the-record conversation with a reporter, argued the crux of the Saudi case: "This guy [Khashoggi] was the link between certain factions in the royal family and Osama. We know that. A journalist? Come on. This was a terrorist masquerading as a journalist."

***

For Jim Mattis, the ever more deeply disgusted secretary of defense, the Khashoggi debacle provided yet another example of the bizarre and inexplicable relationships that Trump and his family had formed with bad guys around the world, from Putin to Kim Jong-un to their entanglement with the never-ending soap opera in the Persian Gulf states, in particular the high-stakes interplay among MBS, MBZ, and the Qatari strongman Hamad bin Jassim—HBJ. Trump's own instincts were weird and confusing, but sometimes even more alarming, and frustrating, were Kushner's incessant meddling and unclear agenda. Mattis had become increasingly convinced that Kushner's continual forays were screwball. And the FBI might seem to have its own concerns: Kushner had failed to pass normal security clearances and had only received a top secret security status due to the almost unheard-of intervention by the president himself (a fact baldly denied by Kushner and his wife).

The Kushner family's financial problems, and their link to the Gulf region, were a source of incredulous discussion in foreign policy circles. It seemed well beyond mere artlessness that someone so overtly conflicted—the president's son-in-law was trying to raise private money from the same people who were involved in complex negotiations and relationships with the U.S. government—could, without universal objection, have a leadership role in those same matters. "The sign of the beast" became a kind of shrugging byword and acknowledgment that Kushner's actions or recommendations might have something to do with his family's efforts to refinance their troubled holding, 666 Fifth Avenue.

The Fifth Avenue office and retail building had been purchased in 2007—on the eve of the world's financial collapse—by Jared Kushner, the deal under way while his father was in prison. The acquisition was part of the Kushner family's grand plan to relocate their holdings and the emphasis of their business from low-profile New Jersey to the spotlight of New York City. The Kushners paid $1.8 billion for 666 Fifth, double the square-foot price record for a building in Manhattan. From the start, the property, needing extensive renovation, had trouble attracting premium tenants. What's more, after several restructurings, a balloon payment of $1.4 billion, cross-collateralized by many of the family's other assets, was due on the mortgage in 2019.

Since before the election, the family had, without much success, tried to secure a refinancing deal. Keeping 666 afloat could be the difference between the family's multibillionaire status and significantly more ignomious circumstances. Adding particular urgency to the situation, the majority of Jared's personal wealth was tied up in his family's business.

Jared's relationship with Steve Bannon, never good after they entered the White House, hit an early flash point when Kushner learned that Bannon was keeping a metaphorical countdown clock for when 666 Fifth would go bust and take the family with it. Certainly Kushner's White House job had made the refinancing efforts vastly more challenging: any lender to the family would invite ethics scrutiny and press attention. Willing lenders, if there were any, had the family in a squeeze and could force a distress deal—unless, of course, there were potential *other* benefits of being in business with the Kushners that a lender might pay a premium for.

As Jared became one of the most significant voices in U.S. foreign policy, the Kushner family tried to obtain financing from the Qataris, Saudis, Chinese, Russians, Turks, and in the UAE, all nations where private monies were invariably aligned with state interests. In each instance, foreign investors concluded that the potential upside of dealing with the Kushners was sorely compromised by the downside of the exposure. But the family pushed on, struggling to find a willing partner in the limited pool of billion-dollar-class high-risk real estate investors.

In August 2018, the Kushner family appeared to save itself by making a deal to bail out 666 Fifth with a Toronto-based investment firm called Brookfield Asset Management. With nearly $300 billion in assets under management, Brookfield fronted for sovereign wealth funds around the world—Qatar was one of its significant investors—that might want high levels of anonymity. In many deals, the anodyne "Brookfield" was better positioned than, for instance, the more overt Qatar Investment Authority. And in this unvirtuous circle of Brookfield, its sovereign wealth funds, and the Kushner family, it was not only Middle East money potentially looking for sway in the Trump White House, but Brookfield looking for White House influence on its behalf in the Middle East.

In the White House, after the announcement of the Brookfield deal, John Kelly lost it. His relationship with Jared and Ivanka, ever a seesaw of him and them trying to oust the other, had reached its lowest point, with Kelly accusing Kushner of having sold his father-in-law's government.

* * *

By mid-October, almost two weeks into the Khashoggi nightmare, every part of it had gotten much worse and much more public. Both the Saudis and the White House seemed wholly unable to adjust to the facts of the case. The Saudis denied the allegations, with mostly harebrained counter-narratives, while the White House rationalized the allegations with half-baked logic.

Strangely, the president's advisers let Trump thread the verbal needle. When speaking or tweeting about the assassination, Trump seemed to be having a public argument with himself, in some sense agonizing out loud about the clash between realpolitik behavior and moral values. For five straight days he offered a variety of opinions and rationales.

"It's being looked at very, very strongly, and we would be very upset and angry if that were the case [that the Saudis ordered the murder]," he said on October 14. "As of this moment, they deny it. And deny it vehemently. Could it be them? Yes," he admitted, seemingly reluctantly, even churlishly.

On October 15: "I just spoke with the king of Saudi Arabia, who denies any knowledge of what took place with regard to, as he said, his Saudi Arabian citizen. . . . I don't want to get into his mind—but it sounded to me like maybe these could have been rogue killers. Who knows? . . . And it sounded like he, and also the Crown Prince, had no knowledge."

On October 16, Trump continued to struggle to find a way out of the subject or a consistent line to adhere to. "Here we go again with, you know, you're guilty until proven innocent. I don't like that. We just went through that with Justice Kavanaugh, and he was innocent all the way as far as I'm concerned."

And later that day: "For the record, I have no financial interests in Saudi Arabia (or Russia, for that matter). Any suggestion that I have is just more FAKE NEWS (of which there is plenty)!"

And still again on that day: "Just spoke with the Crown Prince of Saudi Arabia who totally denied any knowledge of what took place in their Turkish Consulate. He was with Secretary of State Mike Pompeo during the call, and told me that he has already started, and will rapidly expand, a full and complete investigation."

There was more on October 17: "We'll get down to the bottom of it. I hope that the [Saudi] king and the Crown Prince didn't know about it.

That's the big factor in my eyes . . . I'm not giving cover at all. They are an ally. We have other good allies in the Middle East."

That same day the White House announced that the Saudis had just transferred $100 million to the United States as part of an unpaid sum they had agreed to spend on U.S. weapons more than a year before.

And finally, asked on October 18 whether he thought Khashoggi was dead, Trump said: "It certainly looks that way to me. We're waiting for some investigations . . . and I think we'll be making a statement, a very strong statement. It'll have to be very severe. I mean, it's bad, bad stuff. But we'll see what happens."

That week, to one of his after-dinner callers, he put it somewhat differently: "Who gives a fuck?"

Meanwhile, less publicly, Kushner was trying to manage MBS. The effort was not going well, with MBS seemingly incapable of appreciating, on virtually any level, that the world beyond the Saudi kingdom and the Gulf states might demand a different standard of behavior than what was acceptable in the world of a despotic feudal prince.

Kushner suggested to the Crown Prince that he should order the arrest and quick execution of fifteen plotters involved in Khashoggi's assassination. He was considering that, said MBS. Kushner urged MBS to cancel "Davos in the Desert," Saudi Arabia's elaborately staged investment conference, which was scheduled to begin on October 23. Embarrassingly, many blue-chip American CEOs had agreed to attend, in part at Kushner's prodding. But MBS unequivocally refused. He pointed out to Kushner that in Saudi Arabia the press coverage was very positive— nobody cared about Khashoggi!

Publicly and privately, the efforts by the White House to manage the fallout from Khashoggi's assassination merely dug the hole deeper and wider. After several days of pressure from a number of advisers, Steve Mnuchin, the Treasury secretary, finally canceled his plan to attend the Saudi Davos. Trump continued to offer almost daily comments about the assassination, none of them satisfying, until the day the conference began.

By then, the midterm elections were less than three weeks away.

* * *

Jared Kushner came into the White House believing that he could initiate and represent a new generation of cool, Kissingeresque precision in foreign policy—with Kissinger himself encouraging Kushner to believe this.

A few months before the Khashoggi murder, however, Kissinger had attended a luncheon hosted by a small group of influential New York lawyers. Kissinger brought Rupert Murdoch along. Both men had aided the rise of Jared Kushner and, quite despite their better instincts, both had urged an open mind regarding the Trump administration. Kissinger's attitude for most of Trump's first year or so had been that, beyond the nasty rhetoric, and the fact that nothing particularly positive had happened, nothing particularly negative had occurred in this White House's management of the U.S. global role either, so give Trump and his people a chance. But now, at the lunch—and with Murdoch, arms crossed, nodding his approval—a disgusted Kissinger ripped Trump and Kushner in the most fundamental and visceral way. "The entire foreign policy is based on a single unstable individual's reaction to perceptions of slights or flattery. If someone says something nice about him, they are our friend; if they say something unkind, if they don't kiss the ring, they are our enemy."

After the Khashoggi murder, Kissinger, with renewed contempt, told friends that Kushner, in forging a friendship with MBS, had missed the main point about the Saudis. The Trump White House had tied itself to MBS, who had tied himself to his country's economic renaissance. But Saudi Arabia, confronting declining oil prices and ever more demanding royal mouths to feed, was basically broke: its future, or the royal family's future, was tied to the Aramco deal, which was increasingly less likely to happen.

Since Trump's election, Kushner had been developing an elaborate, rose-colored scenario featuring support for Aramco and ever-increasing Saudi-U.S. economic links, a scenario that was coupled with the promise that the Saudis would use their influence with the Palestinians to forge a peace agreement with Israel. This, in turn, would be Kushner's crowning achievement—and this great success would, Kushner believed, help keep his father-in-law in office and also propel Kushner's own political destiny.

Encouraged by Kushner, MBS went on a wide-ranging investment and business outreach tour of the United States. Along the way, David Pecker, Trump's publishing friend, was promised Saudi money for his company AMI; so was Trump's *Apprentice* agent Ari Emanuel, for his company WME; so was Trump and Kushner's favorite businessman, Stephen Schwarzman, the CEO of Blackstone, the private equity group, who got $20 billion from the Saudis for a new investment fund.

Rather than seeing himself as compromised by his family's search for funds in the Middle East and the deals negotiated by various friends and allies, Kushner viewed himself as uniquely positioned to arbitrate the conflicts. He had taken to referring to *Oslo*, a play about the efforts of Norwegian diplomats in 1993 to bring Yitzhak Rabin and Yasser Arafat together. He saw himself as the one person with the sagacity and temperament to effect a resolution among all the players in the region.

During the summer of 2018, Kushner prepared what he thought might be the ultimate initiative, his personal *Oslo* move. His idea was to build a platform for pan–Middle East economic development; through joint-venture lending programs, the platform would lead to political discussion and a conceptual framework for lasting peace. The sheer size of what he envisioned would create a structure of cooperation and codependence. As he described it, the shared platform would be like nothing the region had ever seen before. In pursuing this notion, Kushner was operating outside of diplomatic channels. He was also charging ahead without much involvement from the White House itself, although he promised his father-in-law that his initiative was going to be something "very big."

As the idea evolved, Kushner suggested that the World Bank would stand behind the project, with massive investments from each of the richest states in the region. And the project would be run by someone Kushner had already selected, an investment banker named Michael Klein.

Klein, in fact, was dubious about the project, privately telling people he thought that one of Kushner's motivations, in addition to his pressing desire to announce the initiative in the run-up to the midterm elections, was to sell himself as the administration's indispensable man. Kushner, Klein said, was mounting a PR campaign intended to counter any bad publicity in the event that he found himself facing an indictment: Kushner wanted to appear essential to achieving peace in the Middle East.

This was perhaps not the only aspect of the scheme that failed to acknowledge reality. Indeed, Klein was quite a peculiar choice, one that reflected Kushner's apparent inability to appreciate even a flashing neon sign signaling the appearance of conflict. A former banker with Citibank, Klein was a Zelig-like networker with a vast office overlooking St. Patrick's Cathedral in midtown Manhattan, a pasha-style space occupied only by himself and a handful of assistants. He was one of those people, observed a banker who had participated in a deal with Klein, who seemed to have identified the ten richest people in the world and then made every effort to have a personal relationship with at least one of them. The Saudis were his current key client. He provided investment advice to MBS and was a strategic advocate for the plan to publicly float Aramco for $2 trillion, in what would be the world's biggest public offering. In June 2017, Klein was in Riyadh with the presidential party during Trump's first foreign foray.

Kushner's initiative and Klein's involvement in it highlighted how central MBS was to Kushner's plans and his view of the world. Together, Kushner and MBS's personal banker would make peace in the Middle East. But Kushner's ambitious plan collapsed at the end of summer 2018, not long after the collapse of the Saudi's Aramco public offering.

* * *

Davos in the Desert opened on October 23, three weeks after Khashoggi's murder, with Kushner yet urging U.S. executives to attend the Saudi event. At the same time, Trump dispatched his CIA director Gina Haspel to Turkey. Her brief was to review the evidence held by the Turks about the Khashoggi murder, including the recordings of his assassination.

Haspel confirmed the obvious: just as all U.S intelligence agencies had concluded, Khashoggi died in the manner described by the Turks. What's more, it appeared unbelievable that the murder could have happened without the knowledge of the Crown Prince himself.

Trump, sick of the Khashoggi mess, was privately blaming Kushner for it. "I told him to make peace," said Trump to a caller.

Publicly, Trump openly debated the conclusions reached by his intelligence agencies about MBS's culpability: "[I]t could very well be that the Crown Prince had knowledge of this tragic event—maybe he did and maybe he didn't!"

Once again Trump had needlessly moved the goal posts. It was not just that he had spectacularly mishandled the diplomatic challenge of managing a toxic ally, but that—just as he had done repeatedly with Russia—he had undermined the U.S. intelligence community. In some real sense, he was making this disaster their fault. Not only was he blaming them for inconvenient news, he was doubting the truth of the news they brought.

As a political issue on the eve of the midterms, Trump's public waffling and weakness when discussing an international scandal involving a gory murder would surely not be a plus. But as a practical issue, his handling of the incident might be even more damaging to his future. Many believed that most senior members of the defense, diplomatic, and intelligence communities had now reached the point that they doubted the president's competence or mental stability. What's more, few could be confident that in this instance his logic-defying approach and painful efforts to deny the obvious were not a reflection of side deals or other interests connected to the Trump and Kushner families.

Jim Mattis, for one, had rationalized his place in the Trump government by arguing that, since the president himself could not be trusted or believed, it was vitally necessary for someone with credibility and a steady hand to hold the fort. Now he was telling friends he hoped and assumed that the Democrats would win the House in November—which, in turn, would allow him to at last leave his post.

20

OCTOBER SURPRISES

On October 9, twenty-eight days before the midterm elections, Nikki Haley, Trump's ambassador to the United Nations, and one of the longer-serving and brighter lights of the Trump White House, announced her resignation, effective at the end of the year.

Since she was not leaving immediately, there would be no practical difference between announcing this plan on November 7, the day after the midterms, rather than now. The effective difference, however, was that her announcement became part of the campaign narrative—the negative narrative. During an election season in which Donald Trump was scaring off the nation's college-educated women, the most visible woman in the administration—outside of Trump's own daughter—was choosing this moment to say she was packing up.

Haley's resignation would be one of the closing impressions of the campaign. She had not even supplied enough warning for the White House to name, with fanfare and smiles, a replacement who might lighten the shadow of her exit. The always-scrambling White House staff now had to scramble even more than usual: somehow they had to embrace her resignation so as not to appear surprised or, indeed, openly dissed by it.

The solution was to have her make the announcement in the Oval Office. Haley resisted, forcing the White House to insist, or beg, that she show up in the West Wing. But, in fact, the optics favored her, not the

White House. She was so important and so valued that she was not dismissed in a tweet, as so many others had been. (Even those who quit were usually then fired in a tweet.) Instead, she was fawned over by the president in the Oval. And yet she was quitting. You didn't quit this president, he fired *you*. But now, here—Trump bore a stunned and helpless look as he heaped flattery on her during the staged announcement—*he* was being dumped. "Hopefully you'll be coming back sometime," he said lamely, "maybe in a different capacity, you can have your pick . . ."

An Indian American who was the first woman to be elected governor of South Carolina, the forty-six-year-old Haley—who had, prior to Trump's election, expressed only distaste for him—was Ivanka Trump's personal recruit into her father's largely white male White House. Haley's drive, even among the driven, was already a marvel in Republican Party circles. She told Trump she wanted to be secretary of state. In their initial meeting, she proudly proclaimed her great success, and singular experience, in foreign negotiations: she had persuaded the Germans to put a Mercedes-Benz plant in South Carolina. Trump, usually annoyed by people who spoke up for themselves, seemed charmed by her zeal and not at all bothered by her lack of experience. And unlike many of the others he was interviewing for foreign policy posts, Haley wasn't trying to school him. Secretary of state might be a reach for her first job in foreign policy, but Trump was happy to appoint her as ambassador to the UN.

Connoisseurs of political talent enumerated Haley's skills: she was a quick study, she could read a room, she was fast on her feet, and she combined charisma with toughness. What's more, she was a demographic godsend for the GOP, one of the very few party leaders who broke the Republican mold.

By sending her to the UN, Trump had not only given her national standing and instant foreign policy credentials, he had advantageously relocated her to New York, the country's media and finance capital. Political handicappers began to compare Nikki Haley in New York to Richard Nixon in New York. After his defeat in the 1962 California gubernatorial race, Nixon had moved to Manhattan and, in preparation for a future nobody thought he would have, ingratiated himself with the rich and powerful.

Haley, the quick study, mastered the UN and then mastered the social circuit. She was soon on a first-name basis with Wall Street movers and with the city's power-women strata. In an administration where everyone was tainted by Trump, she used her geographic distance from him, and her ease with the mainstream establishment, to become the contrast gainer, the un-Trump administration figure. Curiously, while almost everybody else in Trump's White House spoke bitterly about him, both privately and not so privately, Haley became noted for her restraint. Or, perhaps more pointedly, she seemed to go out of her way not to talk about him. Her political skills were widely noted: for the small circle of Republican leaders and donors actively trying to strategize a future beyond Donald Trump—the Defending Democracy Together group—Haley had become possibility A.

As Haley settled into her high-profile job and quickly found ways to raise that profile even higher, Trump seemed uncertain about what to make of her. Should he be grateful or suspicious? He spent one Mar-a-Lago weekend in the spring of 2018 polling people on whether he should fire her, while at the same time praising her as the only person in his administration to get good press. The latter was also, obviously, a reason to fire her—she was getting too much attention.

On the most basic level, Trump had no game with executive women. In his orbit, women were either functionaries who tended to him—like Hope Hicks in the White House or Rhona Graff, his Trump Organization secretary and aide-de-camp—or arm candy, like his wife and his daughter. He could compare Haley only to . . . himself. He was fascinated by details of her 2010 race for governor, when she survived accusations by two men who said they had been her lovers. Her survival, he judged, was like his own after the pussy-tape catastrophe.

* * *

In the fall of 2017, Trump told multiple confidants that Haley had given him a blow job—his words. What was true here is that this was what he had said; it was a species of his famous locker-room talk. What was far from the case was that what he had said was true, and few around him gave it much credence.

Haley was enraged by reports of a relationship with Trump, adamantly denying that there was any truth whatsoever to this suggestion. In New York, she had become friendly with several high-profile Republican women who were themselves bitterly opposed to Trump. Now, part of their discussions focused on how Haley could avoid the damage that Trump might surely do to her—not only through her association with him, but as a result of his reflexive need to drag down everyone around him.

By the beginning of Trump's second year as president, Haley had settled on her strategy: carefully but persistently, she would declare her independence. Where so many others in the Republican Party had been cowed by Trump, or were resigned to him, or petulant in the face of him, Haley was determined to think beyond him.

In April 2018 Haley came out in the open. She had pushed for new sanctions on Russia for its role in recent Syrian chemical attacks. The president, urged on by Ivanka as well as Haley and others in the administration, signed off on the plan, and Haley announced it on *Face the Nation*. But then the president—ever second-guessing any move that was critical toward Russia—reversed course and insisted that Haley had to take it back. She refused. At the president's instigation, Larry Kudlow, the new White House economic adviser, was sent to make the correction and, in a comment to reporters, put the blame squarely on Haley: "There might have been some momentary confusion about that."

The most basic Trump White House operating rule was that nobody could talk back to the president—ever, in any sense. If you did, or even if it seemed like you wanted to, you instantly became an enemy or nonperson to Trump. So clear was his inability to take any criticism or to participate in any honest argument about policy that the attempt was almost never made. (Even if you believed you had to say no to something Trump was insisting on, you had to say yes and then trust that, given his short attention span and the White House's chronic disorganization, the issue would at some point disappear.) John Kelly, early in his tenure, had missed this memo and suffered endlessly for it. Even Jim Mattis, as he became more and more disaffected, kept a reliable poker face. Mike Pompeo, Trump's most trusted member of the cabinet, settled into a constant grovel.

Haley, like everyone else in the White House, was well aware that

Kudlow had spoken for the president. Yet she quickly delivered a resounding reproof to Kudlow's comment: "With all due respect, I don't get confused." And then she insisted that the White House make Kudlow publicly apologize to her.

Although Trump regularly became irritated by or bored with the people around him, or contemptuous of them, or tired of them, or jealous of them, this was perhaps the first time he seemed to fear one of his own people. "What does she want?" he kept asking friends and advisers. Haley had gotten under his skin, instead of him getting under hers.

Now, in the final weeks of perhaps the most intensely fought midterm elections in history—a bitter contest likely to come down to how many Republican women the party could hold—Haley, the designated queen of Republican women, by resigning for no known reason at the most damaging time imaginable, effectively announced that she no longer stood with the president. It seemed that her express purpose, which Trump was now helpless to counter, was very much to hurt him. Her resignation was hard to read as anything else but a message that said, "Don't vote for him."

If your pitch was to the Republican establishment, if your goal was to return to the mainstream from the lost cause of Trumpism, if your ambition was to be the leader and embodiment of the Republican reformation, then this was how you did it: with steel and grace. This was how you announced you were running for president. This is how you saved yourself from the ignominy suffered by every other ex-Trumper and, to boot, set yourself up to get a multimillion-dollar book deal, and corporate board seats, and rich consulting gigs.

On October 18, nine days after she announced her resignation and less than three weeks before the midterms, Haley headlined the Al Smith Dinner in New York City. "It's amazing how Nikki Haley has exited this administration with such dignity," said the master of ceremonies in his introduction of her to an audience that included New York governor Andrew Cuomo, Mayor Bill de Blasio, former mayor Michael Bloomberg, Senator Chuck Schumer, former secretary of state Henry Kissinger, and the Wall Street financier Stephen Schwarzman. This annual dinner is a showcase for political talent: on display for all to see is your deftness, acuity, charm, and cunning, plus the great admiration the donor class has for you. In 2016, Trump's own turn as headliner at the dinner had been a disaster; unable to joke about himself, he merely dropped stink bombs on Hillary Clinton. Now, Haley, adroitly landing jokes on Trump, presented herself as a kind of presidential Disney princess—generous, embracing, kind, and, as well, pleasantly sharp and funny.

Joking that Trump had offered her advice about what to say at the dinner, Haley commented that he told her to "just brag about my accomplishments." Then, referencing the president's recent and widely criticized performance at the United Nations, she said: "It really killed at the UN, I've got to tell you." She dead-panned that when Trump learned of her Indian background, "he asked me if I was from the same tribe as Elizabeth Warren," the Massachusetts senator whose claims of Native American ancestry he regularly ridiculed. But it was Haley's closing and most pointed rebuke of the president that brought the house down: "In our toxic political environment, I've heard some people in both parties describe their opponents as enemies or evil. In America, our political opponents are *not* evil."

The president, watching the coverage of her performance, seemed uncertain about how he had come off. In calls to friends, he polled them about whether they thought her jokes were funny and remarked on her "department-store gown."

* * *

Bannon was no fan of Haley's. He found her to be a reliable water carrier of Republican establishment pieties—"not an original thought in that head." But he couldn't help admiring her. "She understands what nobody else seems to," said Bannon. "The odds of Trump not making it are very high. So plan accordingly."

Bannon believed that not only did Haley's carefully choreographed departure provide further indication of the problems the party would have with college-educated women on November 6, but that losing Haley was a precursor to the party's loss of just about everyone with an education. This was uncharted territory for an American political party but, reflecting an essential tenet of Trumpist strategy, you nevertheless doubled down on it. "Here we are, the party of the peasants," said Bannon, not unhappily.

Now, Bannon understood, Trump needed his own exogenous event to fire up the base. *Et voilà*: cometh the caravan.

On October 12, a group of more than two hundred Hondurans (estimates seemed to range from two hundred to one thousand) set out from the town of San Pedro Sula, heading for Mexico and the United States. Most claimed to be fleeing lawlessness and gang violence; upon arriving in the United States, they hoped to be granted asylum.

As the caravan began moving north, Bannon flew to Mexico City to address a conference of hedge funders who were brought together every year by Niall Ferguson, the British historian, writer, and conservative commentator. The trip also gave Bannon an opportunity to seek out information about the man who would soon become Mexico's new president, Andrés Manuel López Obrador, a left-wing populist poised to challenge Trump, the right-wing populist. ("A stoic guy, incorruptible, the former mayor of Mexico City," commented Bannon. "Never took a nickel—*first* guy in Mexico never to take a nickel—lives in a tiny little house, fire-breathing populist, the real thing, whose entire campaign is, 'I'm the guy to stand up to Donald Trump.'") One developing aspect of this anticipated face-off was a potential border confrontation, and during his trip to Mexico Bannon was alerted to the gathering caravan and to Mexico's inclination to let it cross its borders.

Bannon, in constant touch with the conservative media, became a primary purveyor of the caravan narrative. To Bannon the story line was perfectly familiar: he was an admirer of the 1973 French right-wing cult classic *The Camp of the Saints*, by Jean Raspail, a xenophobic, end-of-civilization novel in which hundreds of ships ferry third-world immigrants to France. As the ships reach Gibraltar, the French president sends troops south to stop them—to no avail.

The idea behind the caravan was that immigrants traveling en masse were safer than they would be on a lone trek. By yourself or with just your family, you were an easy target for criminal organizations and the police; furthermore, you were too often dependent on unscrupulous smugglers. But significant numbers would provide some security, media attention, some power. They would also provide the conservative media with a seeming onslaught of alarming images on the eve of the midterms.

In the ensuing days, the caravan grew to more than a thousand travelers—or refugees, or invaders, depending on your point of view. Hannity and Fox took formal notice of the caravan on October 13, the president three days later. Trump posted seventeen tweets on October 16, most of them directly on message, from insults aimed at Elizabeth Warren, to warnings about unaccompanied minors at the border, to a continued defense of the Saudi Crown Prince, to a slap at Stormy Daniels, to attacking the FBI and the "Fake dossier." But to this group of familiar targets he now added the caravan.

> The United States has strongly informed the President of Honduras that if the large Caravan of people heading to the U.S. is not stopped and brought back to Honduras, no more money or aid will be given to Honduras, effective immediately!

> We have today informed the countries of Honduras, Guatemala and El Salvador that if they allow their citizens, or others, to journey through their borders and up to the United States, with the intention of entering our country illegally, all payments made to them will STOP (END)!

> Anybody entering the United States illegally will be arrested and detained, prior to being sent back to their country!

Bannon had focused Hannity on the caravan story, and now Hannity had focused the president.

For Trump and his most dedicated confederates there was only one truly reliable issue: illegal immigration. In Trump's short political history, the issue had never failed to inspire and activate core voters.

The caravan was a Trump-Fox-Bannon play. Every other part of the Republican spectrum was all but writing off the party's ability to hold the House. But the Trump-Fox-Bannon alliance held a different view, and their October surprise was to double down on their most potent issue.

The National Republican Congressional Committee and the Congressional Leadership Fund were continuing to put resources into swing-state moderates like Barbara Comstock, a mainstream party favorite in a tight race in Virginia. They behaved as if Trump did not exist and this election cycle continued to be just business as usual. The Trump camp,

meanwhile, was pushing the immigration issue in a way that might alienate even many mainstream Republican voters.

Bannon was unrepentant. "The establishment party has Nikki Haley,
and we have Donald Trump and the caravan—not ideal, perhaps, but you
work with what you have." By now it was obvious that the Democrats would
be turning out in big numbers (early voting had already started in some
states), and Bannon believed that it was critical to boost conservative—or,
more specifically, deplorable—turnout.

The caravan offered only a binary narrative. You could believe the
Trump version of the story: an invasion was headed this way, gaining
strength and violent passion as it progressed, and it was supported by
insidious forces such as George Soros. Or you could see Trump as a desperate propagandizer, with, even for him, a shamelessly flimsy story, one
that was transparent in its efforts to manipulate the dangerous and toxic
emotions of people inclined to regard it as true.

The Trump political team would shortly triple down on its closing
theme with a nationally aired ad so racially charged that even Fox News,
after several airings, declined to run it further. The spot featured Luis Bra-
camontes, a strangely ebullient murderer who laughed dementedly and
boasted about killing cops—more *Saturday Night Live* than a realistic and
threatening figure. Brad Parscale bragged about how cheaply he had produced it; the president was annoyed about not being featured in it.

* * *

Thematically, the president's obsession with the caravan, and the deep
hatreds that provided the issue's subtext, seemed of a piece with two other
October surprises. On October 22, pipe bombs began to be delivered to
people and media organizations that Trump had regularly singled out as
his enemies. Four days later, fifty-six-year-old Cesar Sayoc, a Florida resident, was arrested and charged with mailing the packages. Sayoc, a cultish
follower of the president, seemed to satisfy every anti-Trumper's certainty
and every swing voter's fear of who the ultimate deplorable might be.
With a foreclosed house, bumper stickers such as CNN SUCKS covering the
windows of the white van in which he lived, and a menacing Trump-
devoted social media account, Sayoc seemed to draw a sharp dividing

line, with rational middle-class Americans on one side and bitter MAGA supporters on the other.

Then, on October 27, eleven days before the elections, a gunman opened fire on the Tree of Life synagogue in Pittsburgh during Saturday morning services, killing eleven and injuring seven. The gunman, forty-six-year-old Robert Gregory Bowers, an anti-Semite who was active on social media, had been aroused by the president's talk of the caravan heading to the United States. "I can't sit by and watch my people get slaughtered," Bowers posted shortly before the attack. "Screw your optics, I'm going in."

The central questions of Trump's new politics seemed ever clearer: How far could he push nativist pride and revitalized bigotry? Could he find enough secret, and not so secret, supporters to challenge the liberal idea of a reconstructed modern world? Or was the modern sensibility, the educated sensibility, the multicultural world now ingrained in pop culture, an adequate bulwark against him?

Before Trump's arrival in the political arena, even Republican dog whistles had arguably become less bigoted; the party's political art had instead focused on how to send a class message while being able to deny a racial message. But Trump, first as a candidate and now as president, was behaving in ways that might otherwise have seemed inconceivable and self-defeating for a national American politician. He was inviting himself to be branded a racist. Indeed, this was the question that pursued him: Was he, in fact, a racist?

Everybody asked it. Not just Trump's enemies, but the people closest to him. In a world in which racism had become a catchall of attitudes and behaviors, his allies often made excuses for him. *The liberals call anyone who disagrees with them a racist.* But in the White House itself, staffers debated about what, actually, was in his heart.

Bannon, too, had given the issue considerable thought. Trump probably wasn't an anti-Semite, Bannon concluded. But he was much less confident that Trump wasn't a racist. He had not heard Trump use the N-word but could easily imagine him doing so.

Trump, speaking about his choice of women, had once told Tucker Carlson that he liked a "little chocolate in his diet."

Trump himself told a story about being ridiculed by friends for sleeping with a black woman. But the morning after, he had looked at himself in the mirror and was reassured that nothing had changed—he was still the Trumpster. He offered this anecdote to show that he was not a racist.

That Trump did not forthrightly disavow racism and racists, that he kept leaving open the issue, that it was his daughter who had to personally assure people that, honestly, he wasn't a racist, left it, days before the election, as a rosebud riddle. Was he one?

21

NOVEMBER 6

By election eve, Steve Bannon had been on the road every day for five weeks. "If ever I thought I'd spend a night in Buffalo *and* a night in Staten Island . . ."

When he arrived in Buffalo, two weeks before the election, the local Republicans were set to charge $25 for a picture of a handshake with him at a campaign event.

It was a dismal gathering, men shuffling into a small, dim meeting hall and standing around the coffee urn. These were hardworking union guys—or they once were union guys. They were smokers. Veterans. In work shirts and work boots. They looked like America the way America looked in 1965, said Bannon, sentimental at the sight of his deplorables.

"I'm not going to have these people pay twenty-five bucks for my picture," Bannon told the event organizers. "My parents would go nuts." Instead, he said *he* would pay the local party organization $25 for each picture and handshake.

During that five-week sprint, Bannon had tried to hit many of the key swing districts in the country. He and Trump might not be speaking, but Bannon, at least in his own mind, remained the best soldier in Trump's army. It was practically a meme—pictures of Bannon, in cargo pants and puffer vest, standing up in an endless series of desultory rooms speaking to a handful of people.

He had reduced the field of play to its existential essence. There were forty-three key House races: of those, twenty were hopeless; twenty others were nail-biters, and the Republicans could afford to lose only five of these; three others would likely flip from Democratic to Republican. If everything broke the GOP's way, the Republicans would lose twenty-two seats and thus maintain a one-vote majority. That one vote provided safety for Trump, but if the GOP lost its majority by even one seat, Trump would be in constant peril. Losing thirty or more seats, however, would be the deluge—and, Bannon believed, the effective end of the Trump presidency.

At one point during the final weeks of the campaign, Bannon visited New York City to check in with an old Trump crony who closely monitored the president's state of mind. What would happen, Bannon wondered, if the Republican loss was truly decisive and the new Democratic majority piled on with subpoenas, aggressive investigations, and constant, hostile oversight? Could Trump hold up under that, especially given that he had already fired or frightened away almost everyone who had once provided his support apparatus? "I think he'll kill himself," said Bannon, answering his own question.

"No, no," said Trump's old friend. "He'll fake a heart attack."

Yes, Bannon laughed, that would certainly be the Trump way out.

For Bannon the stakes were obvious: it would be a two-year presidency or a four-year presidency, an indomitable Trump or a vanquished Trump. In this ultimate battle, Bannon sometimes felt like he was a Republican Party—or a Trump Party, or a Bannon Party—of one. The Trump political operation, led by Kushner's surrogate Brad Parscale, was shrugging off the midterms and, in rosy denial, looking toward 2020.

Significantly, almost nobody from the 2016 campaign remained on Trump's political team except Parscale. A freelance web designer from San Antonio, Texas, Parscale had worked for the Trump Organization, designing on-the-cheap websites, for the better part of a decade before the campaign started. He built the campaign's first website, was promoted to digital media director, and then, under Kushner, was given oversight of data targeting and the online fundraising strategy. (Bannon noted that one of Parscale's initiatives during the run-up to the midterms was to commission a poll about whether Trump should use more inclusive language. "Hilarity ensued," said Bannon.) With Parscale as his chief political strategist at one of the most challenging moments in modern political history, Trump had once again chosen lesser over greater expertise.

This left the White House both ill-prepared for the midterm campaign and, in many respects, indifferent if not hostile to it. In Bannon's estimation, the White House was making almost no contribution to the midterm fight. Kelly said it wasn't his job to help, and he was barely speaking to Trump anyway. Bill Shine, the communications director—and now a primary focus of Trump's taunts and complaints—tried not to be seen. The rest of the White House comms shop was in its usual disarray, with Trump happily ignoring it anyway. Don Jr. and his girlfriend Kimberly Guilfoyle were stumping aggressively, but the one person whom Trumpers believed had a shot at holding female voters, Ivanka Trump, was absent and otherwise occupied.

To the extent that the Republican Party had a strategy, it was to spend vast amounts of media money and skip the more challenging ground game. Bannon believed that in tight races the tie was broken by one side's greater passion and its devotion to manning phone banks, walking precincts, and knocking on doors—"he who grinds better wins," in Bannonese. In this election cycle it was the Democrats who were calling and walking and knocking.

"There has never been an organized plan to save the House," said Bannon. "The troops stayed home—there was never a fight, never engagement." With two weeks to go, the Republican leadership's most optimistic calculation was a loss of thirty-five seats.

Trump remained on the road, continuing to fill stadiums wherever the White House believed they could be filled. For Bannon, these rallies had become utterly routinized, already nostalgic, not so much rousing as familiar. But the rallies allowed Trump to stay inside his happy bubble, content with crowds that were ecstatic at the sight of him even as he ignored the polls.

"He has no idea what can happen, no fucking idea," said Bannon. "Totally la-la. He thinks Nancy Pelosi is an annoying elderly lady rather than a steel-tipped bullet aimed directly at him."

* * *

As Election Day approached, Bannon was glum, but he yet believed in the almost totemic power of the Democrats to fuck things up. And, indeed, just as the Democrats were trying to close their sale, their brightest lights were putting on a remarkable display of ego and avarice. Cory Booker and Kamala Harris had traveled to Iowa to kick off presidential campaigns. Bill and Hillary Clinton were on a moneymaking national tour ("a shake-down tour," in Bannon's words). And Elizabeth Warren had tried to prove she was at least a little bit of a Native American with a DNA test, which ultimately proved quite the opposite.

Even so, Bannon was awed by the Democrats' almost flawless organizational game. Republican incumbents and candidates for open seats had, without urgency, raised the standard cost of a House seat campaign: a well-funded run would set you back $1.5 million, give or take. But vast amounts of money—large money and small money, a great green river of despair and hope—had poured into Democratic congressional races. In some tight races, Democratic challengers had raised as much as four times what Republican candidates had raised.

The midterm elections had produced two separate universes of spending and resources. One was business as usual for the Republicans, with most of the money coming from the typical deep pockets; the other was an explosion of Democratic cash, one that was big enough to neutralize incumbency, overcome the effects of gerrymandering, and introduce a large, energetic class of political unknowns.

In fact, the problem was not that the national Republicans didn't have enough money; they had plenty. The problem was that they were spending it in the sky, not on the ground. They were spending it as though this were a normal midterm election campaign, not a uniquely Trump election. By Election Day, the National Republican Congressional Committee and the congressional PACs, along with other outside groups, would spend as much as half a billion dollars on TV ads, a blitz that paid off, Bannon believed, largely for the consultants who placed the ads. What's more, they were spending a large portion of that money on races that were already lost.

"Sheldon," said Bannon, meaning Sheldon Adelson, the casino and hotel owner and biggest contributor to the Republican Party, "should have taken all his money and just burned it in front of the Venetian," his mega casino and resort on the Las Vegas strip.

* * *

On a rooftop just downwind from the Washington bureau of Fox News, with the Capitol dome in the background, the Bannon/Trump-or-no-Trump/Populist-Nationalist Party, as it were, was throwing its election night bash with hundreds of Dean & Deluca sandwiches and countless bottles of microbrewery beers—"and not a populist brand in sight," noted Bannon.

Bannon's idea was to use this party as a teaching opportunity. It would be both a social occasion and an election night war room, with Bannon, on a social media video feed, explaining election numbers and the mechanics of precinct-by-precinct mobilizing to his hoped-for audience of deplorables. For Bannon, this evening wasn't just about the midterms: "After Donald Trump, be that tomorrow or several years from now, the movement still has to get out the vote."

As darkness fell, and with the party now under way, Bannon was trying to sort out both technical and social challenges. He wanted clear video of the Capitol dome, but the camera would need to shoot it through the heavy plastic sheeting shielding the party from a rainy, windy night. What's more, the feeds to the right-wing pundits and sites that would contribute commentary throughout the evening kept disappearing. Then, too, the curious members of the press—along with Bannon's collection of alt-right partisans and far-right European representatives, not to mention friends and family—all wanted face time with Bannon and were disappointed to discover that, beginning at 6:30 p.m., he had taken to the social media air.

For the next six hours, Bannon would stay on his feet conducting something near a rolling monologue. Sam Nunberg took the chair at his side, feeding him numbers and commentary. "No opinions, please," said Bannon as Nunberg kept trying to interject. "Just numbers."

As the first election results began coming in, the mood turned hopeful. Almost immediately, it became apparent that in the night's marquee Senate contest, the race in Texas between incumbent Ted Cruz and upstart Beto O'Rourke, the challenger was not going to pull off his upset, an upset that might well have shattered the Republican Party. The gubernatorial race in Georgia—featuring Stacey Abrams, a Democrat who would be Georgia's first female and first African American governor—also looked good, and here, too, a loss would have badly shaken the party. And in Florida, the gubernatorial race and the Senate race, both of which had recently been leaning to the Democrats, were tilting back.

Earlier in the evening, Bannon had pronounced Barbara Comstock "the barometer of the night." As Comstock in Virginia's Tenth District went, so would go the party. Virginia 10, which takes in a great swatch of the southern D.C. suburbs, is almost 70 percent white and has a moderate Republican tilt. Since 1980, the district had sent a steady stream of Republicans to the House.

Comstock, a fifty-nine-year-old Middlebury and Georgetown Law graduate with three children, was a kind of ideal Yuppie Republican, business- and women-friendly. Living just outside the Beltway, she was, like so many of her constituents, a wholly inside-the-Beltway figure. Her work on Capitol Hill, as congressional aide, lawyer, and PR adviser, was solidly Republican, yet she knew how to partner with Democrats. Now finishing her second term in Congress, Comstock was well liked by her party, though the rap was that she might not be conservative enough. Overall, however, the party considered her a strong candidate in a swing district, and at the cycle's outset her seat had been seen as safe.

In midsummer, however, as the first wave of worrisome polls began to alarm Republicans, Comstock was down by ten points. Her opponent Jennifer Wexton was, like Comstock, a lawyer and local political figure; the only real difference was that Wexton was a moderate Democrat instead of moderate Republican. For much of the campaign, Bannon thought the GOP should write Comstock off and put its resources into more promising battles. But she was a popular figure in the party, and the prevailing establishment view was that if there was a fight to be waged for swing votes, then as a moderate incumbent woman she ought to be waging it and the party ought to be supporting her.

By October, Virginia 10 had become one of the most expensive Republican House races in the country. But in the days before the election, internal polls had Comstock down by only 4 percent—what once seemed a lost race for the Republicans had become an extremely tight one. As November 6 approached, the Virginia 10 numbers were relayed to the president with the message that the party was doing significantly better with swing voters than anticipated. They were coming back, Trump was told.

"With Comstock at a four percent deficit or under, we hold the House," said a high-spirited Bannon soon after his election night party started. "Done deal."

But the Comstock race was one of the first clear House results of the night. The polls in the Tenth District closed at 7:00 p.m.; by 7:40, with 56 percent of votes tallied, including Comstock's strong districts, she was sixteen points down.

Hearing this early result, Bannon turned to Nunberg. "What's that number?" Still imagining that the night could bring spoils and glory, he was skeptical. "Can that be right?"

"Seems like."

"Check."

"I checked."

Standing on the rooftop, the Capitol dome behind him, Bannon's mood swung, as though in a single moment, from spirited to desolate.

* * *

Depressing Bannon almost as much as the Comstock numbers were the reports he was receiving about another party seven minutes away.

In the ceremonial East Room at the White House, the president's staff had staged a mock Election Day barbecue with hamburgers and hot dogs. It was a big-donor event. Sheldon Adelson, worth $34 billion, was there, along with Harold Hamm, the shale oil mogul, worth $13 billion; Steve Schwarzman, the Blackstone CEO, worth $12 billion; Dan Gilbert, the founder of Quicken Loans and owner of several sports franchises, worth

$6 billion; Michael Milken, the former Wall Street trader and junk bond king who went to jail in the early 1990s for insider trading, worth $4 billion; and Ron Cameron, an Arkansas poultry mogul, and Tom Barrack, the Trump friend and real estate mogul who had managed the president's inauguration, each worth a billion. Also attending the party that night was Franklin Graham, the son of the evangelical preacher Billy Graham, who had been uncompromising in his support of Trump, and Betsy DeVos, the only cabinet secretary in attendance (and a billionaire herself). The vice president and his wife were circulating among the guests, and so was Brad Parscale, representing the 2020 campaign and the president's political operation.

Bannon took the White House party almost as a personal slap. His weeks on the road had brought him back to some metaphysical considerations about the soul of America. As he saw it, almost everything was being taken, day by day, from the country's working people—his deplorables—who yet formed some true heart of the nation. Bannon spoke about their "peasant honesty, peasant wisdom, and peasant loyalty," sounding like Tolstoy speaking of the Russian people. After guiding Trump's campaign to victory, Bannon had hoped to bring a new Jacksonian era to the White House; instead, a retinue of the Republican Party's billionaire donor class was eating hamburgers and hot dogs in the East Room.

It was Trump's tragic duality: he needed either the roar of the crowd or the stroking of billionaires. After they won in 2016, Bannon had met with the president-elect and Trump's friend Tom Barrack to discuss the plan for the inauguration. Bannon argued that they ought to underspend by $1.00 the lowest amount ever spent in the modern age on an inauguration. This was a populist presidency, so a no-frills, homemade inauguration ought to be its first symbol. But Barrack spoke about how easy it would be to raise more money than had ever before been raised. Give him two weeks and he could raise $100 million. Give him four weeks and he could raise $400 million. The opportunity was unlimited.

Trump did not struggle very hard with his decision about what approach to take. Bannon, darkly, understood from what corners of the world that money would come.

"That meeting will be played back many times," Bannon predicted. "It set us on the road to perdition. Nothing good could come out of it. You think you don't know what Trump will do, that it's going to be a head-smacking surprise—radical disruption. But, in fact, no. He does what he's programmed to do."

* * *

Bannon saw the midterm battle for the House as a winnable contest. Equally, he saw what was going on in the White House at that very moment, all the donors cheek-by-jowl in the East Room, as part of another fight. This was the most fundamental Trump battle, one that could also be won—but that, right then, might be lost.

For Bannon, China remained everything. It was the key, and the devil was in the details. And Trump got it: "China bad."

Here was a totalitarian state with a government-run economy that through currency manipulation and public subsidies had reoriented the world's supply chain, and, in just half a generation, turned its 1.4 billion citizens into the world's fastest-growing market, bending the West's capital markets and political class to its will. A dominant China, in Bannon's world schematic, meant a declining United States, ever losing its manufacturing base. For people without a college education—many of them Trump voters—manufacturing jobs represented the single most reliable ticket to the middle class. China's exploding middle class was created at the expense of our own by undermining and then transferring the U.S. manufacturing base.

This, Bannon believed, was the fundamental fight inside the Trump administration. If those who understood the Chinese threat won, or even held their own in this epic battle, that's what would be remembered a hundred years from now.

But from the beginning, the first battle inside the administration had been for Trump's limited and shallow attention span. As soon as the needle moved from "China bad" to "China very complicated," Trump would always wander out of the room. Meanwhile, around him, the fight raged on: for Bannon, it was the populists versus the Wall Street crowd. It was a good day's pay for a good day's work versus global capital accumulation. It was fighting an economic war against a formidable economic adversary versus managing decline. Riding the China train to a new global order was quite a profitable activity for capital markets, but it was devastating for the job prospects of American workingmen and -women.

Yet on this battlefield, Bannon argued, they had succeeded. Here was the accomplishment of the past two years: a nation and a policy apparatus that formerly had been either unconcerned about China or resigned to having to accommodate it had turned fiercely on the country. More and more of the establishment now shared Bannon's (and Trump's) core belief: "China bad."

Each Saturday when Bannon was in Washington, Peter Navarro—the anti-China economist Bannon had recruited to the White House in the fight against Kushner's Wall Streeters—bicycled over to Bannon's Embassy and went upstairs to the dining room. There the two men would spend half the day plotting against their free-trade global adversaries. Sitting at Bannon's table, they had hatched the plan to use emergency measures to levy tariffs on steel, aluminum, and technology. And as they had predicted, an unbeatable China soon became an extremely worried China. In relatively short order, they had pushed their adversary back on its heels.

This crucial change of perspective was what the Trump White House had accomplished. Or, more accurately, this is what the small circle of China hawks battling the Trump circle of bankers and banker friends had accomplished.

Yet the battle was far from over. Schwarzman, whose Blackstone Group was heavily invested in Chinese growth—and whom Bannon and Navarro regarded as a virtual Chinese agent—had, because of his relationship with Kushner and because of his billions, enormous sway over Trump. With persuasion and distraction, Schwarzman could almost invariably swing Trump's "China bad" resolve into something like a lack of interest.

"The two Steves," Trump had once said half-jokingly, as though threatening each with the other.

As Bannon stood on his rooftop that night and watched the election map deteriorate, he knew a Democratic takeover of the House would not help his great cause. The Democrats were the party of Goldman Sachs. Goldman Sachs was the investment bank of China. And if Trump needed to save himself from a Democratic Congress, he would surely make a deal with the Chinese, one that would appease Goldman Sachs.

"He will do a huge deal with China," Bannon said, during a break in his broadcast. "The stock market will go through the roof, Schwarzman will love it, and the media will say Trump succeeded. But it will be disaster in the real war that we're fighting."

* * *

The barbecue in the East Room had been under way for more than an hour by the time the president arrived. The early election results were still bringing enough good news to keep the room light and festive. Trump, one guest noted, always more salesman than politician, seemed to have the capacity to focus only on the good news. For the president, the night's limited positive results wholly supplanted the obviously darkening trend.

To one guest, Trump said: "Great night. Fantastic. Wipe out. Crushed. Big majority. Big. Wave? What wave? Red wave. Total red wave." The guest found himself running through a quick, bewildering progression, first thinking the president was serious, then thinking he was being sarcastic, finally realizing that this was his heartfelt conclusion.

In fact, not only did Trump appear determined to see the results the way he wanted to see them, he simply did not have enough information to make a serious evaluation. Distinguishing himself from almost all political professionals, he clearly wasn't interested in the actual data. As usual, numbers bored him.

Even Brad Parscale, the president's political eyes and ears, seemed only marginally more informed, and, hence, remained optimistic. Every other White House would have had better and quicker data than anyone else anywhere, but this White House seemed slow to collect and process the numbers, or uninterested in doing so. It wasn't that Trump was off his game, one of his guests reflected, but rather that he seemed never to have been in it. The night's success or failure would depend on a few dozen House races, but that was small-bore stuff, beyond his focus. He seemed incapable of understanding that this was a night when his presidency might be won or lost.

* * *

"No fucking way!" said Bannon to Sam Nunberg at 9:33 p.m. Eastern Standard Time.

At that bewildering instant Fox News was the first network to call the fight for control of the House of Representatives. The Democrats, said Fox, would win the majority, with all the subpoena, oversight, and investigative power that went with it.

"Stop," said a genuinely perplexed Bannon. "You really got to be shitting me—they're calling this *now*?"

The other news networks were taking their cues from the polling data company Edison Research. Fox was relying on the AP. The projection of a Democratic victory came at a moment when the news still seemed relatively good for the Republicans. It was just past 6:30 on the West Coast. The continuing belief that the GOP still had a fighting chance to win the House might yet encourage Republicans to cast their votes in a series of tight races in the western states.

Bannon ticked off the races in California and elsewhere that were still up for grabs. Of the twenty he had marked as winnable swing races, the polls were still open in twelve. In his estimation, some of these races could be decided by fewer than a thousand votes.

The decision to call the election with as many as ninety minutes of voting time left in some parts of the country had fallen to Lachlan Murdoch, the new CEO of Fox. The younger Murdoch, now trying to circumvent his more conservative father and exert his authority over the company, had approved the early call.

Bannon, standing at his makeshift broadcast desk and trying to calculate the damage that had been done, especially to the tight California races, was astounded. "The Murdochs," he said, "just blew a rocket up Trump's ass."

Bannon saw Fox's early call as a statement, another cautionary note for Trump's future. The rock-ribbed Trump network wouldn't have choked the remaining Rocky Mountain– and Pacific-time votes unless it wanted to.

* * *

For the next four hours, while broadcasting their social media feed, Bannon and Nunberg sorted numbers and precinct reports. Over the course of the evening, they watched most of Bannon's twenty swing races fall to the Democrats.

The night's emerging theme was about as bleak as could be. Any House race the Republicans could lose, they would lose. To hold a contested seat, they needed an absolute lock on a Republican majority. The undecided, the middle of the road, the ambivalent, anyone who did not feel enthusiastic about Donald Trump—by a substantial majority, they all voted for the Democrats, or against the Republicans. It was so bad that when it was all over the Republicans might lose the House by an 8 or 9 percent margin. Bannon sent Nunberg scurrying to find out what historic ceiling might be broken here.

As a measure of voter sentiment, the House results could hardly have been clearer. The electoral map had solidified. In a sense, little had changed from 2016: there was a Trump country and there was an anti-Trump country. Solid red voters were more intransigent, as were solid blues. Rural white voters were implacably for the president; Trump was consolidating his gains and his power in those regions. Urban and suburban voters, forging a new philosophic and political identity based on their passionate opposition to Trump, were expelling from office even holdover Republicans who sought a middle ground. To the extent that there had once been a middle ground, there might be none whatsoever now. But here was the headline fact: the Trump side, however dedicated, was smaller, by a landslide margin, than the anti-Trump side.

By the time election night was over, Bannon felt reasonably certain that the Republicans would gain two seats in the Senate, possibly even three. But this result cheered him not at all, and he waved it away. There was nothing positive here for Trump. Holding the Senate was not a victory but a grim outcome; it meant only that the exact details and timing of Trump's unhappy fate, the precise portion of cruelty and humiliation that it would deliver, would be in Mitch McConnell's hands.

But the House—holding the House had been life or death. Now Bannon was certain. It would be a two-year presidency.

22

SHUTDOWN

On the morning of Wednesday, November 7, Trump made several phone calls to friends. One recipient described his conversation with the president as "eerie stuff—from another world." Trump seemed unaware that the midterms had gone against him and that he was facing an alarming political setback. He seemed to believe—and seemed to take from his other conversations that morning—that politically he had advanced, with the Senate "such a big win."

The friend did not argue otherwise, and he inferred that no one else the president had spoken to did, either. "Big victory, big victory, big victory," said Trump. "This is what we've been waiting for."

The president went on to tell his friend that the "victory plan" was all set. Sessions—"the shithead"—was out. Mueller would be boxed in.

"How far are you going to go?" the friend asked—that is, would the president now try to shut down the special counsel's office?

"All the way," the president answered.

The president also talked confidently about Nancy Pelosi, the likely new Speaker of the House. He told his friend he hoped she would make it and not "get voted out by the rebels." She was going on seventy-nine, he repeated several times. She looked good, he noted, commenting that maintaining her appearance must take a lot of time. Meanwhile, he said, they got along. Got along fine. They had always understood each other.

It would be great if she got to be Speaker again. That's what she wanted. Everybody, he said, was getting what they wanted. And he knew how to handle Nancy. Not a problem. He knew what she wanted. She wanted to look good. "I know how to set it up," said the president.

Now, with the midterms over, he would finally be able to do everything he had wanted to do. "That son-of-a-bitch Kelly's last day is today," Trump said. "His ass is fired." (Kelly, in fact, would remain in place for another month.)

"Everything is going to be different," Trump insisted. "New organization. Totally new."

As the conversation went on, the friend thought it was possible that Trump felt chastened. Maybe, on the day after the disastrous election, he was mentally preparing himself for what was ahead. But the friend understood it was just as possible that the president—still on something of a high after nearly eight straight weeks of often daily stadium rallies—had no clear understanding of what had happened, and no sense at all of what lay ahead.

* * *

On the morning after the midterms, Bannon reminded several members of the original Trump team—those who had entered the White House nearly two years ago, on January 20, 2017—about a meeting that had taken place three days after the inauguration, the first business day of the new Trump administration. This was a traditional postinaugural occasion: the congressional leadership had been invited to meet the president and his staff.

Reince Priebus and Steve Bannon were sitting to the right of the new president. Nancy Pelosi was sitting across from them. Looking at the House minority leader, Bannon felt a shiver go down his spine. He leaned close to Priebus and whispered, "She *so* sees through us."

Pelosi, the professional, was taking stock of the most ill-informed, ill-equipped, ill-prepared team ever to come into the White House. Bannon perceived that she had to exercise maximum restraint not to break down in open incredulity and hilarity. What she seemed to feel was less scorn, Bannon sensed, than pity. She saw the future.

The establishment might have been rocked to its core by the election of Donald Trump. All the powers that be might be contemplating how to resist and ultimately undo the administration of Donald Trump. But Pelosi, Bannon felt, saw the greater truth: the Trump administration would undo itself. No one in the White House, least of all Donald Trump himself, was capable of succeeding at the complicated dance of holding on to power, a much greater challenge than seizing power.

"She was at peace," Bannon recalled. "Because she knew that in two years she would own us. This was not tragedy to her—it was comedy." Hardly a day had gone by since then that he had not thought about how Pelosi had looked at them from across the table.

* * *

The president's main piece of business on November 7 was to finally fire his attorney general, perhaps the man he most reviled in his government, and who most reviled him. He wasted no time: by noon he had accepted Sessions's resignation and posted a perfunctory thank-you tweet.

He also announced the second part of his "victory plan," the appointment of Matthew Whitaker—a loyalist lawyer who had been shunted around the administration and had few supporters other than Trump—as acting AG. Whitaker, with a host of conflicts and an unimpressive legal record, wasn't a popular choice, even in the Republican Senate. Transparently, he was Trump's latest attempt to undermine the Department of Justice and protect himself from the special counsel's investigation. It was the president's all-too-obvious hope that Mueller would deliver his findings to Whitaker, who would sequester the report while giving Trump the opportunity to launch an attack against it.

Whitaker's new role atop the Justice Department was blessed by the Justice Department's Office of Legal Counsel—the same office that had issued the opinion that a president cannot be indicted. The OLC had helpfully declared that the president could install, on an interim basis, without the advice and consent of the Senate, an appointee who could serve for 210 days, or longer if the confirmation for a permanent AG was in progress. Here was Trump's ultimate work-around: finally, he had his personal attorney general.

Soon after Whitaker was appointed, Kellyanne Conway's husband, George, the Wachtell Lipton lawyer, and Neal Katyal, who had served under Obama for a year as acting solicitor general, published an essay in the *New York Times* in which they argued that the Whitaker appointment was unconstitutional. The article was meant to give a considerable boost to any fight that brought the appointment to the courts. It would also give the new Congress ammunition to resist a Mueller challenge.

That day Trump also heard from Sheldon Adelson, the billionaire who was effectively his principal benefactor. For the $113 million Adelson had spent on the midterm elections, he had only one hope: the election of Danny Tarkanian, his handpicked candidate in Nevada's Third Congressional District. But no dice: Tarkanian had gone down in the Democratic wave. In Adelson's view, he had received zero return on his investment.

"Sheldon seems pretty pissed," a not unconcerned Trump told a caller.

* * *

On Friday, November 9, Trump flew to France to participate in ceremonies commemorating the hundredth anniversary of the end of World War I. (His favorite book, he repeated to several people before leaving, was the World War I novel *All Quiet on the Western Front*, which he had read in high school.) During the flight, British prime minister Theresa May called to congratulate him—she had been told in advance that he regarded the midterm elections as a victory. But as though he had begun to understand that "congratulations" was a way to humor him, and might be, in fact, a kind of mockery, he turned on May in a temper tantrum about Brexit, Iran, and her political abilities.

Trump spent much of that flight on the phone, venting his anger about a number of topics. By the time he reached Paris, a secondary wave of calls had begun to spread from several of the people he had been venting to. They rang the alarm bell: his mood was as bad as any they could remember. Everyone, he was saying, had failed him. He couldn't get rid of Mueller. He felt surrounded. There was no way out.

"It's very, very dark—the darkest," said one caller.

In Paris the next morning, Trump was up early, tweeting and trying to defend Whitaker. He was holed up in his bedroom, stuck in his danger-zone mood. There was no one to talk him through this. In his ever-reduced White House, his travel group consisted of people he regarded as assistants or lackeys or fools—sometimes all three. Among them were his body man Jordan Karem, who was already planning to resign; former Trump golf club manager and now White House social media director Dan Scavino; White House personnel director Johnny DeStefano, who, after so many others had left, had transitioned from marginal figure to senior staffer, and was himself on the way out; and senior adviser and immigration hard-liner Stephen Miller, whom Trump described as "autistic" and "sweaty." As for the two senior-most members of his team, Trump was preparing to fire Chief of Staff John Kelly, and he was mostly not speaking to his communications director Bill Shine.

Lacking someone in his entourage who was tactful enough, or bold enough, or trusted enough to advise him otherwise, Trump decided to blow off the symbolic centerpiece of the trip, a ceremony at an American cemetery outside the French capital honoring the U.S. soldiers killed in World War I. The international backlash to his absence—which his staff blamed on bad weather—began almost immediately, sending him into an even deeper spiral of recrimination and despair.

The Trump baby blimp, which had dogged him on his trip to London over the summer, now followed him to Paris, yet another irritation. And on Sunday, Trump attended a ceremony at the Arc de Triomphe, during which French president Macron delivered what Trump took to be a personal dressing down. "Nationalism is a betrayal of patriotism," said Macron in his speech. "By saying, 'Our interests first, who cares about the others,' we erase what a nation holds dearest, what gives it life, what makes it great and what is essential: its moral values."

In an administration characterized principally by Trump's up-and-down mood swings, his forty-three hours in Paris were, in the estimation of friends charting his emotional course, among the most distraught and angry of his presidency. But after two years of nearly constant instability, this was only the beginning of a new, far more unpredictable mental state. And the Democratically controlled House had not even been seated yet.

* * *

The president's extreme mood swings were alarming for almost everyone. His rages were now greater and his coherence more in question; Sean Hannity told Steve Bannon that Trump seemed "totally fucking crazy."

But this new phase was good for Jared and Ivanka. With Trump spending an increasing number of hours away from the West Wing and cut off from his staff—labeled "executive time" on his schedule—his son in-law and daughter were the only staffers in reliably constant contact with him.

In some sense, here was the triumph of their own relentless political battle. They had sidelined the native Trump forces—Bannon, Bossie, Lewandowski, Meadows—and recently quashed a rump move to have either Meadows or Bossie replace John Kelly as chief of staff. Indeed, on the verge of Kelly's ouster, and thus the dismantling of the organizational structure he had tried to impose on the West Wing and on the Trump family, Jared and Ivanka looked forward to installing their handpicked choice, Nick Ayers, currently the vice president's chief of staff.

The president's daughter and son-in-law seemed somehow—to the amazement of the entire Trump administration, as well as establishment Washington itself—to have prevailed over the political professionals. They truly were, as they had so wished themselves to be, the power behind the throne. Their own feelings about this ascension were suffused with suffering and nobility. They had recently decided to leave their Washington house in Kalorama because their neighbors had made them feel so unwelcome; now they would shop for a new one in, they hoped, a more tolerant neighborhood. This was a particularly bitter pill. After all, hadn't they, repeatedly and single-handedly, soothed and restrained the president?

As well, the administration's major piece of legislation in 2018, one of the few bills wholly created and shepherded through Congress by the West Wing, was their brainchild. The First Step Act, a criminal justice reform bill, passed both the House and the Senate in the weeks following the midterms. The fact that this measure seemed to be at almost incomprehensible odds with everything else the Trump administration sought to achieve was just more proof, they believed, that they were unsung heroes.

Jared and Ivanka were also, as they liked to remind friends, the only people who seemed to be able to talk to the president about his political and legal peril. Trump raged at or dismissed everybody else who raised the subject—or he simply walked out of the room. Kushner, in a view the president liked, told Trump that the best defense was to remain in power.

* * *

Kushner, speaking of the president as though he were a high-strung child needing special cossetting and handling, described the rapidly darkening legal and political clouds to a friend as too much for Trump to fully grasp. "He needs discrete issues," said Kushner as, on an almost daily basis, the threats to Trump and his family increased.

Days after the midterms, the New York State Supreme Court had allowed the New York attorney general's lawsuit to proceed against the Trump Foundation, directly targeting the Trump family. The state's newly elected attorney general, Letitia James, had all but run on a platform devoted to attacking Trump and using her office to help bring him down. Here, if not by other avenues, Kushner told the president, was a highway to that holy grail of the Trump tax returns, since a taxpayer's New York State filing was just a mirror of his federal return. Although the IRS imposed high barriers to accessing a return, the barriers were far lower in New York.

The Southern District of New York, meantime, while privately saying it was not coordinating its efforts with the Mueller investigation, was also privately saying that its investigation of the Trump Organization was largely on a "time track" with Mueller's probe—and that it would let the Mueller report come first. Kushner and his lawyer Abbe Lowell had been following this investigation for almost a year. Both Michael Cohen and Allen Weisselberg, the Trump Organization's CFO, were said to be cooperating—Weisselberg, famous for being cheap, had hired his own lawyer. Robert Khuzami, the federal prosecutor handling the case, was telling people that he planned to leave the Southern District by late spring but hoped to wrap up the Trump case first.

Kushner's catalog of the political crisis facing the president in the wake of the loss of his House majority was no less fraught.

Four soon-to-be-seated Democratic chairs of congressional committees now had the president in their sights. New York's Jerry Nadler—who
Trump, during a fight over real estate development in New York in the
1990s, had called a "fat little Jew"—would lead the Judiciary Committee,
which would deal with any impeachment matters. Elijah Cummings's
Committee on Oversight and Reform would focus on what the Democrats
saw as the Trump administration's abuse of various government agencies.
Maxine Waters, whom the president had repeatedly and publicly insulted,
chaired the banking committee; she would be looking into the president's
financial issues, already singling out his tangled relationship with Deutsche Bank. Adam Schiff, who would chair the House Intelligence Committee and was perhaps the biggest publicity hound in the House, would
be directing an investigation of Russia's involvement in the 2016 election.

Four committees trying to take a slice of the same pie was a recipe
for infighting and disarray, but Nancy Pelosi had drafted no less than
Barack Obama to help her maintain discipline among her troops. They
would not lose this battle by acting precipitously. In an ideal world, she
was telling people, it would be the Republicans pushing for a fast resolution of all these matters and the Democrats slow walking the various
investigations.

* * *

Through it all, Jared and Ivanka yet maintained a kind of otherworldly
confidence. It surely helped that their ally Nick Ayers—who, in everybody's estimation, was the best political operative in the White House—
was about to become chief of staff. In the couple's view, Ayers would be
as much their chief of staff as the president's, thus finally bringing the
White House under their direct control.

With John Kelly's departure at last imminent—the announcement
of his resignation was scheduled for Sunday, December 8, and his last
official day would be January 2—Ayers stepped into the job on Wednesday,
December 5. But Ayers's takeover quickly unraveled: on Sunday, having
spent four days working for, as he told a friend, "Mr. Fucking-out-of-his-
mind-totally-crazy," Ayers informed the president that he would not be
taking the job after all. In yet another head-spinning episode of the West

Wing's soap opera, Ayers was quitting before he had officially started. Hence, by Monday there was no Ayers, no Kelly, and no chief of staff.

On Wednesday, December 11—without a chief of staff, and largely absent a communications director, with Trump continuing to shun Bill Shine—the president invited the Democratic leadership to a televised sit-down in the Oval Office. During the meeting, he threatened, even invited, a government shutdown over funding for the Wall. In a matter of minutes, Nancy Pelosi, the incoming Speaker of the House, was, as Trump tried to hector and bait her, transformed before a national audience into his coequal, and into the leader of a resurrected Democratic Party.

Three days later, at his daughter's insistence, the president took two steps in an effort to undo the damage of the previous few days. He accepted budget director Mick Mulvaney's unusual terms for becoming chief of staff: Mulvaney would not become the permanent chief, just the "acting" one, meaning that he would be ready, it was widely interpreted, to bolt at a moment's notice. The following day, Trump walked back his demand for the Wall and his threats of a shutdown.

* * *

On December 19, the Wednesday before Christmas, the president made two fateful decisions. Early that morning—without preparation or consultation, and bypassing the standard military and interagency review process—Trump sent out a tweet proclaiming that "[w]e have defeated ISIS in Syria," and then announced that he was withdrawing all U.S. troops from that country. The military, diplomatic, and intelligence communities had long ago concluded that Trump's views about foreign policy gyrated peculiarly, and dangerously, on the basis of impulses and mood swings. But this was the topper: declaring that defeating ISIS was "my only reason for being [in Syria] during the Trump presidency," the president tweeted out his announcement and thus kept his promise to his isolationist base.

This, finally, was too much for Secretary of Defense Jim Mattis. The next day, Mattis announced his resignation in a letter that delivered a succinct and devastating critique of Trump's damage to the international community. "We must do everything we can to advance an international order that is most conducive to our security, prosperity and values and we are strengthened in this effort by solidarity of our alliances," Mattis wrote. He also refused to employ the usual anodyne language about his decision to resign, writing: "Because you have the right to have a Secretary of Defense whose views are better aligned with yours on these and other subjects, I believe it is right for me to step down from my position." Bannon's mordant prediction after Helsinki—if Trump lost Mattis, he would lose the presidency—was about to be tested.

On that same Wednesday, the president sent Mike Pence to a lunch on Capitol Hill where the vice president gave assurances that Trump would, as he had done every other time a budget had come to his desk, sign a continuing resolution, known on the Hill as a CR. The CR would continue appropriations at the same levels from the prior fiscal year for an additional set period of time—with no Wall funding provided.

Kellyanne Conway began to publicly recast the wall as "border security," and to say the president would find "other ways," beyond the budget, to build the Wall.

To the base, this sounded like "no Wall ever." To Steve Bannon, it sounded like a five-alarm fire, and he immediately went to work. He called Hannity, he called Lewandowski, and, most especially, he called Ann Coulter.

Trump had long admired Ann Coulter's "mouth," as well as—he always made sure to mention—her "hair and legs." The conservative commentator and performer, with her politically incorrect zingers and signature straight blond hair, had, for more than twenty years, been a right-wing cable voice and bestselling author. (In Kellyanne Conway, a right-wing television personality who also had straight blond hair, Trump had gotten, he often said, the poor man's Ann Coulter.) In fact, Coulter's influence had dramatically waned in recent years. She was far too right wing for CNN and MSNBC, and way too unpredictable for Fox. An early Trump supporter, she had, not long into his term, decided that he was selling out the far-right, anti-immigration, nativist, America First cause. Invited to Trump Tower during the transition, she had lectured the president-elect mercilessly, using frequent f-bombs; she was particularly scathing about his "fucking moron idea" to hire his family. And yet because of her sharp tongue, Trump admired her. "She cuts people down—they don't get up," he said about Coulter with awe. "Great, great television." He also credited her with having some kind of mythic connection to his base.

But now that base was buzzing with anger, and Coulter was about to stir up the hive. On the same Wednesday that Pence made his pilgrimage to the Hill, Coulter, at Bannon's instigation, published a column in Breitbart; its headline was GUTLESS PRESIDENT IN WALL-LESS COUNTRY. Later that day, she recorded a podcast with the *Daily Caller*, and near the top of the podcast she said Trump's presidency was "a joke." And the next day she sent out a blistering tweet:

> The chant wasn't "SIGN A BILL WITH B.S. PROMISES ABOUT 'BORDER SECURITY' AT SOME POINT IN THE FUTURE, GUARANTEED TO FAIL!" It was "BUILD A WALL!"

A friend who spoke to Trump that evening was startled by the intensity of the president's reaction. "Honestly, his voice was breaking," said the friend. "Ann really fucked him up. The base, the base. He was completely panicked."

On Friday, December 21, responding directly to Coulter's taunts, Trump abruptly reversed course and refused to accept any compromise on the budget bill because it contained no funding for the Wall. At midnight, the government shut down.

* * *

During the two years Trump had been president, almost any other moment would have been a more propitious time to force a shutdown. In August 2017, as Bannon was leaving the White House, he had argued that the end of the following month presented the ideal opportunity: with a budget vote coinciding with a vote on the debt ceiling, Trump would have maximum leverage. A shutdown would cause the Treasury to run dry—the perfect time, in Bannon's view, for brinkmanship. Instead, the president blinked, and then kicked the can down the road with another CR, expiring in January 2018. This had happened again in February 2018, then again in September 2018, with that CR now running out in December.

Here, with Coulter baiting him, Trump was finally insisting that the Wall be funded. Just at the moment when the Democrats were about to assume power—and, in their singular enmity toward him, just when they were as united as they had ever been—he had drawn a line in the sand. What's more, he had given Nancy Pelosi, now the de facto leader of the Democratic Party and his most direct antagonist, a dramatic platform. In the past, Trump had demonstrated an extraordinary ability to undermine his opponents, to ridicule and reduce them; in this instance, he was doing exactly the opposite. Over the course of ten days, Trump had turned Pelosi into a political giant.

Trump's decision to shut down the government was virtually incomprehensible to both Democrats, who could hardly believe that they had been handed such a favorable opportunity, and Republicans, who could see nothing but a political disaster for the party and a negative outcome for the president. And no one with any parliamentary experience or political acumen could see how Trump would get out of this.

Mitch McConnell, the Senate leader, famous for his iron-fisted control of everything that happened in the Senate, now merely pronounced that he was just a bystander, an observer awaiting developments. He left town for his home in Kentucky.

In the White House, the president, to general surprise, announced that he would not accompany his family to Mar-a-Lago over the holidays—a confounding, even alarming, turn for anyone who knew how much he valued a golf-and-warm-weather opportunity over any presidential business. Melania certainly had no intention of staying behind. Among other issues, friends suggested that she was still furious about his fireside Christmas Eve chat with a seven-year-old boy, during which Trump had asked the boy if he still believed in Santa. "Melania didn't think that was funny," said one aide. Trump was "clearly a guy who had never dealt with a seven-year-old."

For his part, the stay-behind president became obsessed with the Secret Service detail patrolling the White House grounds, finding them perched in trees in "blackface," he reported to callers, with their machine guns pointed at him. He tried to catch their attention, waving from the windows, but they blanked him. "Spooky," he said. "Like I'm a prisoner."

In an empty White House, a young assistant brought his papers up to the residence, finding him, she told friends, in his underwear. And herein, suddenly, was another subplot.

Trump, who had first taken notice of the woman during the transition, kept repeating, "She's got a way about her," his signature, and creepy, stamp of approval for young women. Now the president was telling friends that he wasn't staying at the White House because of the shutdown—he was staying because, as he claimed, he was "banging" the young aide.

Shutdown bravado? Locker-room talk? Or all part of a new alternative reality that only he seemed to be living in?

23

THE WALL

After the holidays, the House came under Democratic control and the shutdown dragged on. Jared and Ivanka believed that, out of the shutdown, and as part of some new balance in government, there could emerge a grand bargain on the Wall and immigration, including on DACA—Deferred Action for Childhood Arrivals—and the road to amnesty. They seemed to see this imagined resolution as the very basis of a new political equanimity.

Bannon was incredulous. Even more important to the base than the Wall was not bending on DACA or amnesty. Fighting amnesty was the lifeblood of the movement. Besides, the new Congress would not give Trump the Wall even if the White House *could* bend on amnesty—which it absolutely could not, unless it wanted to commit ritual suicide.

To Bannon, therefore, there was only one way out, other than capitulation. The tariffs on China tested little-known and seldom-used unilateral powers of the president. Now, by aggressively using further unilateral powers, the president could emerge from the humiliating corner he had put himself in: he could announce that the government would reopen and, by declaring a national emergency, he could direct the army to build the Wall. Or anyway, facing inevitable challenges, he could fight this battle in the courts rather than caving on the issue in Congress.

"It's not pretty," said Bannon. But it was a solution.

The national emergency rump group—plotting the politics of the move and applying pressure to Trump—consisted of Bannon, Lewandowski, Bossie, and Meadows, who began meeting at the Embassy during the first week of January. The group's pitch was simple: there was no alternative. True, the declaration of a national emergency would be challenged in court—and, yes, the Wall would likely never be built—but here would be a show of strength rather than weakness. This strategy was not so much about finding a way to build the Wall, the four men understood. It was about finding a way out of the shutdown mess—a mess, they acknowledged, that was purely of the president's own making.

The counterargument, coming exclusively from Trump's daughter and son-in-law, was that the Democrats would negotiate. This notion was risible on the face of it, and, as had happened so often over the past two years, none of the men took the couple's plan seriously.

When the president, beleaguered and confused, was presented with the rump group's strategy, he seemed to regain his confidence. The idea of declaring a national emergency had immediate appeal. He began describing the declaration as "this power that I have," as though it were magical.

Trump liked the idea so much that he decided to announce the national emergency in an address to the nation from the Oval Office on January 8. Bannon was skeptical. He warned against both the format and the venue, and said Trump would be judged—and not favorably—against his presidential peers, each memorialized by the Oval Office proscenium. But that, of course, was why Trump was so insistent about announcing it this way: he wanted to show everybody that he was one of them. The border crisis, he declared, was like the Cuban Missile Crisis, when John F. Kennedy faced down the Russians and addressed the nation from the Oval Office.

Well, Bannon thought, at least the president was trying to seize the day. Even if Trump sniffed oddly, as he tended to do when he read from a teleprompter, and even if, in a formal setting, he could never quite match his expression to his words, and even if the stage lights magnified the orange of his hair, the declaration of a national emergency would, Bannon hoped, help him appear to be presidential.

The president's nine-minute speech astonished Bannon as much as anyone. In the hours, and possibly minutes, before Trump delivered the address, it had been entirely recast by Jared and Ivanka. The national emergency disappeared; in its place was a "humanitarian crisis," quite changing the constitutional implications and the political argument of a national emergency. Whatever political advantages Trump offered as counterpuncher, as a strongman, as the buck-and-shock-the-system guy, they weren't here. The speech was, to Bannon, a bad remake of *One Flew Over the Cuckoo's Nest*. Ivanka, improbably playing Nurse Ratched, had subdued her patient.

From this solemn and august pulpit, all the more meaningful in that this was his first Oval Office address, Trump delivered, in one of Bannon's signature expressions, "a nothing burger." He was hunched over, constrained, small—and as the camera moved in, his eyes appeared to become ever tinier. He was a great actor in a belittling role.

No national emergency, no solution, no offer, no progress. Trump was, for the entire nation to see, trapped.

* * *

Mitch McConnell, Bannon observed, had completely distanced himself from the president's standoff with Congress. With no end to the shutdown in sight, McConnell was spending his time and influence trying to convince Mike Pompeo to run for what would be an open Senate seat in Kansas in 2020.

Ever the chess player, McConnell wanted to remain at a remove from the shutdown until there was a deal to be made—and, a not inconsiderable benefit, he wanted to let Trump hang himself. But Bannon believed he also had a second agenda: McConnell, in concert with other Republican leaders and donors—the Defending Democracy Together group already polling for 2020—was trying to get Pompeo out of the way to clear the path for Nikki Haley to be the Republican presidential nominee. Bannon knew that among powerful Republicans it was fast becoming a a best-case scenario that Trump would not be a candidate in the next cycle. But the fear was that by the winter of 2020 Trump would be a mortally wounded figure, with no one of sufficient stature positioned to either challenge him or take over the ticket. Nobody seemed to regard Mike Pence as a reasonable option, even were he to become, in the next year, the default president. The only practical candidate for a party that, under Trump, had almost entirely forsaken the suburbs and college-educated women nationwide was Nikki Haley.

Bannon, meanwhile, was preoccupied with his own chess game. So far, he had appeared five times before the special counsel. (Some Bannon enemies whispered that he had actually had eight sessions.) He had not been called before the grand jury, which might mean that he was a subject or even a target of the Mueller investigation. Emails from the fall of 2016 could be construed to connect him to Roger Stone and Stone's apparent involvement in what seemed like a push by the Trump campaign to ensure the release of hacked material from the Democratic National Committee. Bannon had shooed Stone away, but Stone was another of the Trump denizens who tainted everybody else.

Bannon still could not believe there could be a Russian conspiracy case if it hinged on Stone, an unstable fabulist, one of the many around Trump. Stone began his career as a Nixon hanger-on and then turned, briefly, into a successful 1980s-style international lobbyist and fixer in partnership with Paul Manafort, before a sex scandal in the '90s drove him into caricature and self-parody. He now personified the combination of fanatical lunacy and personal self-interest—he was always selling some book or product—that seemed to more and more exist at the edges of modern politics. Indeed, he was Trumpian, but even more so, often leading Trump to brand him as a nuisance and a nutter. It certainly would be an odd kind of justice, Bannon thought, if the case against the president came down to Stone, Julian Assange, and Jerome Corsi—crazies, conspiracists, bullshit artists, and fringe players all.

Corsi, a right-wing gadfly who had recently become a figure in the investigation, connecting Stone to WikiLeaks and Assange, had once spearheaded the rumors that Breitbart News founder Andrew Breitbart, who died in 2012 from a heart attack, had been assassinated—and that Bannon, in cahoots with the CIA, was involved. (A raging Bannon had confronted Corsi: "I will shit down your neck if you don't stop this. Andrew has a widow and four children. Do not keep saying he was murdered. He wasn't.") Bannon now found it laughable that Corsi might have played a significant role in any sort of actual plot. Likewise, Bannon could hardly believe that Paul Manafort had suddenly become, once more, a linchpin, with the smoking-gun suggestion that he had passed Trump campaign polling data to the Russians. ("The only polling the Trump campaign did was bullshit polling," observed Bannon.)

And yet the small-time-crooks nature of the cast did not change the fact Trump that "was forever giving crazy guys crazy orders," said Bannon, "which he would forget as quickly as he had given them." This might be chicken shit rather than collusion, but in a sense it was just as damning to find the president so hopelessly mired in chicken shit.

In the New York investigations, the key to pick the lock could well be the investigation of the Trump charity, which could implicate the entire family. If it came to that, Trump, as human as anyone, would want to protect his children; even Trump might have to fall on his sword. And beyond the family charity, there was the RICO investigation in New York, which could easily bring about Trump's personal financial destruction— all those loan applications, all that potential banking fraud.

"This is where it isn't a witch hunt—even for the hard core, this is where he turns into just a crooked business guy, and one worth fifty million dollars instead of ten billion dollars," said Bannon, ever on the edge of disgust. "Not the billionaire he said he was, just another scumbag."

For Bannon, then, whether Mueller or the Southern District of New York or the Democrats or Trump's own "psycho" actions provided the engine of destruction, the odds of the president going down remained as great as ever—"and not," said Bannon, "in a blaze of glory."

* * *

Bannon's most urgent internal debate, however, was not about whether the president would go down. It was about when and how he would break with Trump—and save the movement for which Trump, in Bannon's eyes, had never been more than vehicle and agent. He had, he insisted, always seen this moment coming: "Of course, it was obvious from the beginning that the real challenge would be to get this movement past Trump."

And yet, even as Bannon considered his break with Trump, he considered the opposite, too. Trump's misfortune had always been Bannon's opportunity. When, in August 2016, Trump's campaign was flat on its back, Trump had turned it over to Bannon, no questions asked. "He was totally malleable. I did everything I wanted—everything."

Now a similar moment had arrived. Trump was at the bottom without options. Bannon started to poll people. "If they ask me to go back in, should I? Would that be insane? Do you think I could save him, given absolute freedom?"

He was already gaming out the rescue. Not long after Trump delivered his Oval Office address, Bannon sat at his table in the Embassy and described his plan. "Here's the way out of here. It's as plain as day. In the State of the Union, you lay out the case for the national security emergency. You announce, *I am notifying the Joint Chiefs tonight that we are militarizing the border tomorrow morning.* And then you welcome the impeachment process. Bring it on, because Stormy Daniels, obstruction, and Russia are now small potatoes. Now they can impeach him for what they really hate him for—trying to change the system. I mean, would you rather be impeached for trying to overthrow the establishment or for paying Stormy Daniels for a blow job?"

But Bannon's plan was upended almost as soon as it was hatched. On January 16, Nancy Pelosi disinvited Trump from delivering the State of the Union in the House chamber later that month, saying that the address should be postponed until the government reopened. With the greatest élan, she took away the president's platform before Congress and the nation.

Bannon was full of awe. "Even the guys on the right respect her now. How could they not? She's crushed this motherfucker."

* * *

Over the next few days, Jared and Ivanka convinced the president that a group of Democratic senators would join the Republican majority and vote out a compromise bill that would contain, in language that always seemed to soothe Trump, a "substantial down payment for the wall." Cory

Booker was in. So was Bob Menendez. Even Chuck Schumer. But this was delusion: there was no break in the Democratic ranks, far from it.

The shutdown—now the longest in American history—continued, with most polls blaming, by dramatic margins, the president and his party for the disaster. Finally, on January 25, thirty-five days in, Trump capitulated on all issues and signed legislation that temporarily reopened the government, claiming that the bill "was in no way a concession." For the next twenty-one days, the government would be funded while congressional negotiators tried to work out a deal on border security, though the Democrats immediately drew a red line, declaring they would reject any deal that contained funds for the building of a physical wall.

The corner in which Trump had trapped himself required something that nobody believed he could summon: a political master stroke. He was once again in a familiar fix. He wanted what he wanted but lacked any clear understanding of how to get it. The Wall—to which he had sworn absolute commitment, unmindful of its logistical and political complications, and then, over the past two years, quite neglected—was now hung hopelessly around his neck.

Flailing, Trump declared that if the budget negotiations continued to go nowhere, he would close the government again, an option no one believed the rest of his party would ever accept. He was left with only the same threat he had been issuing, and then beating a hasty retreat from, for more than a month: he would use emergency powers to build the Wall. But his turnarounds had already undermined the nature of the emergency—he had sacrificed both logic and high ground. The Republican leadership warned that any declaration of a national emergency might well be overturned by a congressional majority—in which case he would have to veto a bill supported by some in his own party. Whatever the outcome, he certainly would not be endearing himself to fellow Republicans.

Bad went to worse; one rebuke followed another. On January 29, the director of the CIA, Gina Haspel, the director of the FBI, Christopher Wray, and the director of National Intelligence, Dan Coats—each of them Trump appointments—went to Capitol Hill and said, in effect, that the president had no idea what he was talking about in his assessments of threats against the United States. Never before had intelligence chiefs so publicly contradicted a president. Trump was living, they seemed to say, in another reality.

In early February, Senate Republicans, en masse, broke with Trump and opposed his plan to remove troops from Syria. Since retaking the House, the Democrats had been proclaiming Congress as a coequal branch of government with the White House. Now the Republicans were making the same point.

The Southern District of New York, its RICO case unfolding, leaked word that it was interviewing Trump Organization executives. And federal prosecutors in New York suddenly issued a new, wide-ranging subpoena relating to the funds that Trump's inaugural committee had raised and spent, meaning the feds were now following Bannon's certain road to perdition.

The president, listening to Kushner, continued to somehow believe that the Democrats would yet offer him a face-saving deal. Chuck Schumer, he kept saying, was someone he could talk to.

Lou Dobbs, a mainstay of Trump support and philosophy, told Bannon he could not believe how delusional Trump had become.

* * *

Three days after the shutdown ended, Nancy Pelosi invited the president to deliver the State of the Union on February 5. In the days before the address, Jared and Ivanka's allies began to leak reports that Trump would deliver a "unity" speech. This was part of the continuing Kushner plan to cultivate a new atmosphere and a new "cordiality," he told confidants, with Democrats. Kushner was even suggesting that Trump might pivot from the Republicans and make several key deals with Democrats—on infrastructure, on drug pricing, and on Kushner's fond notion of a far-reaching immigration reform bill.

Just as he had been from the beginning of his presidency, a fundamentally self-obsessed and otherwise uninterested Trump was willing to accede to his daughter and son-in-law's desire for establishment status. At the same time, he was—and he usually, if not always, understood this—utterly dependent on his hard-core supporters' belief that he stood for what they stood for. He would reliably tilt back and forth between these divergent poles, but by what degree depended on the hour of the day.

A few days before the State of the Union, Bannon was in New York having breakfast with one of Trump's old friends. The discussion was, with a sense of growing urgency, about the fate of Donald Trump.

"I think he'll revert back to us," said Bannon, predicting the tenor and thrust of the State of the Union speech. "He's a vaudeville actor. He can't lose his audience. He can read a room." But Bannon also understood that Trump was now operating in a world of quickly diminishing returns. "The whole apparatus is cutting him loose," he observed.

Trump's old friend, enumerating all the ongoing investigations and anticipating an eventual endgame, wondered, "Who does he negotiate with? How does he step down?"

"Well, he won't go out classy," answered Bannon. "Nixon was classy even though he was Nixon—and he was smart. We don't have smart and we don't have classy. If you think about it, American history doesn't have that many unseemly moments. Even bad guys, looking at the end, take their medicine. This is not going to be like that. This is going to be very . . . unseemly."

"Romney? Maybe it's Romney who goes to him," said the friend about the former presidential candidate who had recently been elected to the Senate. "Or McConnell?"

"Romney—hated," said Bannon. "Mitch? Hated, too, but Mitch is a deal guy. You can't go to Trump and walk him through a process. You've got to go to him with a deal; the only way Trump leaves is with a release. DOJ, State AG, Labor Department, all the RICO stuff, no prison time— and he keeps all his money. It's got to be clean."

"Not going to happen," said the friend. "There's no clean deal. Nobody to give him one. So, okay, it's got to be Ivanka and Jared who go to him. Like Julie and David Eisenhower, who went to Nixon."

"David Eisenhower was Eisenhower's grandson," said Bannon. "Jared and Ivanka are coming from very different stock. They are grifters"—a word that Bannon had been using since the early days of the administration, introducing it into the modern political lexicon. "They understand that if he's out, the grift is over. The grift only keeps going as long as he's around. That's the scam. That's how they get their phone calls returned from Apple, that's how she gets her trademarks from the Chinese. Come on, they are nothing burgers. If he's gone, nobody's gonna rally around them. What, Jared and Ivanka will keep Camelot alive?"

* * *

After two years in the White House, Trump still had no speechwriters. When preparing for the State of the Union, the president's staff farmed out much of the writing to Newt Gingrich and his people. Other parts of the job were managed by Jared and Ivanka, although neither actually wrote; instead, they threw out strategic thoughts. Stephen Miller played a role, too, but he wrote only in PowerPoint and was, to say the least, a limited wordsmith. Also involved were Lewandowski and Bossie, who had, between them, written two books—even though, practically speaking, neither of them had done any of the writing.

This was the team. The early drafts of the speech were so flowery that Trump could barely make his way through them. He couldn't follow the abstract messaging and stumbled over the wordy, warm-tummy unity stuff.

On the night of the speech, the president was, strangely, unaccompanied in the limousine from the White House to the Capitol. The staging that evening was telling as well. White House staffers traditionally wait backstage as the president speaks, but Jared and Ivanka—now reverting to family status—joined Don Jr., Eric, Tiffany, and Melania (absent Barron) in pride-of-place guest seating.

Bannon, getting ready to watch the speech in New York—"I usually hate watching this stuff, so cringe-worthy"—was cautiously optimistic. He had been slipped pieces of the final text and said, with considerable satisfaction, "Unity is off the table."

The address went on for a long hour and twenty minutes, often sounding rather like the result of a high school assignment to write a State of the Union speech. The president divided his time almost evenly between bland words about the importance of accommodating different points of view and an implacable throw down. Warming to his favorite topics, he offered a surly censure to the threat of oncoming investigations. He renewed his expostulations about the Wall and his promise that he would build it. And the immigrant hordes, he said, were once again heading in our direction.

"There it is," said Bannon. "That's the headline. Come on. Where else do you go? If you put yourself in a corner, you've got to be ready to come charging out of it. How many times can you announce that you'll take nothing less than a big, beautiful Wall—and then take less?"

Politics favors the nimble. If the worst goes down, you need to have another card to play. But here was Trump, his hands empty

* * *

"If you put Trump in the Republican Senate caucus and turned out the lights and counted to ten, he'd be dead," said one Trump ally. The Republican Party, feeling both sorry for itself and ashamed, was also out of cards.

The twenty-one-day negotiating period was almost over, and the new shutdown clock ticked toward February 15. The Senate and House conferees were hard at work; they evinced little doubt that they would accomplish their task and showed limited concern for the White House's reaction. The president would agree or the Congress would vote without his support and overrule him if he attempted a veto. Jared Kushner was happily telling people that everything was under control. No worries: the government would not close down and the Wall would not be funded. All good, everybody on board.

Except: the man who had spent his life making his personal brand about winning was now losing. Calling more attention to his loss, Trump showed up for a rally at the U.S.-Mexico border and insisted that the Wall would be built, that in fact it *was* being built. Look, over there, do you see it?

Back in Washington, Kushner continued to provide assurances that his father-in-law would take the negotiated deal, which was now less advantageous to the president than what had been on the table before the shutdown. They would revert to the old language; the new bill would make a "down payment" on some kind of barrier at the border. "He'll go for that," said Kushner.

But hostile armies surrounded him. On one side, Trump faced a majority of the electorate that believed he had abused his high office and soiled the country, its views ever hardening. On another, he faced, only days or weeks away, an array of investigations that were now set to enumerate his crimes and overwhelm his presidency. On the third, he faced a brewing rebellion by his own party, if not its open contempt. And on the fourth, he faced a Democratic House majority that was effectively pledged to his destruction. Could he escape yet again?

* * *

On February 14, William P. Barr was sworn in as attorney general. Among other duties, it was now his job to oversee the federal prosecutors and grand juries investigating the president. Barr replaced Matthew Whitaker, Trump's hand-picked acting attorney general. In the days after Whitaker's appointment, Mitch McConnell had let the president know that his plan to bypass Senate approval wouldn't work. Trump needed to nominate someone acceptable to the Republican majority—and he had to do it within weeks, not months.

The GOP leadership was anticipating that the attorney general would need to be a broker between the DOJ investigations, including Mueller's, and the president. Looking further down the road, the attorney general was a likely point person in the complex and very delicate negotiations that might need to be conducted with the president to avoid a constitutional crisis.

Bill Barr was McConnell's suggestion. He was a safe choice: Barr had served once before as attorney general, from 1991 to 1993 under President George H.W. Bush. He was embraced by Pat Cipollone, the White House counsel, and even by the president's lawyer Rudy Giuliani, suggesting something of a consensus about the way things might need to go if, in fact, push came to shove.

Barr was sold to the president as a respected attorney who had a record of believing in a strong executive. He had publicly expressed misgivings about the Mueller investigation, especially its emphasis on obstruction of justice. In June 2018, Barr had stated his opinion in an unsolicited memo to the Justice Department; the memo struck many legal observers as little better than an effort by a first-year law student, its purpose solely to curry favor with the president.

But in a larger sense, Trump had missed the point. What Barr represented was the establishment view. He was not only a Republican fixture and a Bush-family loyalist, he had worked for the CIA and had long-standing ties to the intelligence community. All these details were gently obscured when describing his bona fides to the president.

Barr, meanwhile, was telling friends that he was looking for a payday. If he somehow succeeded in navigating this combustible situation—an unpredictable and possibly unstable president, an uncompromising Democratic House majority, and an unhappy Republican leadership—and at the same time managed to satisfy some ineffable GOP establishment ideal, there were many, many future millions in it for him.

Barr's mandate was to avoid both a constitutional conflagration and the destruction of the Republican Party. In Barr's view, a successful navigation past a naked showdown with Donald Trump ought to yield a big payday—one he would deserve.

* * *

Trump spent the night of February 14 making calls. Trying to talk his way out of his corner, he rehashed the serial disasters of the past few weeks.

Nobody was defending him, he bitterly complained. Nobody was out there on his behalf. The Feds were making Weisselberg talk, he declared with great agitation. Michael Cohen was the puppet of the Clintons; Jared had prevented him from making his stand on the Wall. And by the way, he said, it was a done deal—Jared would be indicted. That's what he was hearing.

So here was an idea: What if he pardoned everybody? Everybody! For the good of the country! He returned once again to the magic of his pardon powers. "I could pardon El Chapo," he said.

All of the Democrats were weak, he said with sudden determination. Weak! He could destroy them all. But Mitch was fucking him. What a fucking snake McConnell was.

He had another bold idea, too: a new vice president. Boom! Pence goes out the door. Fresh blood. Big. Surprise. "Probably have to pick Nikki Haley," he added, a bit more glumly.

He knew he was going to get killed on the national emergency. But what else could he do? He had to do it. Should he do it? He had to. The Wall, the Wall, the Wall. The fucking Wall.

"He's like a deer that's been shot," said a surfeited Bannon.

The next morning, panicked, irrational, stuck in the loop of his own stream of consciousness—more, it seemed, just to get it over with, since the fun was now gone—he declared his national emergency.

Epilogue

THE REPORT

After January 3, when the new Democratic majority in the House was seated, every day was a possible or even likely day for the delivery of the special counsel's report on his investigation of the president. Weeks went by, yet there was still no sign of the report; by late February, its already magical properties as a potential game changer and Trump killer seemed compounded beyond all reason. Many felt the delay must mean that Robert Mueller had found a bottomless landfill of misdeeds, forcing him to dig ever deeper into the dark character and twisted dealings of Donald Trump.

For Trumpers, the fact that the report remained undelivered sat uneasily in the pit of their stomachs, their sense of foreboding increasing as time went by. A telling gauge was Jared Kushner's lawyer Abbe Lowell. For months, Lowell had been saying with absolute certainty that his client was safe—that he had gotten him off—but now Lowell appeared to have gone to ground. The silence seemed eerie.

Kushner, meanwhile, was painting a grim scenario. Even if, in the absolute best case, no high campaign officials—Kushner himself, Flynn, Manafort, Donald Trump Jr., not inconceivably even the president—were indicted for conspiracy, they could almost certainly expect a devastating critique of the campaign's careless conduct and its casual willingness, if not eagerness, to accept Russian help. Mueller's report was equally likely to enumerate, in painful detail, the Trump family's craven pursuit of its own interests during the campaign. As for obstruction, Kushner was yet hoping he would escape, but he assumed that his brother-in-law, Don Jr., would not, and that the president would, at the very least, be named as an unindicted coconspirator. Even without indictments, the report would weave a damning narrative bearing directly on Donald Trump's fitness to be president.

Where you were when the report was delivered would, Steve Bannon had begun to think, rank up there in a historic context with where you were when 9/11 happened. Here was, after all, a systematic review of the Trump presidency. Here would be Donald Trump reduced to existential essence. In a way, the judgment that Donald Trump had avoided all his life was finally to be rendered. And no one, least of all Bannon, believed that Trump would be found to be anything but Trump.

The runaway train was about to hit the wall.

The wings were about to come off the aircraft.

* * *

But where was the report?

In fact, it was all but complete by early January. Most members of Mueller's staff were already planning their exits. The once collegial mood among the nineteen attorneys who had worked on the investigation had turned, at best, sullen. Two years of investigation and internal debate had reduced the special counsel's broad mandate to a prudent, carefully defined pair of issues. Had the president or members of his inner circle conspired with Russian state agents to influence the 2016 U.S. presidential election? And if that "predicate event" did not occur, could the president—no matter how determined his attempts to disrupt the investigation of him—be fairly accused of obstructing justice?

Bob Mueller did not want to file his report with Matthew Whitaker, the acting attorney general. He decided to wait for William Barr, the president's nominee for attorney general, to be confirmed and seated. Shortly after Barr took up his new post on February 14, he conveyed his view that the protocol was for the attorney general to request the report from the special counsel—and he wasn't yet requesting it. Barr did not want the report until after the president held his summit with the North Koreans in Vietnam at the end of February. He might not ask for it, in fact, until after the planned summit with President Xi of China at the end of March.

The consideration here was the new attorney general's desire to put the nation's critical business first. But the reality was, too, that Barr was bracing himself and looking to get situated in his new office before facing the anticipated Mueller explosion.

On Capitol Hill, breathless anticipation was turning to frustration and irritation. On March 4, the House Judiciary Committee ran out of patience and decided to issue information requests to eighty-one individuals and organizations. The committee would begin its own investigation without further delay.

The move by the Judiciary Committee, with the clear message that the Democratic House was now setting its own timetable, forced Barr's hand. On March 5, the attorney general and the special counsel conferred, with Mueller spelling out his report's conclusions.

On March 14, the prospective Trump-Xi summit at Mar-a-Lago was postponed. The attorney general then officially requested the report by the end of the following week: the hard deadline was now Friday, March 22.

That same day, the fourteenth, Andrew Weissmann, Bob Mueller's key deputy, announced that he was leaving the special counsel's office. Weissmann had promised to see the investigation through to the end. But now, bitterly disappointed, he would tell friends, by how narrowly Mueller had come to focus the scope of the investigation, he wanted to stay not a moment longer.

* * *

Robert Mueller, the stoic marine, had revealed himself over the course of the nearly two-year investigation to his colleagues and staff to be quite a Hamlet figure. Or, less dramatically, a cautious and indecisive bureaucrat. He had repeatedly traveled between a desire to use his full authority against Donald Trump and the nagging belief that he had no such authority. He could be, he knew, the corrective to the louche and corrupt president; at the same time, he asked himself, what right did he have to correct the country's duly elected leader? On the one hand, you could indict the president for acting as if he were above the law; the secret draft indictment outlining the president's casual abuses had been on Mueller's desk for almost a year. On the other hand, a reasonable man might, in certain nuanced ways, see aspects of the presidency as indeed above the law.

In some sense, here was an unintended result of the exceptional silence of the special counsel's office: it had lived entirely inside its own head. Setting itself apart from public discussion, it had come to dwell in its own ambivalence—or Bob Mueller's ambivalence. For the special counsel, doing the right thing became doing as little as possible.

Mueller let it be known that as concerned as he was with Donald Trump, he was equally concerned with Ken Starr, the independent counsel who investigated Bill Clinton. As Mueller kept reminding his staff, there were substantial differences between a special counsel and independent counsel. The special counsel's office was not independent: it worked directly for the Justice Department. Moreover, Mueller believed that Starr, with his leaky office, agenda-driven investigation, and visceral hatred of Bill Clinton, had undermined the office of the presidency.

Ken Starr had forced Bill Clinton to testify before the grand jury. Deciding whether to subpoena the president became perhaps the central fault line in the Mueller investigation—and when the special counsel decided *not* to subpoena the president, he overrode the will of much of his staff. Here, part of Mueller's analysis was not just about the special counsel's limited authority; it was also a recognition on his part that it would somehow not be a fair fight to make the president testify, because Trump would surely incriminate himself.

In a way, Robert Mueller had come to accept the dialectical premise of Donald Trump—that Trump is Trump. It was circular reasoning to hold the president's essential character against him. Put another way, confronted by Donald Trump, Bob Mueller threw up his hands. Surprisingly, he found himself in agreement with the greater White House: Donald Trump was the president, and, for better or for worse, what you saw was what you got—and what the country voted for.

* * *

But the president did not know any of this yet. A heads-up about the contents of the report was reaching some in the White House, but there was a careful effort to keep this intelligence from the uncontainable president, lest his celebrations begin before the process was complete. He remained, in the same description offered by three different allies, "batshit crazy" right up until the end. His tweeting, always barely under control, reached obsessive-compulsive levels during the weekend before the report's deadline, his mental agitation on vivid display. And yet he remained convinced that he was going to prevail, or, anyway, that Bob Mueller did not have the guts to stand up to him. His enemies might have elevated Mueller to a hero, but Trump still regarded him as a zero.

Curiously, in the days leading up to the formal delivery of the report, one of the people with whom the president frequently spoke was his old friend and campaign contributor Robert Kraft, the owner of the New England Patriots. In February, Kraft had been charged with soliciting a prostitute while visiting a massage parlor in Palm Beach, Florida.

Trump seemed to find comfort in counseling his friend on his legal peril, offering him copious amounts of advice and maintaining that he was much better at this than any lawyer. He knew what to do. He knew how to handle it. They always wanted you to plead out. But don't give an inch. "You're innocent," he said, even though the police claim they have Kraft on a video tape at the massage parlor.

* * *

At the close of business on March 22, the Mueller report was at last delivered. The grand jury, sitting on this Friday, issued no indictments, and the special counsel's office confirmed that its investigation would not yield any new indictments.

It was unclear how long or how involved the report was. It was unclear how much of the work product of the twenty-two-month effort had been sent to the attorney general. But almost immediately after accepting the report, Attorney General Barr wrote a letter to Congress expressing confidence that he could quickly provide a summary of the special counsel's findings, possibly within forty-eight hours.

A chill went through the establishment. Perhaps there wasn't all that much to the report.

In a sense, this was the central question: How much had Bob Mueller reduced the scope of his inquiry? What if his two years had been spent not working to build his investigation, but working to limit it?

On Sunday, late on a spring-like afternoon, sixty-four degrees in Washington, the attorney general sent his summary of the report to Congress. In a four-page letter, Barr said that the special counsel had failed to find evidence of a conspiracy to influence the 2016 election between Trump or his aides and representatives from the Russian government. Further, while the special counsel had found evidence of possible obstruction of justice, he had left it to the attorney general's discretion whether to pursue the issue. In his letter, Barr said he had made the determination that the evidence did not warrant prosecution.

Elliptically, the letter added, "During the course of his investigation, the Special Counsel also referred other matters to other offices for further action." Indeed, there were now as many as a dozen other federal and state inquiries involving the Trump White House, the Trump Organization, various Trump family members, and Donald Trump himself. The potential crimes being investigated included money laundering, campaign finance fraud, abuse of the president's pardon power, corruption involving inaugural funds, lying on financial disclosures, and bank fraud.

But for now, Donald Trump seemed to have slipped his pursuers. As an amused Steve Bannon commented, "Never send a marine to do a hit man's job."

By Sunday evening, a feeling perhaps most reminiscent of election night 2016, desolate and confounded, spread through the mainstream media, the liberal establishment, and among all those who were confident that they had surrounded Donald Trump and left him nowhere to run. This was—and there could hardly be any better illustration—defeat snatched from the jaws of victory.

* * *

Almost immediately, Trump was publicly proclaiming his "complete and total exoneration." Soon he was on the phone seeking congratulations, taking congratulations, and congratulating himself.

"Who's the man? I'm the man. I am the man," he said to a well-wisher. He went on about his toughness, ferocity, and strategic acumen. He restated his constant point: "Never, never, never give in. Weakness is what they wait for. Fear. I am fearless. They know that. I scared the shit out of them."

He continued with imprecations against the Democrats and the media, and again launched a long and bitter recapitulation of the pee-tape accusations. And then he delivered a scornful critique of Robert Mueller: "What an asshole."

And there, perhaps, Trump had something of a point. If this was the result—a pass on conspiracy and equivocation on obstruction—how could you not have hastened it along, or, worse, how could you have fostered the exact opposite impression? For two years, the secret tribunal had let the nation assume Trump's peril and guilt. How had it taken twenty-two months to grill a nothing burger?

"Am I safe?" Trump persisted in asking the caller. "Am I safe?"

He answered his own question: "They are going to keep coming after me."

Here was one of the most seismic reversals in American political life—and yet, for Donald Trump, it was not out of the ordinary at all. Once again, he had dodged a potential death blow. But his "exoneration" changed little because he was still guilty of being Donald Trump. It was not only that his very nature would continue to repulse a majority of the nation, as well as almost everybody who came into working contact with him, but it would lead him again and again to the brink of personal destruction.

His escape, such as it was, would be brief.

Acknowledgments

Immediately after *Fire and Fury* was published, the president publicly and furiously broke with Stephen K. Bannon, the man arguably most responsible for making him president, over remarks he had made in the book. Donald Trump's wrath helped cost Bannon the backing of his patrons, billionaire Bob Mercer and his daughter Rebekah, and forced his departure from Breitbart News, the news site that Bannon led and the Mercers controlled.

It is a measure of Bannon's character that he stood by his remarks in *Fire and Fury* without complaint, quibbles, or hurt feelings. In all my years in this business, I have encountered few sources who, after revealing themselves, didn't blame the person who exposed them.

Steve Bannon, as the most clear-eyed interpreter of the Trump phenomenon I know, as the Virgil anyone might be lucky to have as a guide for a descent into Trumpworld—and as Dr. Frankenstein with his own deep ambivalence about the monster he created—is, in this volume, back again, and on the record, with my thanks for his trust and cooperation.

* * *

Stephen Rubin and John Sterling at Henry Holt are the kind of publisher and editor most writers have only ever dreamed about. Steve's full-speed-ahead enthusiasm and confidence has driven this book. John's meticulousness and insight informs every page; his good grace brought it over the finish line, once again. Holt's Maggie Richards and Pat Eisemann have taken this book to market with passion and deftness.

Writing about an unpredictable and vengeful president of the United States involves uncommon publishing risks. My great thanks to John Sargent and Don Weisberg at Macmillan, Holt's parent company, for their unwavering, indeed ringing, support.

My agent, Andrew Wylie, and his associates, Jeffrey Posternak in New York and James Pullen in London, on top of providing almost daily advice and service, have coordinated a complex and seamless international publication.

The lawyers on this book, Eric Rayman and Diana Frost, both of whom weathered the president's legal threats after the publication of *Fire and Fury*, have remained ever cool, cheerful, unafraid, and steadfastly on the side of publishing the full story.

I have, as always, depended on Leela de Kretser for her friendship and counsel. My great thanks to Danit Lidor who fact-checked this manuscript, Chris de Kretser who checked the check, and to Edward Elson and Thomas Godwin, my able research assistants.

Michael Jackson, John Lyons, Jay Roach, and Ari Emanuel, my partners in trying to render the Trump White House in dramatic form, have helped me think through key aspects of how to tell a political story that is much less about traditional ideas of power than it is about one man's extraordinary public battle with almost everyone—and perhaps most of all with himself.

My great appreciation to the unsung sources here, many of whom have counseled me on a regular, if not daily, basis throughout the writing of this book.

My wife, Victoria, has been my rock and inspiration.

Index

To buy any of our books and to find out
more about Abacus and Little, Brown, our authors
and titles, as well as events and book clubs,
visit our website

www.littlebrown.co.uk

and follow us on Twitter

@AbacusBooks
@LittleBrownUK